Diversity in Italian Studies

EDITED BY
Siân Gibby and Anthony Julian Tamburri

JOHN D. CALANDRA ITALIAN AMERICAN INSTITUTE
QUEENS COLLEGE, CITY UNIVERSITY OF NEW YORK

STUDIES IN ITALIAN AMERICANA
VOLUME 14

©2021 by the authors
All rights reserved
Printed in the United States of America

John D. Calandra Italian American Institute
Queens College, CUNY
25 West 43rd Street, 17th floor
New York, NY 10036

ISBN 978-1-939323-11-8
Library of Congress Control Number: 2020952026

CONTENTS

i   Introduction
ANTHONY JULIAN TAMBURRI

1   Why LGBTQIA+ Inclusivity Matters for Italian Studies
SOLE ANATRONE AND JULIA HEIM

13   African Americans and the Future of Italian Studies: Teaching Italian in Historically Black Colleges and Universities in the United States
NICOLINO APPLAUSO

25   AIDS in the Italian and Italian American Canon: Death as Metaphor for a Profession in Peril
RYAN CALABRETTA-SAJDER

45   Fear and Nostalgia in Italian Studies
ROSETTA GIULIANI CAPONETTO

57   The Value of Cross-Cultural Studies
MARY ANN McDONALD CAROLAN

65   Italian Studies, Queer Possibilities
JOHN CHAMPAGNE

79   What's So Different about "Diversity"? Reflecting (on) Plurality of Italian Experience in Teaching and Research
MARK CHU

91   Race and Ethnicity in Italian Film Studies
SHELLEEN GREENE

97   *Roma: arte, cultura, identità:* Diversity and Study Abroad
KRISTI GRIMES

109	"Un uom nasce a la riva de l'Indo": Expanding the Field of Medieval Italian Studies AKASH KUMAR
125	A Voice from the Margins: Reflections of a Sister Outsider on Her Voyage to Italy and through Italian Studies KENYSE LYONS
149	Hybridize or Decline: Practical Solutions toward a Sustainable Future for Italian Studies VETRI NATHAN
157	Transforming Italian Studies DEBORAH PARKER
169	Diversity and Inclusion in Italian Studies Curricula DEANNA SHEMEK
177	Reflections of and on Diversity: (Re)Discussing Course Materials ALESSIA VALFREDINI
193	From Roots to Routes: Italian Studies Between China and Italy via North America GAOHENG ZHANG
199	Contributors
205	Index

Introduction: A Call to Action

ANTHONY JULIAN TAMBURRI

> [P]eople who imagine that history flatters them (as it does, indeed, since they wrote it) are impaled on their history like a butterfly on a pin and become incapable of seeing or changing themselves, or the world.
> —JAMES BALDWIN

> [Blackface] is a practice where the black body is used as a dress to wear.... White is never worn. Black is always worn to ridicule.... [I]n addition to the colonial heritage there is also the usual southern issue. In one fell swoop through the figure of the minister the color black and the South has been ridiculed.
> —IGIABA SCEGO

I feel compelled to open this introduction with the following chronology: We held our symposium in January 2019, a year and one-half after the tragedy of Charlottesville, VA (August 12, 2017), and almost a year and one-half before George Floyd's murder in Minneapolis, MN (May 25, 2020). It is an uncanny chronology, for sure; almost halfway between these two terrible and paradigm-shifting events, our conference took place with its specific regard to Italian studies. As might society at large, we of the Italian studies community should ponder such serendipity and, in our own academic semiosphere, respond *post quem* in the most constructive manner possible.

We need to be cognizant of the effects of systemic racism at large and its insidious infection in specific arenas throughout society, which include the academy. That said, we must interrogate further our own field with regard to diversity, equity, and inclusion. In so doing, we are then compelled to complete the second half of the symposium's stated formula ("Diversity and Inclusion and Equal Opportunity"); while there is, for sure, diversity and inclusion in the field, there is also the second element, equal opportunity, which is truly the more challenging of the two.

Whereas diversity entails the recognition and appreciation of difference and its value, it is, for the most part, an expression that serves to urge the effecting of some form of transaction or change; it is primarily a rhetorical act, we can readily say. Equal opportunity, in turn, is more constitutive as the performative part. It requires that we take certain steps in the hiring process so that fair and equitable consideration is extended to all potential candidates regardless of race, ethnicity, sexuality, ableness, etc. Such consideration, I would further contend, needs to have its origins early on in the hiring process. Indeed, it must be employed at the inception of the hiring process; the wording of the ad, the clearly stated requirements, and the places in which ads appear constitute the primary steps in this process. Years ago, the lamentation was that there were no specific outlets for diversity hiring. When the early newsletters for all aspects of affirmative action—including placement of ads—began to appear, a subsequent lamentation was budgetary. Today, with the highly advanced electronic processes readily within reach, any complaints about the difficulty of advertising job opportunities are now unfounded.

Another issue with specific regard to Italian studies is that there are no surveys and studies that speak to a general, statistical make-up of the population of Italian studies, save one that is curricular in nature.[1] We surely do not have any record of the demographics of the faculty in Italian studies; anything we might have, to date, is anecdotal. That said, this much I am confident in stating as an embroidery of the faculty of yesteryear, while recognizing still its unscientific valence: Historically, the faculty of Italian studies has been populated predominantly by men, markedly by Italians, some Italian Americans, and less still by those not of Italian origin. Women, for the most part, seem to have held the title of lecturer or instructor,[2] depending on the institution's preferred nomenclature. Minorities, in turn, well, that is why the symposium took place and why this book now exists!

In point of fact, as we tenured members of the academy move forward, we truly can no longer remain silent about the prejudices and biases that undergird this part of our profession and that have contributed to over the years in a closed system based significantly on race and national origin. In her article titled "Race and Foreign Language," Deborah Parker, a professor of Italian, pondered the issue of being "a minority (Asian) in a field (Italian) in which there are very few minorities." The symposium from which this book is born was organized as an expanded conversation to Professor Parker's article. As the subtitle of the symposium signaled, the binomial of race/ethnicity is just one of the issues pertinent to the notion of diversity in Italian studies. Gender, sexuality, ableness, and—to a notable degree as well—class are also significant concerns within Italian studies. Hence, our use of the term *diversity* in this context includes all of the above and then some.

With specific regard to the symposium, "Diversity in Italian Studies" is the first organized event to deal with the overall issue in the field. I believe, in addition, that it could not have taken place at a better research institute than one under the umbrella of The City University of New York. CUNY is one of the most diverse institutions of higher education in the United States, and it is proud that its faculty and student populations reflect said diversity. In turn, the John D. Calandra Italian American Institute is one of the best research centers, anywhere, dedicated to the history and culture of Italians outside of Italy, and in our case, with specific focus on Italians in New York. Further still, there is, unfortunately, a history of discrimination against Italian Americans within the hallowed halls of CUNY,[3] which led to the founding in 1979 of the Italian American Institute to Foster Higher Education, which subsequently became the John D. Calandra Italian American Institute.

One of the many glaring factors about our profession that comes forth from Deborah Parker's essay is that ample data are still lacking in order to grasp a better picture of diversity within world language programs. Thus, precisely for this reason alone the symposium and the research now published herein are all the more significant. The challenges are surely numerous, and each essay in its own right attends in a cogent and provocative manner to many of the trials and tribulations that originate in an institution's reluctance to embrace fully a constructive philosophy of diversity and equal opportunity.

The issues of race and ethnicity within the field of Italian studies are very much tied to a canonical notion of literature, a dominant cultural thought process that often dictates for the reader how a novel might be constructed and what themes it should, or should not, include. Given the changing demographics of Italy over the past forty-plus years of immigration, which have turned the country into a point of arrival for many, diversity becomes a *sine qua non* in our further attempts at a greater understanding of the field of Italian studies, past and present. For example, as we consider some of Italy's current writers of color, given the likes of Pap Khouma, Igiaba Scego, and Amara Lakhous, to name just a few, how are we to read and analyze said literature, and according to whose semiotic?

A number of essays in this volume deal directly with curricular matters. The methodologies of teaching and the philosophies of what we teach all have an impact on the success of a course, its department, its college, and, in the end, on the students' achievements. Thus, in this age of greater awareness of diversity, the re-examination of course materials and more profound reflections on plurality in the classroom can only promise a more conducive environment for learning, in which students and educators alike may develop more rigorous and nuanced perspectives and analyses of curricula and its relationship to everyday life.

The fostering of all communities in our classrooms must be one of our primary pedagogical goals; it constitutes the "how" of "what" we teach, both of which go hand in hand in their own symbiotic relationship. Hence, creating a comfortable—

and yes, a safe—space for all members of our society is one of our singular duties. In that vein, we open the volume with an essay on LGBTQIA+ concerns and notions of inclusivity in the classroom.

Furthermore, there are those contributors who offer here their personal reflections with regard to gender, race, sexuality, and their own experiences fraught with challenges as a member of the academic community. Our world is changing notably, almost from day to day in certain ways. Hence, as our readers ponder the contents of this volume, we are hopeful that it will leave an indelible mark and, in the end, have an everlasting impact on the field of Italian studies, specifically, as well as on the academy as a whole.

As instances of violent expressions of systemic racism unfortunately abound in our nation (Breonna Taylor [Louisville, KY; March 13, 2020] and Rayshard Brooks [Atlanta, GA; June 12, 2020], among others still), it is abundantly clear that what we must ultimately question is the overriding notion of whiteness, heterosexuality, dominant-cultural thought processes, other exclusionary social categories, and their amalgamate power that aggregates various groups into one vast cluster of, in our case, professors and intellectuals. What we consequently need to do is to dismantle such long-held notions, and in so doing, we need to destabilize, first and foremost, "white privilege" with the specific goal of "affirm[ing] commonalities and confirm[ing] differences" in order to promote, in the end, "a network of scholarly entanglements instead of isolated nodes of inquiry" (Anagnostou 2013, 122). Networks of this type, per force, stimulate communication among an integration, to varying degrees, of such "isolated" thought processes.

A first step in the promotion of "a network of scholarly entanglements" would require a greater awareness of the histories of other racial and ethnic groups as well as people of other categories mentioned above, for example. This is the beginning of a desire to engage in a paradigm shift that would lead us away from the so-called "conventional" center of dominant cultural thought. Second, we need to create a platform in which all voices are heard and free to discuss both differences and commonalities. Third, we must calibrate our own individual suffering, or lack thereof, against the backdrop of African Americans, Jews, Muslims, women, LGBTQIA+, able-bodied people, and others. "Whiteness" surely remains within the general conversation of racial/ethnic/other discourse, but it undergoes along the way a series of interrogations and analyses that eventually underscore its malleability of signification. In some corners, the ignorance of such histories, unfortunately, seems still to clamor oh so loudly.

Overall, the essays included within this volume will guide the reader in negotiating this terrain from a broad perspective. They do so through a variety of lenses:

from the analytical to the personal, from the curricular to the pedagogic, from the racial to the ethnic, as well as from an international and intercultural perspective. In the end, this collection constitutes a preliminary blueprint of how, why, and where we need to begin in order to effect substantial change in Italian studies.

Those of us who are not Black, those of us who are not of African origin (specifically, in the United States and in Italy), those of us who are not queer, not differently abled, nor representative of other human characteristics not deemed "conventional" by dominant cultural thinkers, truly cannot, viscerally, comprehend what it means to live on the other side of "whiteness," "convention," and all that they entail. Often, regrettably, we simply do not see ourselves as privileged. Thus, unless we struggle to recognize our own privilege, which means questioning our own socio-moral measure of evaluation, we shall fall into that trap, run the risk, of seeing things always at a distance and through a semiotic lens of gender and racial privilege, which, while so doing, we do not recognize.

Notes

1. See Anonymous in *Voices in Italian Americana*. Deborah Parker stated as much in her 2019 essay in *Inside Higher Ed*, the stimulus for this symposium.
2. I am reminded of Cecilia Ross, PhD in Romance Philology (1953) from the University of California, Berkeley. In U.C. Berkeley's Italian Department, Dr. Ross spent her entire career as senior lecturer. From the very beginning, she was an active member of the professoriate and dedicated to professional development. In 1951, while still a doctoral student, she was one of three co-founders of the Foreign Language Association of Northern California (FLANC). Apropos of our symposium, the theme of FLANC's 2020 conference is "Diversity and Languages."
3. In 1978, the late New York State Senator John D. Calandra completed a study on discrimination against Italian Americans at CUNY. The alleged claims of discrimination were divided into two categories: faculty and students. For faculty, they involved concerns regarding appointments, promotions, tenure, and major committee assignments and lack thereof. For students, the claims revolved around ethnic-studies programs, student counseling services, allocation of student fees for Italian American groups, and support of Italian American centers on college campuses.

Works Cited

Anagnostou, Yiorgios. 2013. "White Ethnicity: A Reappraisal," *Italian American Review* 3.2: 99–128.

Anonymous. 2018. "Italian Graduate Programs in North America," *Voices in Italian Americana* 29.2: 3–8.

Calandra, John D. 1978. *A History of Italian-American Discrimination at CUNY*. Albany, NY: New York State Senate.

Parker, Deborah. 2018. "Race and Foreign Language," *Inside Higher Ed*. June 21. https://bit.ly/2PMBbqt (accessed January 10, 2019).

Why LGBTQIA+ Inclusivity Matters for Italian Studies

SOLE ANATRONE AND JULIA HEIM

LGBTQIA+ students may regularly experience verbal or physical harassment, threats, and misgenderings in all aspects of their lives, be it at home, at school, or in public. At school specifically, as the Human Rights Campaign (HRC) reports, the result is often absenteeism, higher dropout rates, mental health issues, and academic underachievement (HRC 2018). There are also more subtle issues of microaggressions and invisibilities that occur whose consequences are much more commonly swept under the rug. Our words and behaviors can significantly impact the experience these students have. As Italian-language, literature, and culture instructors, we may often neglect to consider LGBTQIA+ inclusivity, labeling it as outside the framework of our course content. The normativity embedded in our texts and the shape of our pedagogical materials, however, are both isolating to our LGBTQIA+ students and ignore, and thus erase, LGBTQIA+ Italian literature, history, and culture, pushing it outside the bounds of "legitimate" disciplinary study. We founded Asterisk, a diversity taskforce, as a way of responding to this crisis by offering workshops and trainings that aim to promote practices of inclusivity within institutions of higher education, with a specific focus on gender and sexuality. In this essay we discuss some of the reasons for this type of pedagogical formation and some of the specific tools for building intentionally inclusive learning spaces.

CAMPUS CLIMATE AND INSTITUTIONAL STRUCTURES

The history and current structure of universities have a direct effect on the daily lives of students on campus; the policies, hiring and admissions practices, course offerings, and campus culture and traditions all come together to shape a student's experience. The frameworks upon which institutions of higher learning are built reflect larger societal systems of power and oppression and are thus necessarily marked by a current and historic politic. Take, for example, current efforts to reform Title IX (an educational amendment meant to foster gender inclusivity and protect against gender-based discrimination). According to Steven Petrow (2016), many religious schools are seeking exemption from Title IX so that they may more easily discriminate against LGBTQIA+ students. In a letter to the U.S. Department of Education, for example, Spring Arbor University in Michigan states that they are "requesting exemption on religious grounds from Title IX . . . to allow the University religious freedom to discriminate on the basis of sex, including gender identity, and sexual orientation, in regard to housing, living arrangements, restroom, locker rooms, and athletics" (Petrow 2016). By taking this kind of position, institutions can inflict negative psychological and physical harm on LGBTQIA+ students; this represents one blatantly discriminatory decision that can determine the campus climate and condone acts of hate against these students. Given the degree to which campus climate is informed by the institutional structures, it is easy to see how the ramifications and the history of those structures may often be much more subtle than the example elaborated above. We are adopting Susan Rankin's (2005) understanding of campus climate, which she defines as "the cumulative attitudes, behaviors, and standards of employees and students concerning access for, inclusion of, and level of respect for individual and group needs, abilities, and potential" (17). Without a conscious push toward structural inclusivity, professors, administrators, and staff have significantly less potential to provide resources and aid to LGBTQIA+ students, regardless of their personal stances and affiliations. Furthermore, professors, administrators, and staff who identify as gender and sexual minorities experience their own discrimination, lack of resources, and lack of institutional support and may thus experience many of the same physical and psychological repercussions that these minority students face.

In 2018 students at the University of North Carolina, Chapel Hill, took matters into their own hands and pulled down the Confederate soldier Silent Sam statue, refusing to accept the lack of institutional action against this monument to discrimination. Events like this show that not only are students often forced to take action on their own when universities refuse to acknowledge or respond to hateful events, symbols, or structures, but also that a university's history is often still deeply felt by the current student body. The impact of such histories—and the tacit support historic injustices receive by way of a university's inaction—can be particularly taxing on precarious students whose identities and existences are threatened by the narratives, values, and ideologies these histories perpetuate. The refusal to provide medical support or safe spaces or to allow gender nonconforming and transgender people to use the bathrooms in which they feel most comfortable represents instances of discrimination and shows a lack of support for LGBTQIA+ students. These institutional choices have a direct and daily impact on individual students and shape the campus climate in such a way as to if not encourage, at least condone other discriminatory behavior aimed at these individuals.

We have offered particularly American examples to begin our discussion because, although we are talking about Italian studies, the experience, structure, and flexibility of higher education in the United States and Italy are dramatically different, especially when it comes to questions of gender and sexuality. Faculty teaching in Italian universities are cautious when using terms that reference non-hetero, non-binary, non-cis existence; this caution is a reaction to institutional bans and social condemnation for teaching things like gender theory.[1] The difference between this attitude and the type of institutional support things like Title IX represent, even when that support is purely nominal, is significant as it points to a potentiality we need to seize.

While the university as a whole creates top-down policies and dictates much of what departments look like, how they operate, and what they prioritize within their discipline, there are departmental structures and standards that are unique in their disciplinary specificity, and these too impact the comfort, safety, and overall health of minority students.

On what level does the professorial body contribute to diversity of the campus community and the diversity of scholarship within the discipline? How do our hiring practices represent or erase gender variance in terms of the scholarly focus (and not just identity politics) of the people hired? What are we reinforcing when we prioritize certain areas of study within Italian departments? How might this contribute in certain ways to the marginalization of LGBTQIA+ people within the field of study, the invisibility of gender and sexual variance within the subdisciplines studied, and the negative impact for the minorities that belong to the educational communities doing the studying? What are we consciously or unconsciously reinforcing if we neglect to incorporate LGBTQIA+ literature and culture, queer methodologies, and LGBTQIA+ scholars within Italian studies?

INCORPORATING LGBTQIA+ CONTENT IN THE ITALIAN CLASSROOM

It should never be a given that a professor or researcher in a specific disciplinary field has the threshold concepts necessary to foster LGBTQIA+ inclusivity.[2] Often because of their own privilege or lack of experience in this regard, professors do not feel they have the proper tools necessary to even begin to address these issues; as a result, many people shy away from or ignore these topics—not out of malice, but from fear, self-doubt, or lack of knowledge. The consequences of this extend to their LGBTQIA+ students most directly but also to other students, the department, the campus climate, and society more broadly. When we do not represent minoritarian identities and elide sexual and gender differences, we are communicating—intentionally or not—our support for the continued invisibility of these peoples. When we omit these stories from our syllabi, we reinforce a practice of devaluing these experiences, a practice that can be internalized to harmful effect by our students and colleagues.

There are also those instructors who do not feel that LGBTQIA+ issues pertain to the discipline of Italian studies. This mentality and the resulting behaviors reinforce dominant heterosexual norms, erase LGBTQIA+ histories and cultures, and effectively marginalize minority student experience by not reflecting diversity in course content. In the face of this kind of erasure, LGBTQIA+ students (and faculty) may be forced to closet themselves in order to feel any semblance of belonging within the classroom or create a connection with the material being studied. Closets are a response to a lack of sociopolitical and religious acceptance; they are a strategy for self-preservation and point to an embodied fear in the face of the structures at the root of homophobic oppression. Eve Kosofsky Sedgwick (2008) reminds us that "homophobic oppression . . . has resulted from its inextricability from the question of knowledge and the processes of knowing in modern Western culture at large" (33–34). More specifically to our context, she elaborates: "[S]imply existing as a gay person who is a teacher is in fact bayonetted through and through . . . by the vectors of a disclosure at once compulsory and forbidden" (70). It is not and should not be solely the responsibility of those oppressed minorities to insist that these oppressions get addressed within our institutions; it is the responsibility of everyone within these structures to recognize how we participate in the forced liminality of these people when we fail to introduce language, culture, and literature that reflect their lived experience. To acknowledge is to interpolate and begin to provide a pathway toward acceptance, whereas silence "depends on and highlights more broadly the fact that ignorance is as potent and as multiple a thing there as is knowledge" (4).

ITALIAN LITERATURE AND CULTURE COURSES

What are we told to focus on—and what do we assume we *must* focus on—when preparing to teach an Italian literature or culture course? Much depends on the scope of the class, which is often determined by temporal markers and organized around events of social, political, and/or technological significance. At other times the class scope is determined by a theme like genre, race, or gender, as in the case of courses on Italian women writers or Italian modernism; while these two titles are both examples of thematically organized courses, they are by no means on equal footing, as "women" are still too often considered a nonlegitimate area of investigation within Italian studies. Though in most universities our discipline has expanded to "studies," courses are still largely organized around literary content, and the assumption and dominant expectation is that instructors must first and foremost teach to the canon, canonical texts having been both academically legitimized and woven into the cultural fabric of national studies disciplines ("If you don't know Dante you don't know Italy and you don't know Italian culture"). We do not need to spend time here reifying this hegemonic belief; instead we would like to reiterate that the canon is comprised predominantly of straight White men—and often those with less-straightforward identity categories are simply stripped of their alterity and passed off as "one of the boys." At times this list is speckled with moments of difference, as professors add a woman-identified writer or a person of color to the syllabus. This act of inclusion, while political, is not radical. These small gestures help, but we must not risk tokenizing our content (one woman does not and could never speak for all Italian women writers); we must ensure that our teaching strategies refuse the universalization of one person's lived experience, or body of work, even as we make efforts to diversify our material. This act of inclusion is important and should not go unacknowledged, but we must more consistently and intentionally make room for LGBTQIA+ works and authors within Italian studies. As the sample syllabus in Figure 1 demonstrates, current norms omit these voices entirely.

Introduction to Italian Literature From 16th Century to Present, Syllabus	
Boiardo, *Orlando inamorato*	Castiglione, *Il cortegiano*
Ariosto, *Orlando furioso* (selezioni)	Machiavelli, *Il principe* (selezioni)
Machiavelli, *La mandragola*	Bembo, *Rime* (selezioni)
Tasso, *Gerusalemme liberata* (selezioni)	Vico, *Scienza nuova* (selezioni)
Goldoni, *La locandiera*	Foscolo, *Dei sepolcri* (selezioni)
Leopardi, *Operette morali* (selezioni)	Manzoni, *I promessi sposi* (selezioni)
Verga, *I malavoglia* (selezioni)	Pascoli, *Myricae* (selezioni)
D'Annunzio, *Il piacere* (selezioni)	Ungaretti: *L'allegria* (selezioni)
Pirandello, *Sei personaggi in cerca d'autore*	Montale, *Ossi di seppia* (selezioni)
Svevo, *La coscienza di Zeno* (selezioni)	Saba, *Il canzoniere* (selezioni)
Calvino, *Il barone rampante*	

FIGURE 1

This required-reading list is from a City University of New York (CUNY) course whose syllabus is available online, but it is by no means unique. In fact, we selected it because it could be from any North American university offering a survey course on Italian literature; the authors listed are some of the most frequently found in the online samples we studied. What is unfortunately not surprising is that the list is made up exclusively of straight White men. It is true that some of these texts touch on queer topics, as Mary-Michelle DeCoste (2004) points out with regard to Fiordispina's love for Bradamante in Ariosto's text.

Teaching canonical texts like Ariosto in this way could open the door to discussions about queer topics; however, the reality is that even this kind of potential for transforming our discursive practices goes too frequently overlooked. To practice an intentional pedagogical inclusivity does not necessarily mean teaching texts that explicitly represent gay sex or that make lesbian politics the focus of discussion. As the sample syllabus we have created in Figure 2 demonstrates, there are many "safe" texts written by LGBTQIA+ authors and texts with LGBTQIA+ characters or content that fit within or on the margins of contemporary notions of the Italian canon.

Some fairly well-known ("safe") names you can add/substitute	
(These authors make diversity, alterity, and disenfranchisement central to their work.)	
Colonna, *Rime amorose*	Pallavicino, *Retorica delle puttane*
Colombi, *In risaia*	Serao, *Il ventre di Napoli*
Aleramo, *Una donna*	Bassani, *Gli occhiali d'oro*
Morante, *L'isola di Arturo*	Pasolini, *Ragazzi di vita*
De Cespedes, *Quaderno proibito*	Maraini, *Donna in guerra*
Tondelli, *Camere separate*	Ferrante, *L'amore molesto*
Abdel Malek, *Fiamme in paradiso*	Scego, *La mia casa e dove sono*
Ghermandi, *Regina di fiori e di perle*	Marcasciano, *Antologaia*

FIGURE 2

We offer this list not as alternative, but rather as a series of supplemental texts that could quite easily be incorporated into a course syllabus such as the one in Figure 1. Not only do these texts address diversity and alterity in their work, the authors' lives also represent sexual, gender, and racial diversity. This list is in no way meant to be comprehensive; instead, it is a way of creating a moment of reflection for those instructors tasked with composing and teaching Italian literature courses. We are calling these authors and these texts "safe" because of the recognition they have received within academic and cultural spheres. Using one or more of these texts represents a move toward LGBTQIA+ inclusion in the classroom, a move that, as we have said, is not radical but is, unfortunately, still politically necessary.

Italian studies courses offer students a lens into the cultural landscape and sociality of Italy and its diasporas. From courses on food culture, to fashion, to music and cinema, there has been a clear attempt to showcase the breadth of Italy's cultural expression, but within this framework too we have seen a very limited and marginalizing engagement with LGBTQIA+ populations and topics. What little representation we see is typically limited to the incorporation of mainstream cinematic LGBT representation (specifically and almost exclusively limited to Pier Paolo Pasolini, Ferzan Ozpetek, and more recently Luca Guadagnino); there is much opportunity here to push beyond. While there should definitely be a place within this vast field to include these internationally acclaimed and financially successful filmmakers, such representations hardly do justice to the legacies of LGBTQIA+ lives and cultures in Italy.

There is also opportunity to incorporate Italian literature courses in our curricula that more explicitly prioritize difference, alterity, and marginalized peoples' voices.[3] Furthermore, there is potential to incorporate some of this literature into other cross-disciplinary classes, or classes within gender and sexuality departments; this kind of interdisciplinary development is beneficial for both sides. While we have discussed the reasons why it is essential that more texts discussing LGBTQIA+ subjectivities be incorporated into the Italian studies classroom, we must also acknowledge that departments that house the study of gender and sexuality in the United States too often study exclusively anglophone lives and literatures; this not only prioritizes anglophone voices and experiences but also universalizes them, which is inherently damaging for both anglophone cultures and those cultures whose voices remain unheard and unstudied. We have the opportunity to counter this by making room for those subjectivities that go unseen and by occupying our own space within an academy that tends to reinforce tradition if it is not continuously questioned and redirected.

ITALIAN-LANGUAGE CLASSES

For Italian-language classes, which generally make up the bulk of Italian course selections any given semester, the integration of LGBTQIA+ materials may appear less obvious on the surface, and the task may seem more difficult than the insertion of texts and discourses into a syllabus; the impact, however, is significant. The two primary areas that must be addressed when considering LGBTQIA+ identities in these courses are the approaches to teaching grammar in all its gendered structure and the basic vocabulary units (family, professions, etc.). Because, up to this point, Italian textbooks (often mandated by universities) have been heteronormative and minority exclusionary to an alarming degree, it is up to individual instructors to reshape the language surrounding the activities and lessons in a text and to rethink their approach to the particular content being studied. The importance of making LGBTQIA+ content an integral part of the curriculum cannot be overemphasized, as it both acknowledges that these people and experiences exist in Italy[4] and allows for LGBTQIA+ students, or students from rainbow families, to see themselves included and considered within the language and the discipline as a whole.

When we talk about textbooks being heteronormative we are referring to an array of characteristics, from the imagery and vocabulary, to the grammatical and cultural examples. Discussions of family, for example, reproduce ideals of straight coupling, gender-stereotyped roles, and procreative futurity. Take for instance the section on "la vita di tutti i giorni" (everyday life) in Lazzarino, Dini, and Peccianti (2007). Here an exercise about the passato prossimo (present perfect) asks students to recount the romantic progression of Alessia and Riccardo as they move "dalla festa alla chiesa" (from the party to the church) (148). This kind of example reinforces the idea that proper coupling is between a man and a woman and necessarily leads to religiously sanctioned marriage, as the title of the exercise makes clear. In the sixth edition of *Ciao* (Riga and Dal Martello 2006), we find an informative textbox about the family tree that laments the dissolution of the so-called traditional family:

> Oggi, a causa della lontananza, è più difficile dare un aiuto ai genitori anziani, che si ritrovano soli e sono spesso costretti ad andare nelle case di riposo. Inoltre, i nonni non possono badare ai nipotini che devono stare negli asili d'infanzia quando i genitori sono a lavoro. (127)

> Today, due to distance, it is more difficult to help elderly parents, who often find themselves alone and forced to stay in nursing homes. Furthermore, grandparents can't care for their grandchildren who must go to daycare facilities when their parents are at work.

Here readers are guilted by way of implications into thinking that a family in which both parents work leads to neglect of elderly parents and young children; this kind of messaging not only reaffirms heterosexual family structures, but also works to alienate students who do not see themselves or their families represented here.

To counteract/repair the kind of damage done by this type of teaching tool (that tacitly reinforces norms and codes of acceptable behavior and existence), we must demand better from publishers, we must build our own materials that put our goals of intentional inclusivity into practice, and we must share with each other, breaking down outdated notions of pedagogical propriety and working instead to create networks of supportive and innovative teaching practices. We are thinking, for instance, of the kind of collaborative lesson planning Lillyrose Veneziano Broccia discussed at the John D. Calandra Italian American Institute's Diversity in Italian Studies conference (January 17 and 18, 2019).

As we work to create these intentional teaching practices we must also take stock of our own positionality and the biases we bring to the classroom and the discipline. The assumptions that are reinforced and that effectively police and silence our students and colleagues come from standard textbooks, established canons, and repeated/reused syllabi but also from the language and behavior we as individuals use and the language and behavior we as professors tolerate in our classrooms.

INSIDE OUR CLASSROOMS

Before we begin to teach course content, and often before we even speak to our students, we have already begun judging them and determining our expectations of them based on our perceptions and assumptions about their outward appearances. As Melissa Garcia (2018) explains, "These subconscious thoughts and feelings are known as implicit biases. Whether our perceptions are positive or negative, they have an impact; they determine expectations, and these expectations dictate how we teach. Studies show that teacher expectations are closely linked to student achievement and success." These assumptions are, on some level, unavoidable; what we can do is manage how they influence our expectations and interactions. When students internalize our treatment of them or our expectation of them, they respond accordingly. We must monitor our own behaviors to ensure that all students are given equal possibility and equal respect in our classrooms. Our assumptions about students often stem from these implicit biases, whether positive or negative. Often these biases also have to do with our expectation of their social and cultural knowledge rather than with their academic performance. Similar to the tokenization of minorities we spoke of with regard to selecting texts and course content, we must be wary of asking students from minority backgrounds to speak for "their kind" and resist assuming that they could or would want to universalize their individual experiences. Asking an openly gay or lesbian student, for example, to speak about marriage equality assumes that this gay or lesbian student has any knowledge on the matter, that this knowledge will be in support of a liberal homonormative position on the subject, and that this student would like the chance to speak out about a topic that they *clearly* must have an interest in because they are gay. The consequences of this kind of ask can be many and can be significant: By asking, you may unwittingly out a student who is not ready or does not feel safe being openly gay and thus expose them to psychological, social, and physical harm; or, put on the spot, the student may feel they need to take a position on a topic they are uninformed or ambivalent about and may, consequently, feel insecure or resentful toward the classroom environment, resulting in missed classes, limited participation, and less-engaged learning.

At the same time, we must work on asking students when we need them to help us understand their positionality. While asking a person's sexuality should never enter the realm of acceptable classroom discourse, asking someone's preferred gender pronouns and name is a sign of acknowledgment and respect for that student. If you make a mistake, acknowledge that you have misspoken without being dismissive. Furthermore, it is not OK to ask a trans or gender-nonconforming student what their "real" name is, thereby implying that the name with which they identify is less valid that the one they were assigned at birth. In the Italian-language classroom we need to make space for (de)gendering in ways that may, at first, sound incongruous; for instance, if a student mentions a same-gendered partner or family structure or uses a pronoun that does not match your assumptions about their appearance, you might think it is a grammatical "mistake" that needs "correcting," but to assume error in a circumstance such as this would be to reaffirm heteronormativity and be dismissive of this person's identity or life experience. Moments like this should be seen as a discrete opportunity to talk about difference and to provide all students the language needed to talk about themselves, without making them feel like their personal or home lives are grammatical (and social) errors. It is our job as educators and classroom leaders to make space for these conversations, to build pauses and flexibility into our lesson plans and rehearse the kind of language we can draw upon to invite generous, inclusive discussion.

As pedagogues, we act as models in our classrooms; as such, the ways that we act and react change the shape of our learning spaces and influence the ways our students act and react to one another. We must recognize this position of power and authority, both by acknowledging that our pedagogical practices matter and by understanding that it is also our responsibility to be perceptive and responsive to microaggressions that may be happening between students in our spaces. As Derald Wing Sue (2010) clarifies, "Microaggressions are the everyday verbal, nonverbal, and environmental slights, snubs, or insults, whether intentional or unintentional, which communicate hostile, derogatory, or negative messages to target persons based solely upon their marginalized group membership." He continues, "Microaggressions reflect the active manifestation of oppressive worldviews that create, foster, and enforce marginalization." When it comes to LGBTQIA+ people, microaggressions might, for example, look like a student referring to something as "gay" when they mean they did not enjoy it or find it interesting; or the assumption that a lesbian or gay student is attracted to everyone of the same sex; or casual references to stereotypes such as gay men being into fashion, lesbians being butch, or that bisexuality does not exist. As Wing Sue (2010) concludes, "These everyday occurrences may on the surface appear quite harmless, trivial, or be described as 'small slights,' but research indicates they have a powerful impact upon the psychological well-being of marginalized groups and affect their standard of living by creating inequities in health care, education, and employment." It is our responsibility to recognize our power in the face of these acts and to teach and show students that no form of discrimination, no matter how small, is acceptable inside or outside our classrooms.

HOLDING OURSELVES ACCOUNTABLE

As we stated at the beginning of this essay, HRC (2018) reports that for our LGBTQIA+ students, issues of discrimination, violence, threats, misgenderings, and microaggressions often lead to absenteeism, high dropout rates, mental health issues, and academic underachievement. There are ways these issues may be and must be directly addressed by us in our classrooms. It is clear that this kind of discrimination is prevalent in Italian studies, whether by way of the campus climate, discipline or departmental expectations, or classroom leadership and social dynamics. To combat the negative effects of these structures of bias and exclusion, we must educate ourselves and our students and take steps toward creating inclusive curricula and learning, research, and work environments. Do it now!

Notes

1. One need only look at the organization of the Thirteenth Annual World Congress of Families that took place in Verona on March 29–31, 2019, to understand the precariousness of gender and sexuality studies and activism in and outside the university. As the statement put out by the Italian Network of Gender, Intersex, Feminist, Transfeminist, and Sexuality Studies makes clear, "The institutional support to the Congress is alarming, as is the participation of Matteo Salvini, Minister of Home Affairs and Deputy Prime Minister, and of Lorenzo Fontana, Minister for Family and Disability. Equally worrisome is the participation of Marco Bussetti, Minister for Education, University and Research. Since the start of his mandate, Minister Bussetti, through his continuing support to the demands of those 'anti-gender' movements that are now promoting the 13th

World Congress of Families, has been delegitimizing the democratic principles upon which a public, secular, and democratic education system is built" (Politesse, Facebook post, March 21, 2019).

2. The term *threshold concept* refers to certain key ideas necessary for the comprehension and development of a discipline or idea. In the case of Asterisk and the work we do around LGBTQIA+ inclusivity and pedagogy, some of the key concepts we believe must be addressed are the difference between gender and sexuality, the meaning of the LGBTQIA+ acronym, gender roles and gender identity, microaggressions, implicit bias, and the significance of pronouns to identity.

3. As the broad array of topics addressed in this volume suggests, there is too much being overlooked, work that is often being studied and researched but not published, or work that is delegitimized (a move, we should mention, that often forces scholars who focus on these issues to remain in liminal and tenuous positions in relation to the university), or work that is published and never addressed in our classrooms.

4. Many LGBTQIA+ Italians, in fact, choose more gender-neutral language, substituting, for example, an asterisk or a "u" at the end of a word instead of the gendered "o" or "a."

Works Cited

DeCoste, Mary-Michelle. 2004. "Knots of Desire: Female Homoeroticism in Orlando furioso 25." In *Queer Italia: Same-Sex Desire in Italian Literature and Film,* edited by Gary Cestaro, 19–34. New York: Palgrave Macmillan.

Garcia, Melissa. 2018. "Why Teachers Must Fight Their Own Implicit Biases." *Education Week,* July 25. https://www.edweek.org/tm/articles/2018/07/25/why-teachers-must-fight-implicit-biases.html (accessed July 4, 2019).

Human Rights Campaign. 2018. "Student Non-Discrimination Act." https://www.hrc.org/resources/student-non-discrimination-act. Accessed December 21, 2018.

Larese Riga, Carla Dal Martello and Chiara Maria Dal Martello. 2006. *Ciao!*, 6th ed. Boston: Cengage.

Lazzarino, Graziana, Andrea Dini and Maria Cristina Peccianti. 2007. *Prego! An Invitation to Italian,* 7th ed. New York: McGraw Hill.

Petrow, Steven. 2016. "Some Colleges Can Discriminate against LGBT Students. Here's How to Check If Your Top Choice Does." *The Washington Post*, September 19.

https://www.washingtonpost.com/lifestyle/style/some-colleges-can-discriminate-against-lgbt-students-heres-how-to-check-if-your-top-choice-does/2016/09/19/73673d46-7e7c-11e6-8d0c-fb6c00c90481_story.html?utm_term=.e4f912e43969 (accessed July 4, 2019).

Rankin, Susan. 2005. "Campus Climates for Sexual Minorities." *New Directions for Student Services* 111: 17–23.

Sedgwick, Eve. 2008. *Epistemology of the Closet.* Berkeley, CA: University of California Press.

Wing Sue, Derald. 2010. "Microaggressions: More Than Just Race." *Psychology Today,* November 17. https://www.psychologytoday.com/us/blog/microaggressions-in-everyday-life/201011/microaggressions-more-just-race (accessed September 16, 2019).

African Americans and the Future of Italian Studies: Teaching Italian in Historically Black Colleges and Universities in the United States

NICOLINO APPLAUSO

Is there enough diversity in Italian studies? If not, why is this issue relevant to teachers and students of Italian in universities and local communities across the United States? These questions have been addressed by Deborah Parker in her influential essay "Race and Foreign Language," which sparked numerous reactions in the academic community since its first publication in June 2018. By providing testimonials from a sample group of minority graduate students and faculty members, she ventured to assert that the field of Italian studies (in comparison with other Romance-language programs) has currently very little diversity. Such a lack is reflected both in the demographics of faculty members (the great majority of whom are of Italian ancestry) and students (who rarely are of African American or Asian American heritage) in various university programs nationwide. Overall, the most thought-provoking thesis raised in this article is that there might be a correlation between this lack of diversity and the decline in Italian studies. Such a possibility is further supported by testimonials given by minority faculty members and students, who linked their lack of motivation to remain in the field to their exclusion from academic circles. By juxtaposing Italian studies with language programs with more diverse students and faculty, Parker finally proposes to broaden the field in order to secure growth and minimize the current decrease in foreign-language enrollment. She states this strongly in the closing challenges: "Can this sentiment be converted to action? Can Italian enact a bold and more inclusive vision for its future or will we be left with managing a decline?" These questions are appropriate because they call for a self-evaluation of our current state of affairs alongside a plan of action on how to move forward for the future. Are changes possible in this difficult situation? If so, what can we do to implement more diversity in Italian studies?

I agree with Parker's assessment, which has been confirmed throughout my fifteen-year career in Italian studies in an academic setting where I have found very little diversity in the field. This could be related to the lack of a practical vision and purpose that I observed in the numerous Italian programs with which I have been involved. These institutions ranged from large public-research universities to medium and small private liberal-arts colleges located across at least six states. Because of students' limited exposure to foreign language outside the classroom, Italian programs promoted activities with student associations in which I noticed the centrality of food and recreational pastimes that were supposed to promote Italian as a fun language to study. However, these events lacked the acknowledgment of a deeper purpose that linked academia to our diverse local communities. They involved mainly students and their personal interests in food or sports, and over time I noticed that foreign-language activities started to be exclusive to the social aspect of the college environment. This situation effectively discouraged students who did not focus on recreational activities and were interested in getting an education for the purpose of obtaining employment outside the university and were thus less attracted to the social college experience. These social-oriented gatherings often simply do not attract minority students. While these recreational activities are important, I think that they should not be the only available outlet outside the classroom for students interested in foreign-language study.

Although it is challenging to find solutions to these central questions on the issue of diversity in Italian studies, I will augment discussion of my personal experience with that of something I believe constitutes a rather exceptional opportunity and occurrence: the creation of a new Italian course of study at the institution where I currently teach, Morgan State University, Maryland's "Preeminent *Public Urban Research* University" and one of the largest historically Black colleges and universities (HBCU) in the United States. Because this initiative is new, it offers the possibility to develop an original working model for learning foreign languages that could perhaps revive the field. This new model could include recreational activities with student organizations but above all would center on students' academic interests and on the needs of specific institutions and local communities. Through this new offering we could find constructive ways to foster more diversity in Italian studies and attract minority students from different socioeconomic backgrounds.

In view of the existing national trend of decline in enrollment in foreign-language education at the university level (Flaherty 2018), this new academic endeavor should be further examined. One notable fact is that its success is in contrast with what happened in Maryland in early 2019 when various foreign-language programs and majors were cut from several university curricula in at least two major private liberal-arts colleges.[1] So, how is it possible that when more than fifty Italian offerings are no longer in existence and the national trend shows a decrease of 9.2 percent in enrollment in language courses other than English, we can somehow experience the birth of new Italian studies from scratch (Looney and Lusin 2018)? Is this an isolated case or perhaps the sign of a new trend in language education? These questions are pertinent especially if we consider the fact that this new Italian course has emerged from a space where we do not traditionally find Italian-language study: Its historical importance should be stressed because (to my knowledge) it is the only Italian course of study currently offered at an HBCU anywhere in the United States.

Before focusing on the specific elements of this new offering, I will first talk about how it originated and share some insights on my experience in teaching Italian at an HBCU. I will reflect on the positive elements as well as the challenges I faced in introducing Italian to minority college students by emphasizing both the question of diversity and the reality of being "a minority" in Italian studies. This contribution will conclude by adding some reflections about the significance of teaching Italian at an HBCU in relation to the current situation of decline in Italian studies. I will also introduce some suggestions about possible ideas for the future of studying Italian in the United States.

Let's first start with the question: What exactly is a historically Black college and university? HBCUs are institutions of higher education in the United States that were created mainly to support the African American community. The first HBCU was created in 1837 when "Northern philanthropists and Black Church leaders established what is now Cheyney State University" (Newkirk 2012, 13). After the Civil War the number of HBCUs gradually increased to nearly a hundred as they sought to provide education to the growing freedmen population, which amounted to "more than four million formerly enslaved people" (Gasman and Tudico 2016, 1). The intention was to offer accredited, high-quality education to African Americans for an affordable price, and "for nearly 150 years, these institutions have trained the leadership of the Black community, graduating the nation's African American teachers, doctors, lawyers, scientists, and college faculty" (1). There are in total 107 HBCUs in the United States with about 300,000 students, the majority of whom are African Americans.[2]

Unfortunately, HBCUs do not always receive the exposure they deserve. Relegated to appendices in college guides under their own category, they have not always been duly represented in national academic circles. The case of one of the world's largest scholarly associations, the Modern Language Association (MLA), seems typical. As Jamal Watson eloquently puts it: "While there was never an official policy to exclude Blacks from participating in one of the world's largest academic organizations, they [the MLA] concede that for decades its membership was less than eager to embrace African Americans into their scholarly ranks" (Watson 2013). This divide between HBCUs and predominantly White institutions (PWIs) and associations has been acknowledged in recent studies (Prince and Ford 2016) and documented by the creation of the College Language Association (CLA), founded in 1937 to support HBCU educators and students of English and foreign languages. Although the relationship between the CLA and the MLA has improved in recent years,[3] there is still much work to be done to promote the visibility and good reputation of HBCUs around the United States, especially in connection to foreign languages. This promotion is needed more than ever given the rise in popularity of HBCUs. According to recent polls, enrollment in HBCUs is up 20 percent, which has led some observers to coin the term: "Black-College Renaissance" (Harris 2018).[4] Successfully competing with predominantly White, private liberal-arts colleges or large public-research institutes, HBCUs like Morgan State University (MSU) are attracting record numbers of students due to their affordability and academic excellence. MSU has marketed itself through prominent programs like its Music Department (which has been ranked among the top three in the nation) and its Engineering Department (considered one of the best in Maryland) and is a Carnegie-classified doctoral research institution, the largest historically Black college and university in Maryland, and one of the ten largest HBCUs in the nation.

Although only a handful of studies exist on foreign languages in HBCUs, it is safe to say that MSU is one of very few (if not the only) HBCUs in the United States to currently offer courses in Italian. Available data show that Italian-language classes experienced a steady decrease in HBCUs throughout the twentieth century. Italian was first offered in three institutions (in the 1930s), then in no institutions (during and after World War II), and finally in only one institution (from the 1950s to perhaps the 1980s).[5] The small presence of Italian at HBCUs is also confirmed by the fact that currently the CLA offers panels in various foreign languages (i.e., Spanish, Portuguese, German, and French) but not in Italian.[6] It is possible that the interest for this language study could be approached not so much in terms of a general new trend in HBCUs, but rather as serving a more personal need best applied to a specific case. This is confirmed by the interim chair of the World Languages and International Studies Department at Morgan State University, Helen Harrison, who stated, "We became aware we had a demand at Morgan for Italian. I teach French and German, and over the years, I've heard especially from music students in my German class that they really wanted to take Italian" ("Morgan State University in Baltimore . . . " 2019). According to Morgan State University Public Relations writer Eric Addison, "Morgan's renowned music programs include study and performance of many Italian-language songs. So, Dr. Harrison asked Dr. Eric Conway, director of the MSU Choir and chair of Morgan's Department of Fine and Performing Arts, for his thoughts about whether the new courses could be filled. Dr. Conway replied that his voice teachers would be delighted" (Morgan State University 2018). This shows how Italian courses were adopted to fulfill an immediate need, which is related to a particular institution in a way that differs from other HBCUs. For this reason, this new program is even more exceptional. The rarity of this circumstance sparked the interest of the university administration. On December 1, 2018, Morgan State University President David Wilson posted on his personal Facebook page the following statement, which supported the establishment of Italian for the first time in the university's 152-year history:

> While we currently offer numerous African and other language courses, we have never offered Italian—until now. These courses will greatly strengthen our voice program where Morgan is already known for producing some of the most impressive young opera singers today like Issachah Savage, Soloman Howard, Ben Taylor, Leah Hawkins, and the list goes on and on! Don't sleep on The National Treasure. #growingthefuture #leadingtheworld. (Wilson 2018)

On January 4, 2019, the news received national coverage through the *Journal of Blacks in Higher Education* ("Morgan State University in Baltimore ..."). In addition, on June 20, 2019, news about the new Italian program at MSU has been announced by the Honorable Angela Fucsia Nissoli Fitzgerald and it was released by the Agenzia Nazionale Stampa Associata (Associated Press National Agency) via various media outlets throughout the United States. Finally, on December 2019, this new program received a $1,000 donation from the Associated Italian American Charities of Maryland to support the study of Italian at Morgan State University.

Italian 101 started in the fall of 2018 and had an enrollment of about fourteen students, the majority of whom were music majors fulfilling the foreign-language requirement for the BA, while others were English or biology majors who chose Italian for personal academic growth. Italian 102 was also offered the next semester in the spring of 2019 with an enrollment of almost ten students.

Although currently small, the courses show some potential growth. A good portion of Italian 102 students continued with Italian 203, Intermediate Italian I in the Fall 2019, and are currently enrolled in Italian 204, intermediate Italian II, in Spring 2020. These courses may very well be the first time Italian has ever been offered in the second year in the history of HBCUs.[7] Having introduced this development and its history, I will now offer some reflections on the positive elements as well as the challenges I faced in introducing Italian to minority college students by emphasizing both the question of diversity and the reality of being "a minority" in Italian studies.

The principal positive component to teaching Italian to mainly minority students is the creation of new trends in the United States that could revive and enrich a field that is currently stationary and that often does not reflect the contemporary changes in place in our modern society. This is particularly relevant in a city like Baltimore where the African American population has been expanding and now makes up about 63 percent of the total population.[8] By creating new connections between African American communities and historic Italian American communities established in downtown Baltimore in Little Italy and Belair-Edison or in other neighborhoods in Baltimore County alongside the rest of the surrounding populace, we will foster what has already been done by other Italianists and activists to strengthen this multidisciplinary perspective beyond the classroom and in connection with American life and society.[9] I introduced these new courses to the African American student community with a flyer that illustrated my focus on Italian language and grammar as well as culture. In doing so I incorporated "cooking, music, and visual arts into the lessons," seeking to encourage student engagement in "a fun, supportive environment" (Morgan State University 2018).

The development of Italian courses geared toward minorities could foster new opportunities for the creation of innovative study abroad tailored for different majors (e.g., music, English, medicine, political science, engineering, or architecture), thus bringing about interracial dialogues among students and faculty coming from different socioeconomic and cultural backgrounds to meet students' individual needs and adding purpose to their foreign-language experience. As studies show, the majority of students do not always feel prepared to go abroad because they do not feel adequately fluent in the language studied, and they regard foreign-language study as not fundamentally related to their majors and minors (Moore 2005). These findings should encourage instructors to develop a more practical approach so as to connect the language studied to specific disciplines throughout an entire institution.

Another important component in the courses is mentorship outside the classroom. Through my involvement with the Baltimore and Baltimore County Public

Schools, I offer guidance to MSU graduate and undergraduate students interested in seeking a career in music education at primary and secondary schools, thus exploring ways through which they are able to utilize their acquired knowledge of Italian for their postgraduation experience. According to data provided by the Department of Education pertaining to elementary and secondary schools, bilingual education and foreign language are both high-demand fields (especially in schools that serve low-income students). In Maryland, Italian is currently offered in several middle and high schools, including Montgomery County, Prince George's County, and Howard County.[10] The Italian consulates in Washington, D.C., and Philadelphia have been involved in managing the growth of Italian study in Baltimore, Baltimore County, Montgomery County and Prince George's County, but this endeavor has faced several challenges, including the consistent shortage of Italian-language teachers. This critical need for teachers could engender interest in connecting the disciplines of education with the study of world languages in various HBCUs, particularly at large urban and public universities like MSU.

In some cases, primary education promotes more inclusive language programs that could be replicated at the university level. For example, both at the elementary and middle-school levels teachers are implementing full-immersion STEM (science, technology, engineering, and math) programs through which different foreign languages are used "as the main language in Mathematics, Science and Social Studies and Reading/Language Arts."[11] It seems that primary and secondary schools are implementing a more comprehensive approach to foreign language—learning that better integrates the foreign-language experience to the entire institution than ones found in many universities, which, as we have said above, are closing down language programs. All these possibilities could establish new openings for approaching Italian studies as a more inclusive and global discipline, thus bridging the gap between the academic and vocational environments.

These Italian courses at Morgan State do face obstacles. The main challenge in teaching Italian to a body comprised mainly of minority students is generally the lack of diversity within the primary material of instruction available on the market. Although in Italy there is an emerging population of young native Italian speakers who are not of Italian or European descent, they are scarcely represented in teaching materials. Textbooks of Italian language for English speakers are often geared toward a less diversified representation of Italians. For example, vocabulary sections rarely feature pictures, videos, or content related to Italians from different backgrounds, like Italians of African or Asian descent.[12] In most cases, the models of native Italian speakers in audiovisual material very rarely feature Italians of darker complexions, who are typically presented exclusively in connection to controversial topics pertaining to immigration, violence, or crime, a practice that discourages minorities. A richer diversification is present in other romance-language-based textbooks like French or Spanish, where in dialogues students can hear and see native French or Spanish speakers who belong to different ethnic backgrounds involved in a variety of everyday situations. For example, Spanish textbooks sometimes include native speakers from Equatorial Guinea describing their daily routines (see Blanco and Donley 2016). Minorities of African and Caribbean descent are also well represented in various French instructional materials, which devote ample space to francophone language and literatures (see Wong, Weber-Fève, and VanPatten 2017). It is interesting to note that other language textbooks, like Chinese, manage somehow to include a more inclusive vision of diverse speakers than most Italian textbooks do (see Kubler 2014). There is much work to be done to develop a wider vision and a more accurate portrayal of Italians, especially considering that the percentage of Italian native speakers who are from African descent is on the rise.[13]

A more inclusive representation of Afro-Italians could also serve to encourage African American students to embark more frequently on study abroad programs. In HBCUs the number of students who have ventured abroad has been gradually decreasing (Mullen 2013). One of the main reasons for this has to do with financial-aid issues (Mullen 2013), but students also feel disinclined to venture abroad because of documented cases of prejudice and discrimination. One recent source of this information, and one that had a great impact on educators and students, is an article written by Nicole Phillip (2018) for the *New York Times* titled "My Very Personal Taste of Racism Abroad" in which she describes her negative experience as an African American woman in a study abroad program in Italy. In addition to reports like these, other sources can be useful to learn about important opportunities for African Americans currently traveling and living in Italy (Martin 2013). There are several YouTube blogs made by African Americans (some of which have several million views) in Italy that are excellent resources for students to learn about the potential of studying, living, and working in Italy.[14] All these sources provide a comprehensive approach to traveling abroad and could be integrated into the academic curriculum for students interested in seeking more accurate information about experiences and opportunities in study abroad programs in Italy or elsewhere.

The introduction of new Italian-language classes offers both hope and room for reflections. It is important to keep in mind that even though Italian-language classes have experienced a steep decline in enrollment, Italian is still among the most-studied foreign languages in the United States. And the decline is not reflected on a global scale, because Italian is still enormously popular, ranked number four among the world's most-studied languages (Agencia Italia 2016). Despite all this, Italian studies in universities nationwide continues to struggle. The current generation of Italianists must promote change. This change could involve the establishment of new language courses tailored for different institutions and individual minority students, more direct mentorship between students and teachers in a supportive environment in the classroom, more basic training to prepare minorities for study abroad experiences, and more direct and practical connections to draw between the students' academic interests and the need of local and international communities.[15]

By building a more solid connection between the students' interest in foreign language and viable and varied career paths, we could inject this much-needed change. The question posed by Deborah Parker in relation to the future of Italian studies remains relevant: "Can we enact a bold and more inclusive vision for its future?" I see change coming, but we cannot afford any longer to simply observe the shrinking enrollment numbers without ourselves becoming agents and active participants for a new beginning. In the case of Morgan State University, this initiative flows parallel to and is a part of the historic Black college renaissance that is shaping the future of Baltimore and our nation right in front of our eyes.

ACKNOWLEDGMENT

I would like to thank Anthony Tamburri and the John D. Calandra Italian American Institute for putting together this very lively and engaging symposium. I am particularly grateful to Deborah Parker, who suggested I take part in this important event. This article is dedicated to my mentor, Raymond Fleming, who has inspired and encouraged me to pursue my interest in Dante and Italian studies in the United States. He had a crucial impact on my decision to enter into this field. Fleming is one of the first African American scholars to graduate at Harvard with a PhD in comparative literature and a concentration in Italian studies.

Notes

1. See, for example, Goucher College, which has cut several majors, among them the Italian, Russian, and German language programs (Tkacik 2018); and see also the similar curriculum reduction implemented at McDaniel College, where French, German, and music will no longer be offered as majors for future students (Jaschik 2019).

2. According to recent governmental data from 2017, 76 percent of students enrolled at HBCUs are African Americans, while "non-Black students made up 24 percent of enrollment at HBCUs, compared with 15 percent in 1976," cited from https://nces.ed.gov/fastfacts/display.asp?id=667. The current number of HBCUs is cited from http://www.thehundred-seven.org/hbculist.html.
3. For more about the relation between these entities, see the CLA website from a shared event in 2018, https://www.clascholars.org/cla-at-mla-in-nyc-january-5-2018.
4. A more recent article on this subject was written by Alina Tugend (2019).
5. Napoleon Rivers (1933, 491) documents that in 1933 Italian was offered at three institutions. Virginia Simmons Nyabongo (1946, 155) shows that only French, Spanish, and German were offered in all major HBCUs right after World War II. This might be related to historical and political circumstances, as Italy declared war on the United States in 1941, and Italians in the United States were considered enemy aliens. K.C. Miller (1954, 42) reports that by 1954 "Italian was offered in only the largest of the institutions," which at the time was likely Howard University, as also confirmed by Vernessa White-Jackson, the chair of the Department of World Languages and Cultures at Howard University, who reported to me (via an email) that "Howard University definitely offered Italian courses in the 1970s and perhaps into the next decade." According to the list of top five HBCU World Languages Programs in the United States, provided by the Penn Center for Minority Serving Institutions at the University of Pennsylvania, no Italian program is included in the list of offered courses in 2016; see https://msilineup.com/2016/10/31/5-hbcus-for-world-language-lovers/.
6. To see more about this, visit the CLA website https://www.clascholars.org/convention/convention-archives.
7. This might be the case, considering that when Italian was most frequently taught in HBCUs during the 1930s, Rivers (1933, 491) reported that no HBCUs "offered two years of Italian."
8. For more on this, see https://www.census.gov/quickfacts/fact/table/baltimorecitymarylandcounty/AGE295217.
9. See, for example, Dennis Looney's (2011) *Freedom Readers,* John Gennari's (2017) *Flavor and Soul*, Samuel F. S. Pardini's (2017) *In the Name of the Mother*, as well as recent works by the Italian filmmaker Fred Kuwornu, i.e., *Inside Buffalo* (2010) *Blaxploitalian* (2016), and the *Blaq Italiano* project (2019–2020). Most recently it is important to mention the pioneering work by Bellamy Okot and Grazia Sukubo, who created in 2015 the first digital platform on Afro-Italians, that is, the blog http://www.afroitaliansouls.it/.
10. For the Italian program in Montgomery County, see https://montgomeryschoolsmd.org/curriculum/languages/italian/. For the Italian program in the World Languages Program in Prince George's County, see https://www.pgcps.org/worldlanguages/index.aspx?id=20530. As reported by Joe Burris (2013), Italian is particularly popular in Howard County, where "Italian is taught at Wilde Lake, Marriotts Ridge, Hammond and Reservoir high schools. And though the offerings pale in comparison to those in Spanish and French—which are offered in all county high schools and middle schools—they make Howard a rarity among local schools when it comes to teaching Italian."
11. This system is in effect in many schools in Prince George's County and also includes a STEM program. In some cases the full immersion is implemented throughout the entire curriculum, as is the case for the Chinese-language program in Prince George's County, where STEM and math are taught 100 percent in Chinese. For more on this, see https://www.pgcps.org/immersionprograms/.
12. See, for example, the textbook that I am currently utilizing for my Italian 101 and 102 classes at MSU; that is, Cozzarelli (2016) or other recent textbooks like Melucci and Tognozzi (2015).
13. Sources show that it could make up about 14 percent of the total Italian population; see http://www.afroitalian.it/identikit_di_un_afroitalian/comunit_nera_in_italia:_limportanza_di_essere_rappresentati/. Governmental data show that almost 1 million Afro-Italians are now living in Italy; see http://noi-italia.istat.it/.
14. One of the most viewed blogs is the one by Tia Taylor, whose YouTube Channel currently has about 306,000 subscribers and posts several videos about the African American experience in Italy that have several million views. See https://www.youtube.com/channel/UCOXyfKNF2mAIV-sYMASNSyg.
15. On June 20, 2019, news about the new Italian program at MSU was announced in Rome at the Italian Parliament by the honorable Angela Fucsia Nissoli Fitzgerald in the chamber of deputies.

Works Cited

Agencia Italia (AGI). 2016. "Tutti pazzi per l'italiano, è quarta lingua più studiata." October 18. https://www.agi.it/cultura/tutti_pazzi_per_litaliano_quarta_lingua_pi_studiata-1174983/news/2016-10-18/ (accessed May 5, 2019).

Blanco, José A., and Philip Redwine Donley. 2016. *Vistas: Introducción a la Lengua Española*, 5th ed. Boston: Vista Higher Learning.

Burris, Joe. 2013. "Italian language instruction taking hold in Howard County schools." *The Baltimore Sun*. https://www.baltimoresun.com/news/maryland/howard/bs-xpm-2013-02-28-bs-md-ho-italian-teachers-20130228-story.html (accessed April 29, 2019).

Cozzarelli, Julia M. 2016. *Sentieri: Attraverso L'Italia contemporanea*, Boston: Vista Higher Learning.

Flaherty, Colleen. 2018. "MLA Data on Enrollments Show Foreign Language Study Is on the Decline." *Inside Higher Ed*. https://www.insidehighered.com/news/2018/03/19/mla-data-enrollments-show-foreign-language-study-decline (accessed April 29, 2019).

Gasman, M., and Christopher L. Tudico, eds. 2016. *Black Colleges and Universities: Triumphs, Troubles, and Taboos*. New York: Palgrave Macmillan.

Gennari, John. 2017. *Flavor and Soul: Italian America at Its African American Edge*. Chicago: University of Chicago Press.

Harris, Adam. 2018."Black-College Renaissance Students Are Once Again Flocking to HBCUs." *The Chronicle of Higher Education*. https://www.chronicle.com/article/Why-Many-Black-Colleges-Are/242671 (accessed April 28, 2019).

Jaschik, Scott. 2019."McDaniel College Eliminates 5 Majors and 3 Minors." *Inside Higher Ed*. https://www.insidehighered.com/quicktakes/2019/02/25/mcdaniel-college-eliminates-5-majors-and-3-minors (accessed April 28, 2019).

Kubler, Kornelius C. 2014. *Basic Spoken Chinese: An Introduction to Speaking and Listening for Beginners*. North Clarendon, VT: Tuttle Publishing.

Looney, Dennis. 2011. *Freedom Readers: The African American Reception of Dante Alighieri and the Divine Comedy*. Notre Dame, IN: University of Notre Dame Press.

Looney, Dennis, and Natalia Lusin. 2018. "Enrollments in Languages Other Than English in United States Institutions of Higher Education, Summer 2016 and Fall 2016: Preliminary Report." Modern Language Association. https://www.mla.org/content/download/83540/2197676/2016-Enrollments-Short-Report.pdf (accessed April 29, 2019).

Martin, Joanna Brett. 2013. *Involuntary Racism: Reflections of an African-American Woman in Italy*. CreateSpace Independent Publishing Platform.

Melucci, Donatella, and Elissa Tognozzi. 2015. *Piazza: Luogo di incontri*. Stamford, CT: Cengage Learning.

Miller, K. C. 1954. "*Modern* Foreign Languages in Negro Colleges." *Journal of Negro Education* 23(1): 40–50.

Moore, Zena. 2005. "African-American Students' Opinions about Foreign Language Study: An Exploratory Study of Low Enrollments at the College Level." *Foreign Language Annals* 38(2): 191–200.

Morgan State University. 2018, "New Italian Courses Set Morgan Apart," November 30. https://news.morgan.edu/new-italian-courses-set-morgan-apart/ (accessed April 27, 2019).

"Morgan State University in Baltimore Now Offering Courses in Italian Language." 2019. *Journal of Blacks in Higher Education*, January 4. https://www.jbhe.com/2019/01/morgan-state-university-in-baltimore-now-offering-courses-in-italian-language/ (accessed on April 27, 2019).

Mullen, Sarah. 2013. "Study Abroad at HBCUs: Challenges, Trend, and Best Practices." In *Opportunities and Challenges at Historically Black Colleges and Universities*, edited by Marybeth Gasman and Felicia Commodore. New York: Palgrave Macmillan.

Newkirk, R. Vann, ed. 2012. "The Origin and Development of the HBCU." *New Life for Historically Black Colleges and Universities: A 21st Century Perspective*. Jefferson, NC: McFarland & Co., 13–36.

Nyabongo, Virginia Simmons. 1946. "Achievement in Modern Foreign Language in Negro Colleges of America." *Journal of Negro Education* 15(2): 153–160.

Pardini, Samuel F. S. 2017. *In the Name of the Mother: Italian Americans, African Americans, and Modernity from Booker T. Washington to Bruce Springsteen*. Hanover, NH: Dartmouth College Press.

Parker, Deborah. 2018. "Race in Foreign Languages." *Inside Higher Ed*. https://www.insidehighered.com/views/2018/06/21/paucity-asians-and-other-minorities-teaching-and-studying-italian-and-other-foreign (accessed April 29, 2019).

Phillip, Nicole. 2018. "My Very Personal Taste of Racism Abroad." https://www.nytimes.com/2018/10/23/travel/racism-travel-italy-study-abroad.html (accessed April 29, 2019).

Prince, Charles B. W. and Rochelle L. Ford, eds. 2016. *Administrative Challenges and Organizational Leadership in Historically Black Colleges and Universities*: Hershey: IGI Global, 2016.

Rivers, W. Napoleon. 1933. "A Study of Modern Foreign Languages in Thirty Negro Colleges." *The Journal of Negro Education* 2(4): 487–493.

Tugend, Alina. 2019. Seeking a Haven in H.B.C.U.s and Single-Sex Colleges." The New York Times. https://www.nytimes.com/2019/02/21/education/learning/hbcu-womens-colleges-haven.html (accessed April 30, 2019).

Tkacik, Christina. 2018. "Maryland's Goucher College eliminating several majors, including math." https://www.baltimoresun.com/news/maryland/education/higher-ed/bs-md-goucher-majors-eliminated-20180815-story.html (accessed April 29, 2019).

Watson, Jamal. 2013. "Fueled by Rejection, Black Scholars Built College Language Association to Last." https://diverseeducation.com/article/61449/ (accessed July 4, 2019).

Wilson, David. 2018. Facebook post, December 1. https://www.facebook.com/david.wilson.14268/posts/2068037556587566 (accessed May 3, 2019).

Wong, Wynne. 2017. Stacey Weber-Fève, and Bill VanPatten. *Liaisons: An Introduction to French*, 2nd ed., Boston, MA: Cengage Learning.

AIDS in the Italian and Italian American Canon: Death as a Metaphor for a Profession in Peril

RYAN CALABRETTA-SAJDER

According to the most recent Modern Language Association (MLA) "Enrollments in Languages Other than English in United States Institutions of Higher Education, Summer 2016 and Fall 2016: Final Report," Italian enrollments have declined 20.1 percent from fall 2013 to fall 2016 (Looney and Lusin 2019, 4). As a surprise to many, Dennis Looney and Natalia Lusin point out that the MLA's 2013 report should have been a warning sign to Italianists that issues had been persisting. As evidenced from the article, Italianists did not heed the 2013 alarm. Although the report is exhaustive in nature, it focuses primarily on data and numbers, even though a bit of reflection is intermingled throughout. As part of the reflective piece, the authors targeted programs that demonstrated successful growth in certain languages to share fruitful ideas and generate discussion across languages, an activity that rarely, if ever, occurs and should be done frequently so that common goals can be projected and launched together. From their general research, those programs that have been illustrating growth have been unique from a curricular standpoint. What has not been properly addressed to date, it seems, is a thorough study of the concept of diversity within Italian studies, both in faculty and curricula, for which this publication aims to address and offer various possible solutions. Through considering less commonly taught texts and themes that are often overlooked in Italian studies curricula, this essay will introduce new ideas that could be adopted to rejuvenate Italian but also modeled for other modern language programs.

Since the first awards of the Nobel Prize in 1901, fifty-one women have received this momentous recognition, Marie Curie being the first, the only female to date to win it twice (for physics in 1903 and for chemistry in 1911), and the only person to be awarded a Nobel in two different sciences. Of the fifty-one Nobel Prizes awarded to women, fourteen have gone to women for literature, the second of these being Italy's Grazia Deledda in 1926—who is noted among the likes of Toni Morrison, Doris Lessing, and Nelly Sachs, to underscore a few international literary names. Significantly before Deledda enters the international stage, however, Italy had already produced talented modern female authors including Maria Messina (1887–1944) and Sibilla Aleramo (pseudonym of Rina Raccio, 1876–1960).[1]

Sibilla Aleramo completed her semiautobiographical novel *Una donna* as early as 1901, but scholars claim that she contemplated the ending of the novel for a few years, unsure if she should use her autobiography to end the story.[2] In 1906, Aleramo published the first feminist awakening novel in Italy, sharing some but not all aspects of her autobiography; in the end she leaves her abusive husband, and consequently her son, behind.[3] Noted as one of the earliest "feminist awakenings" in Western literature, along with Henrik Ibsen's *A Doll's House* (1879), which is cited within the novel, and Kate Chopin's *The Awakening* (1899), *Una donna* is considered a masterpiece of Italian literature; for the feminist canon, it is an essential milestone, yet it is almost unknown to the anglophone world. Within our globalized world, the fact that this work remains mostly unknown seems unfair. An English translation, by Mary Lansdale, titled *A Woman at Bay*, dates back to 1908, only two years after the original. Therefore, an edition for the anglophone world had been available for an extensive period. It was the only English translation available until the 1979 version by Rosalind Delmar published by Virago. However, 1950 marked a new edition of the novel in Italian, published in the Universale Economica series. According to Valerio Ferme, the discovery of the text by editor Feltrinelli and its republication reintroduced the work to a growing culture of Italian feminists and allowed the novel to experience a certain rebirth (for more on this see Ferme 1999). Ironically, the work as a whole has not been given just attention. The last milestone afforded the English translation occurred in 1980 when Richard Drake wrote an introduction to Delmar's translation, and it was published by the University of California Press.

Una donna, however, is not Aleramo's only novel. In fact, she has written a few, and even more noteworthy for the discourse on diversity is her *Il passaggio/The Crossing* in 1919, which recounts her one-year affair with Cordula "Lina" Poletti, whom she originally met at a women's congress. Through this later publication, Aleramo overtly challenges the sexual norm in contemporary society by recounting her lesbian affair. In the 1920s, Aleramo was taking a great risk concerning her personal and professional life. One hundred years later, almost no attention has been afforded *Il passaggio* (for more on this see Luciano 1996). Aleramo's novels, along with her autobiography, highlight a critical aspect of sexuality studies; she changes the manner in which sexuality is understood and appreciated. She demonstrates early on that sexuality is always in flux and not a fixed concept; this realization at the beginning of the twentieth century was not commonplace. This work therefore represents strides in understanding sexual behavior and orientation roughly thirty years prior to Alfred Kinsey's famous *Sexual Behavior in the Human Male* (1948). When considering the avant-garde nature of the work from a sexuality standpoint, it is mind-boggling how this work has not been afforded more serious attention, even if it may not have the stature that *Una donna* has assumed over the years.

During my master's degree coursework, I first learned about Aleramo's *Una donna* by chance in a course on Italian novels. The class was taught as a traditional, chronological "review" of the canon in which we studied only male authors; not one female writer was ever even mentioned throughout the semester except when I gave my final presentation on *Una donna*. Apart from my discussion, there were no other female authors addressed in my entire master's program. During my examination, there was not a single question related to female writing or even the representation of women within the field, which as we know is not equivalent but may be considered a half-step in the right direction.

Why is this personal experience worth mentioning? First, it is imperative to note that this story is not an isolated event at that university, nor is it isolated within Italian studies. I also use this incident as the premise to open a much larger discourse on the role of the canon in the future of our field. In his *No Future: Queer Theory and the Death Drive*, Lee Edelman states:

> Fuck the social order and the Child in whose name we're collectively terrorized; fuck Annie; fuck the waif from *Les Mis*; fuck the poor, innocent kid on the Net; fuck Laws both with capital ls and with small; fuck the whole network of Symbolic relations and the future that serves as its prop. (Edelman 2004, 29)

Edelman's unique citation draws attention, albeit in a bit of a grotesque manner, to the importance of the future and what we are collectively doing, or not, in the present, to preserve it for future generations. Edelman, whose theoretical approach calls to mind that of Leo Bersani, points out the differences between the heterosexual and what is now considered the queer community. Both theorists have argued and demonstrated the importance of the various and varied needs of the queer community and the dire necessity to fight for its own needs, culture, and language. This radical approach suggested by Bersani and Edelman highlights how diversity studies are critical in understanding cultures and societies. As elaborated by Dennis Looney, director of programs at the Association of

Departments of Foreign Languages of the MLA, during the Diversity in Italian Studies conference hosted by the John D. Calandra Italian American Institute, enrollment in Italian studies is declining. Italian studies remains a rather traditional field into which many educators find it difficult, or maybe useless, to incorporate new theoretical and/or pedagogical approaches.

The theoretical foundation for Edelman's work forces the reader to reconsider the role of the Other in society. His wild metaphor of "killing off the child" is just that, a metaphor, which he adopts for various readings. In this moving work, he fights to disrupt all efforts to produce a self-sufficient wholeness. Therefore, Edelman calls us to disrupt the past, break the cycle; only then can we queer the future. Before queering the future, however, it is critical to recall the past.

An illustrative example: Three significant female scholars graduated from a noted Ivy League university together. Their adviser suggested that they write on the *tre corone* (three crowns) for their dissertation because being women in Italian studies afforded more difficulty regarding perspective careers, and strong knowledge of the canon would be the best way to combat that mentality. All three followed their beloved professor's advice, at least to a certain extent: One focused on Petrarca, another on Boccaccio, and the last, although she did not write further on Dante (she had previously published on the *Vita Nuova*) instead wrote her dissertation on a contemporary poet. Although this professor's advice sounds harsh, in the end it was prudent and fruitful because all three women went on to have robust and important careers, and all eventually studied exactly what they wanted. Two of the three became noted scholars of feminism and gender studies. All three of these strong female scholars left the medieval world to study modern and contemporary Italy, and one probably no longer considers herself an Italianist at all, similar to Teresa De Lauretis, who became a noteworthy name in the realm of critical theory at large, another aspect in which Italian studies is still lacking.

Through her early work, De Lauretis attempted to queer the field, long before she coined the term in academia (1991), even though at that time no one else was willing to accept it. In her early work, *Alice Doesn't: Feminism, Semiotics, Cinema* (1984), De Lauretis analyzes various Italian texts, most important of which are Italo Calvino's *Invisible Cities*, Umberto Eco's *Theory of Semiotics*, Pier Paolo Pasolini's *Salò, or the 120 Days of Sodom* and *A Cinema of Poetry*, Federico Fellini's *Satyricon*, and Liliana Cavani's *The Night Porter*. In her subsequent manuscript, *Technologies of Gender: Essays on Theory, Film, and Fiction* (1987), the queer-theory scholar spent much time discussing Italian texts including Eco's *The Name of the Rose* and Calvino's *If on a Winter's Night a Traveler*.

These two volumes demonstrate De Lauretis's dedication to expanding the scope of Italian studies from a theoretical standpoint. These works incorporate numerous feminist and semiotic approaches to cinema and the narrative and introduced new theoretical models, particularly for film studies at large. By the time she wrote *The Practice of Love: Lesbian Sexuality and Perverse Desire* (1992), her interests in Italian studies had almost completely fizzled; there is only the briefest mention in this book of Eco, her mentor, along with extremely short citations of two Italian films: Pasolini's *Oedipus Rex* (1964) and Lina Wertmüeller's *Sotto . . . sotto* (1984). In this regard, it can be argued that she attempted to destroy the child, as Edelman has said, yet no one else supported her drastic reexamination of Italian studies; consequently, she left and established herself in gender studies.

The beauty of De Lauretis's entire opus however, at least from a critical standpoint, is that she believed, or at the very least her writings demonstrate, that critical theory, like sexuality itself, is always in flux. De Lauretis tried to push Italian studies ahead of the curve, but the field was not quite ready yet, possibly because it was not prepared to accept cultural studies as a whole. In fact, she organized the first ever queer-theory conference in 1990, published the introduction to a special volume of *Differences* in 1991—"Queer Theory: Lesbian and Gay Sexualities. An Introduction"—and within a few years after its publication, she became disappointed at the capitalist turn queer theory had taken, arguing that it had become too commercial, saying, "This commercially motivated choice reflects the banality and shallow trendiness that has characterized the mobilization of queer in North American academic studies and so-called alternative media" (De Lauretis 1991, 258). De Lauretis quickly became disillusioned by the importance of her work because it evolved in a manner that lost value; her goal was to combine forces, which in the end worked against her. She has argued,

> This theory, I hoped, would remove the hyphens from "lesbian-and-gay," restoring specificities, i.e. exploring "the respective and/or common grounding of current discourses and practices of homosexualities in relation to gender and to race, with their attendant differences of class or ethnic culture, generational, geographical, and socio-political location," and thus restore the possibility of effective alliance across differences instead of uneasy cohabitation under a label. (1991, 257)

The notion of the hyphen proves noteworthy here as well. De Lauretis's goal by removing the hyphen was to bring the field together, to focus on the commonalities of the LGBTQIAA+ experience. Anthony Julian Tamburri adopts an analogous discourse to argue for a reevaluation of the concept of Italian American by removing the hyphen and replacing it with the backslash. Both theorists are fighting to emphasize the similarities of the shared community rather than the differences. Unifying fields instead of separating them encourages growth and camaraderie, which serves a higher end goal.

Even though De Lauretis attempted to theorize the field, philology is still the dominant critical lens most Italian studies scholars adopt. Moreover, huge periods of Italian studies and numerous authors are consciously being ignored by students and scholars alike. Many female authors have been overlooked or pushed aside, considered not a worthy read often due to their lack of formal training, which was only provided to men of the day.[4] If research exists on these authors, it often does not represent the true sense of the text; scholars are not applying the most appropriate critical theories to these works. Many are just as good as their male counterparts, others may not be, but this does not taint the importance of the text, particularly from a sociohistorical, sociopolitical, or socioeconomic perspective. As scholars, but even more importantly, as teachers, we need to incorporate these works into the classroom and offer them the attention they deserve. More often than not, these are the texts that students can more easily relate with because the Otherness found within these works more appropriately reflects their own personal and professional experiences; these stories become real for our students. It is equally critical to examine issues of segregation, integration, diversity, and inclusion because through studying these themes, students obtain a more rounded, interdisciplinary grounding in the subject.

The 1990s opened the doors to a richer, more well-thought-out approach to analyzing female literature. The academy also began to welcome more women with PhDs into the field, which changed the discussions of Italian studies greatly. Unfortunately, these discourses almost solely were undertaken by female scholars. Rarely do we encounter heterosexual male scholars plunging into the study of women, even today.[5] Even though the 1990s brought a newfound respect for female authors and the importance of a diverse authorship, these interests are not represented in that generation's PhD students. A grand concern still plagued a large portion of Italian studies regarding the then-referenced "women's studies" and the ability to publish and find a job.

Within the last fifteen to twenty years, the field has begun to open up, and much more attention has been afforded female voices, even if huge blocks of space are still rather untouched, particularly Italian female poets and Italian women directors, which (ironically within the Italian tradition) dates back to Elvira Notari from Salerno, Italy, who made more than sixty feature films and about a hundred shorts and documentaries. Notari truly changed the manner in which film was made and produced in Italy; ironically, only one major project has been dedicated to her life's work, Giuliana Bruno's *Streetwalking on a Ruined Map: Cultural Theory and the City Film of Elvira Notari* (1992). So, if we cannot grasp one of the most important figures of Italian cinema, how can we admit and invite diversity into our classrooms?

Beyond the scope of pedagogical training, I examined the MA and doctoral reading lists of the graduate institutions in North America that offer either a terminal PhD or else an MA and PhD combined program.[6] The purpose of this research is to explore the required texts and authors for preparation to pass the PhD examination in Italian. My focus was female and LGBTQIAA+ authors; I paid particular attention to Aleramo's *Una donna* and the works of Pier Vittorio Tondelli. The results were not all that surprising.

This study considered twenty-nine programs. Before reviewing the actual results, it is important to note that of the twenty-nine universities that I explored, seven had no information on their websites regarding the PhD examination process. Of the twenty-one schools that remained, ten programs no longer require the traditional exam given from a reading list; instead, students create a primary and secondary list with their adviser and are examined solely on texts selected together. One school has a two-part exam; the first half is based on a list of texts representative of the student's main research field, and a secondary exam is comprised of works particularly important to the student's primary research interests/the focus of the dissertation. Of the eleven remaining schools, eight, which is roughly 73 percent, require Sibilla Aleramo's *Una donna* for the comprehensive exam, and one made it an optional text for the examination. That being said, it is logical to say that *Una donna* has finally found its place in the canon. However, is it an accomplishment to just have it added to a reading list? How many professors actually teach the text in a graduate seminar? Besides teaching diverse texts in canonical courses and offering seminars focusing on the representation of and by women, what else can be done to diversify the curriculum?[7]

When we move the study further to examine the coverage of LGBTQIAA+ texts or even authors, the situation becomes dismal. I was particularly interested in the role of Pier Vittorio Tondelli's *Camere separate* but was able to make various observations while studying these reading lists. *Camere separate* appeared on just three reading lists, a fourth university required his *Altri Libertini*, which is still better than excluding him completely, and another institution required *Un weekend postmoderno*. Thus, out of twenty-one schools with a PhD reading list, only five had a work from Tondelli on the list, roughly 45 percent, 27 percent requiring *Camere separate*.

Moving beyond Tondelli, Aldo Palazzeschi, another noteworthy author who was homosexual, even though not necessarily considered a queer writer by most critics, was a name that appeared on a few reading lists. Most programs required, more often than not, *Il codice di Perelà*, but one had *Sorelle Materasse*, and even his poetry was mandatory for two schools. Although he was a homosexual author (noted in both his biography but also clearly seen in his texts, particularly *:riflessi* and *Il codice di Perelà*, but also his poetry) noted literary critic Gino Tellini (2011) prefers to call him a "omosessuale celebate" ("Ri-leggere Aldo Palazzeschi" [2011]). Palazzeschi has been studied at length, and in fact numerous conferences have been organized on the beloved author over the years. Due to the former director of Palazzeschi's archive (which was donated to the University of Florence), the collection does not seem to serve the general populace. In fact, while I was a Fulbright Scholar in Italy in the spring of 2017, I had plans to visit the archive, but when I arrived in Florence, I was surprised to learn that I would not be granted access and that "everything was online and I should access whatever I needed there."

I share this anecdote for a few reasons. In Italian studies, scholars have continuously modeled what I, and some of my positive mentors, have called, "bad behavior," which very often is passed from professor to student. One of these "bad behaviors" is the concept that scholars "own" authors, periods, and so forth, and that junior colleagues must beg at the "Godfather's" table to be permitted to study a particular writer. This exact situation revolving around Palazzeschi has occurred to numerous scholars over the years, and the prejudice crosses the gender and sexuality lines. For instance, I was blocked from studying queer theory in a seminar on critical theory with the same professor; had I been allowed to proceed, I am confident I would have studied in greater depth Palazzeschi as a homosexual author, a fact that is already well-established.[8] I would have worked to introduce newfound approaches to his bibliography and literary works. What some traditional-thinking professors seem unable to grasp is that by allowing someone to develop further their intellectual inquiry of such a rich author who struggled at length with his sexual identity, I could have very well succeeded in opening a unique approach to Palazzeschi, which could then in turn be adapted to other homosexual authors. Nonetheless, Italian studies prefers to run on power and fear rather than dialogue, collaboration, and forward thinking.

This distrust of cultural criticism within the large scope of Italian and Italian American studies is detrimental to the growth and cultivation of the field on the international stage. Both Italian and Italian American studies have a lot to offer cultural studies, yet too many of our senior scholars are blocked in the mindset of philology, which although important is a method that has already been perfected. The field needs to be liberated from the past and allowed to consider the wealth that it already has but by encouraging new creative and scholarly voices. The curriculum must shift as Italian-language study has dipped so drastically, and it was our only decrease in numbers historically (Looney and Lusin 2016).

In addition to women writers, I would like to continue to draw attention to LGBTQIAA+ authors worthy of serious consideration. Italian American studies boasts the first AIDS novel in the U.S. canon. Although it was not the actual first novel to ever discuss AIDS, it has been granted the recognition. Robert Ferro, an Italian American who was part of the famous Violet Quill gay writing group in New York City penned five novels, the last of which, *Second Son*, was published in 1988 only months before Ferro's death from AIDS complications. The Violet Quill had two Italian American writers, Ferro and Felice Picano,[9] and met on eight occasions from March 31, 1980, until March 3, 1981, most meetings being hosted at the Ferro-Grumley apartment.[10] Robert Ferro was born into an upper-middle-class Italian American family from Cranford, New Jersey, on October 21, 1941. He graduated with a BA in English from Rutgers University in 1963 and went on to complete an MFA from the prestigious University of Iowa writing program, where he studied under Chilean author and activist José Donoso. While studying at the University of Iowa, he met his lifelong partner and fellow Quill author, Michael Grumley, who also died of AIDS complications within two months of Ferro's death.

Second Son recounts the story of a man, Mark Vallerian, attempting to grieve his mother's recent death at the family's beach house, the same house in which she died, where Mark cared for her, and where he currently lives. Similar to his mother, Mark too is suffering from an incurable illness that is unnamed and only referred to as *It* throughout the text and that is understood to be AIDS. The Vallerian family, particularly Mark's father, wants to sell the summer home due to economic straits his company is facing. Thanks to Mark's friend, who is introduced through an epistolary exchange throughout the novel, Mark is set up with Bill Mackey, who is also infected with It, and the two deal with the frustrations associated with living with AIDS in the late 1980s. In the end, Mark and Bill are faced with a choice: Try an experimental drug to help them face their illness or go to the planet Splendora where there is a colony of folks infected with It. Although the novel sounds rather bleak, when published it was described and reviewed as a novel of hope. In addition to confronting the topic of AIDS directly, the novel addresses themes of death, mourning, survival, and family relations. In the end, Mark and Bill attempt to have exactly what all the other characters have, a healthy loving relationship. Robert Ferro has stated, "The major point I had in writing this book is often missed. And that's that hope *has* to be injected into this situation, hope has to be injected into the epidemic" (Hoctel 1988, 17). Hope was an aspect left out in AIDS literature during the period, and it is what attracted so much attention to Ferro's work, particularly in the late 1980s. In fact, Ferro claims the significance of *Second Son* is "that belief in the healing power of love is a proper response to catastrophe, and that there can be no survival without hope and an underlying belief in survival" (Reed 1988, 45).

Similarly, in *Italianistica* we have Pier Vittorio Tondelli's *Camere separate* (1989), which to a certain extent discusses a similar story to that of *Second Son*. Leo and Thomas are a homosexual couple. Thomas is depressed and dealing with issues of solitude. He subsequently falls in love with a woman, even though he remains in love with Leo. Thomas unexpectedly dies from complications of an incurable illness, which many read to be AIDS. At the end of the novel, Leo continues to search for his own happiness, and soon the reader learns that he too is infected with an incurable disease. The sexual orientation of the characters in the novel is noteworthy both directly and indirectly from the discourse of sexuality studies. The triangular relationship between Leo, Thomas, and Thomas's girlfriend recalls Rene Girard's triangular conception of love. Once Thomas introduces a third person into the relationship, many critics have argued that Leo becomes jealous (for more on this see Capirossi 2017). Through adding a third inhabitant to the "separate bedrooms" of the book's title a power dynamic is broken, causing the two male protagonists to reconsider gender identity, sexual orientation, and in the end the conceptualization of love.

Unlike *Second Son* and Robert Ferro, much has been written on Pier Vittorio Tondelli and on *Camere separate* in particular. Scholars have examined its place in the evolution of the Italian narrative, studied his style in relationship to that of Umberto Eco, and considered it a post-modern work. Critics have also examined it as a gay text, and some interesting and eye-opening interpretations concerning its worth as a LGBTQIAA+ text have been published (Bolongaro 2018, 11–34). Writings like that of Arianna Capirossi (2017) are imperative works on Tondelli and even shape the way he could/should be read through contemporary queer theory, although many of the theoretical modes adapted in pieces like it are now dated. Furthermore, the most recent Tondelli scholarship does not advance the discourse or adopt current theoretical models appropriate for a strong queer reading; rather, it returns to older, less nuanced critical thinking (see Cestaro 2008, Ferme 2007, Pispisa 2013, Bolongaro 2007a, b, Burns 2000). Academically, it is compelling to recognize all the critical work Tondelli's writings have drawn and continue to draw; however, it would be even more significant if new, more adequate theoretical approaches were utilized in the analysis.

Robert Ferro died of AIDS complications in 1988, and Tondelli died in 1991; they are considered contemporaries and although they come from diverse societies, they offer similar perspectives. It is also noteworthy that Robert Ferro spent significant time in Italy with his partner.[11] He often stayed in Rome's Trastevere neighborhood and was familiar with Italian culture. In fact, in his earlier novels, the protagonist always embarks on his gay *Bildungsroman* after/during an Italian experience. *Second Son* functions a bit differently. It is clear from the beginning of that novel that Mark is diagnosed with It and is currently single. He travels to Rome for work as an interior designer. While in Rome, Mark meets Bill, and they start a serious relationship, first in Rome and then in Venice. For Mark, this relationship signifies new beginnings, as he had not been intimate with a man since being diagnosed with It. The cultural allure and romantic atmosphere of idyllic places like Venice may have its influence on the couple, but I would argue that being in a new physical space allows Mark to reassess his current life and try new experiences. Being with Bill in Italy leads to a committed relationship; upon returning to the United States, Bill moves into the beach house with Mark, and they turn the beach house into their home.

Both of these authors have changed the way AIDS is examined in the literary world, and both authors and texts are rarely studied; Ferro has almost been completely removed from the map. In fact, I have never formally studied him in any class. I learned about his importance through a senior scholar who knew I was interested in gender studies and queer theory. Thanks to this professor, I was able to enter this world and have even researched Ferro's archives. Teaching texts like these is not easy as the new generation of students is completely removed from the AIDS epidemic, how it quickly became so destructive, and why people were so afraid. Yet these novels fill a sociohistorical gap that today's generation needs in order to fully grasp how and why the LGBTQIAA+ looks and acts the way it does. I am not necessarily suggesting one teach a course dedicated to AIDS in Italy, or anywhere, for that matter. I do however challenge the reader to reconsider what texts one teaches and how one presents them.[12]

As Julia Heim, Sole Anatrone, and Dennis Looney all addressed throughout the symposium, there is a serious importance related to curricular decision making, both on the macro and micro levels. And our courses need grounding in the classics or the canon, but rather than teaching to the canon *in sè*, Italianists, and quite honestly humanists at large, must think thematically and then chronologically or through another method when recreating courses and the curriculum. The previously mentioned texts, for example, would easily fit into any course on the novel, on the evolution of the *Bildungsroman*, illness, or trauma theory, definitions of family, and so forth. For instance, Rebecca West argues against teaching women's literature outside of the canon because by doing that we only create a secondary canon, thus recreating our own problems. It is time, therefore, to get creative. I once taught a successful course on the concept of love in the Italian tradition, beginning with the troubadours, through the *tre corone*, to love of country in the eighteenth century and onto the family with Natalia Ginzburg and ended with homosexual love between two women in Rossana Campo. The course was successful not only because it reinvented the traditional "survey" course, but because it touched something that was relatable to the students in many manifestations; it is a course that they still recall eight years later.

I would like to end with a few responsibilities that all faculty collectively share, whether they identity as part of the queer community or not. When it comes to gender identity issues and discourse, it falls on all our shoulders to create safe spaces for dialogue both inside and outside of the four walls of our classroom. Names and pronouns are just the beginning steps to make the classroom a space where a student feels comfortable being him/her/theirself. In addition to asking students their chosen name and the pronoun they identity with, it is crucial to explain to all students the importance of these two items, otherwise the class as a whole does not grasp its significance and society cannot evolve as it needs to.[13] This does not need to even come from an Italian cultural background but from another; the importance is discussing identity and its place in one's classroom. Another meaningful discussion point for the beginning of the semester is pointing out the nearest gender-neutral bathroom, which is something that we often overlook if we identify with the binary. For language programs, the classroom *in sè* is just one of the many facets of our courses. Students need to feel comfortable meeting for office hours, which sometimes means meeting in a public space, or a more private one. Similar ice breakers should also be adopted for language club activities to create a welcoming, safe environment for all involved.

Considering what some may define as a militant stance on "ungendering" the classroom, I often hear stories and am asked advice regarding students who do not identify on the binary scale. One colleague of mine recently informed me that she has a transgender student in her class. At first, she was not sure if the student was in fact transgender or not, but her teaching assistant informed my colleague of the student's pronoun and then it became clear to my colleague. Those situations can easily be defused by addressing them early and head on and not only for the instructor but the entire class. Again, as instructors, we create the classroom climate, and there is much we can do to make it a safer, more comfortable learning environment with just a little preparation and creativity.

When we recruit students to study world languages, we also proclaim that language is culture, particularly in Western European languages, but it is true across the board. We often cite examples that in Italian we have formal and informal, which are utilized with different people and depending on the situation. Additionally, we introduce North American students to the concept of gender in Italian, which at first is a challenging concept for our students to grasp, as English functions in a diverse manner. So, what happens when a transgender student takes Italian and that student identifies with the pronoun *they*? It becomes increasingly complicated when we want to use the past tense, for example, to say "They (singular) went to the park with their friends/ È andat_ al parco con i suoi amici/i loro amici." The Italian phrase causes confusion, and Italian linguists have yet to fully rethink the paradigm. That is not to say, however, that the discussion is not active in Italy; it is. The queer community has been pushing for a more inclusive language structure for a while; yet, we need to push forward and fight louder with our nonbinary friends and colleagues to afford them the space needed to feel recognized and appreciated.

The American Association of Teachers of Italian has granted more space to these discourses in recent years. In fact, at our last conference at Marist College, an entire panel was dedicated to this theme, and we even heard an undergraduate deliver her undergraduate thesis, which unveiled many myths concerning gender within the Italian language. In reality, this is not a new topic at all and has been around since the 1980s, just another one that has been swept aside. Linguistically, Italian has had a "gender neutral" that ended in -e, which was common for vocabulary dealing with occupations, even though it has fallen out of contemporary use. (See the following: Sabatini 1986, 1987, Robustelli 2019, Fresu 2008, Sapegno 2010, Luraghi and Olita 2006.) This topic of gender in language must be addressed quickly and seriously as it affects not only the field as a whole but the way people live and identify. It is a much larger situation that needs activism and not just academic input. This is an opportune moment for academics to be collaborating with activists, and maybe even politicians, to force the discourse.

Similarly, Italian studies needs, formally and publicly, to open a discourse that mirrors what is going on in German studies. Roughly two to three years ago, two untenured German professors organized an advocacy forum titled Diversity, Decolonization, and the German Curriculum, which, as the subtitle states, is a Forum for Ongoing Scholarly Inquiry Regarding Advocacy and Access to German Studies.[14] The group has organized a formal listserv and a serious blog where scholars may submit blog-length pieces that contribute to the general theme. Additionally, the group hosts a conference every other year. These conferences are extremely well attended, and it has been conceived as a space for those interested in re-thinking German studies, from materials chosen, to how to better recruit and welcome the so-called minority or nontypical German student to study German instead of other languages, to calling for more respect for those who research noncanonical texts and movements. Within three years, my German colleagues have made an impact on the field, receiving national recognition from the MLA, and are continuing to do so, bringing their mission into the discussions of larger organizations such as the Society for Cinema and Media Studies, the American Comparative Literature Association, and the MLA. The German colleagues involved in that organization have done a terrific job in re-thinking the place of German in the university curriculum and how to demonstrate the importance of German studies across fields. Many colleagues collaborating with this group have been chosen for tenure-track positions because during the interview process they are able to develop engaging ideas to build and maintain these programs. These groups should be a model for all language programs currently experiencing declines in enrollment.

Another way of de-colonizing Italian studies is removing the importance established on the traditional PhD and acknowledging the equality and prestige of other terminal doctorate degrees. Many colleagues who have earned degrees such as doctor in education, doctor of music arts, or the doctor of modern languages, to highlight only a sampling, are not only considered less educated or less qualified for positions in Italian studies, but are also quite frankly dismissed from searches. If they do have teaching jobs in academia, many are allowed to teach only language, blocking them from tenure-track, research-focused roles. This fixation with PhD programs and even Ivy League education needs to be rethought, particularly because the entire movement of cultural studies, which directly includes Italian American/Italian diasporic studies, primarily grew out of public institutions. Even today very little attention is provided Italian American and Italian diasporic studies at those top Ivy League institutions. It is noteworthy that Peter Bondanella, along with Ben Lawton, initiated the study of Italian cinema in North America in the state of Indiana: at Indiana University Bloomington and Purdue University.

Leo Bersani, another theorist who changed the way we study gender in the 1980s, argues for a queer culture that is in fact queer, and proud to be so. He pushed for gay culture to move away from the dichotomy and rather create new language and culture that more properly defines it. In this vein, students want to read about situations familiar to them. I am not proposing the removal of the canon, per se; Dante and many other authors secure a prominent position in Italian studies at large. Instead of teaching Dante in the traditional, chronological method to undergraduates, however, why not flip the perspective and offer a course on retro-reading Dante, introducing the primary texts but paying more attention to how Dante has been re-invented over the centuries and throughout various cultures, mediums, and so forth, including the literature of African Americans (see Baraka 2016, Morrison 2007, Naylor 1986, Looney 2011) or Dante and the Arab world (for more information see Cappozzo 2009)? Nonetheless, it is past time to add writers such as Amara Lakhous and Dario Bellezza into the curriculum. As teachers we[15] must attempt to introduce students to the multifaceted aspects of the culture, including non-normative realities.

Continuing with Bersani's theory present in "Is the Rectum a Grave?", our theorist pushes the status quo of those identifying as queer to act queer. Although there is not time nor space to delve here into Bersani's conceptualization of the Other, I would like to return to something mentioned during the symposium. In general, some professors claim that teaching "off the beaten path," those non-canonical texts, is activism. As I have stated in past presentations on queering Italy, I do not share that same belief; in fact, as professors, I believe that it is our responsibility to present these other perspectives of Italy or the field at hand. One of the issues of the current state of the humanities, it seems, is that professors no longer (probably due to added service, research, and teaching requirements, but also in part due to the political climate we find ourselves in) have a civic sense. We cannot expect our students to learn this on their own; we know that modeling is key. Even within my own career, I have observed a heavy decline in true political discourses within the walls of academia. As the university continues to rely more heavily on adjuncts for instruction, I have noticed dwindling attention to politics on the micro and macro levels. Except for the recent #MeToo moment, caused in part by the state of affairs related to Donald Trump, students and faculty alike are rarely organizing.

Therefore, to conclude, I do not buy the general belief that sexuality *should not* be brought into the classroom. I know that I will receive pushback on this from both heterosexual and queer colleagues alike. I also do fully understand that the "coming out" process is unique, and each person must confront that on his/her/their own terms. It is not easy. Yet there are plenty of us who are already out, and one would never realize that they are out. I do not teach in a major metropolitan city but in Fayetteville, Arkansas, and teach not only Italian courses cross-listed in gender studies but also courses in the PhD in comparative literature and cultural studies for the Gender Studies Program: Queer Theor(ies), The Representation of AIDS through the Arts, Media, and Literature, and Queers on Screen. Through these courses, I am able to cross-pollinate; I can bring my Italian minors into the realm of gender studies but also bring *Second Son* and *Camere separate* into the queer classroom. I can attest that being out helps to create an environment of inclusion, particularly in courses cross-listed with gender studies. Although gender and sexuality are fluid concepts, always in flux, and one's story is always unique, the old wise tale still holds true; there is strength in numbers, strength but also comfort. Through teaching Queer Theor(ies) this past May, the proposal to launch The Lavender Society emerged, which will host a Lavender Graduation, a pre-graduation ceremony aimed at celebrating students who identify as queer. Lavender, a color that was used in Nazi Germany to denote homosexual individuals, has been reclaimed, and students will be awarded a lavender stole to be worn during the commencement procession and ceremony.

To return to Edelman's conceptualization, we need to "kill off the child," but also the Lacanian "fathers." We must queer the Italian curriculum, from questioning or leaving behind the canon, to pursuing courses focusing on Italy as an economic European power, like MADE IN ITALY,[16] commercial Italian, and internships. Italian studies must explore culture with a little "c," courses like Italy through pop culture, that is, Contemporary Italian Culture through Rap or Street Art,[17] or Italian for Engineers, collaborating and grounding the importance of Italian across the university; remember the engineering and business professors *do not need* us, unfortunately, we need them. More so we must offer students a representation of their own makeup, that is, queering it up. We need to add LGBTQIAA+ writers to the curriculum: Sandro Penna, Dario Bellezza, Rossano Campo, Aldo Busi, and many more. If we do not start taking ownership of the curriculum and begin tailoring it to the twenty-first century, our future will be bleak. Thus, we are posed with a similar decision from *Second Son*: to take the safe road, trying the experimental drug for those infected with AIDS *or* take the risk and journey to the planet Splendora, not certain of the risks but relying solely on the rumor of its benefits.

Notes

1. At this point, I am focusing on modern female authors. I am by no means ignoring the wealth of important women writers as far back as the Renaissance and Early Modern periods. See Letizia Panizza's (2011) *A History of Women's Writing in Italy*.
2. It was her then partner, Giovanni Cena, writer and journalist, who encouraged Faccio to write her story into what many categorize as a fictionalized memoir.
3. It is critical to remind the reader that the narrator of *Una donna* is actually raped and forced into marriage with her rapist. Although she does choose to leave her husband, aware that she will never see her son again, she believes that she has no choice. Moreover, Rita Faccio did attempt to gain custody of her child, but never succeeded. Lastly, when Rita Faccio left her husband, she was already involved with another man; this aspect is left out of the novel.
4. See Julia Heim and Sole Anatrone's piece in this volume for a more robust list of understudied authors.
5. The one exception might be the collection edited by Santo L. Aricò (1990) in which the scholars included are divided between women and men. I would also point out that Aricò (1998), in addition to this collection on women, also published a monograph on Oriana Fallaci.
6. There are eight stand-alone PhD programs and twenty-one MA/PhD programs in North America. I did not look at master's-only programs due to the diverse nature between the two groups. Often, master's-only programs are forced to cross-list undergraduate and graduate courses, and curricular decisions in those types of programs are distinctively different. This information comes from the following publication: "Italian Graduate Programs in North America," in *VIA* 29(2 (Fall 2018): 3–10.
7. To clarify, Sibilla Aleramo's *Una donna* was not the only text written by a female author on the comprehensive examination lists. Other names that appeared on *some* include Grazia Deledda, Natalia Ginzburg, and Elsa Morante. Being a female author, however, does not necessarily make a text feminist; the importance of *Una donna* is the fact that it is a feminist awakening novel, one of the first in the Western canon.
8. Palazzeschi's homosexuality was an object of study as early as the late 1980s by Giorgio Marconi and Dario Trento (1988). Soon thereafter Anthony Julian Tamburri (1990) briefly discussed Palazzeschi's homosexuality in *Of* Saltimbanchi *and* Incendiari: *Aldo Palazzeschi and Avant-Gardism in Italy* and later (1992), in more depth, in "Aldo Palazzeschi's :*riflessi*: Other Reflections of Reading and Writing."
9. Felice Picano is an interesting Italian American homosexual author who still teaches on occasion in California. For more information, visit his personal website: www.felicepicano.net.
10. Michael Grumley was Robert Ferro's life-long partner. He was also a member of The Violet Quill and co-author with Ferro of *Atlantis*. In addition to being an author, although he was much less known for his writing, he was an artist and actor, both in the United States and in Italy. They had met at the University of Iowa's Summer Writing Program.
11. Michael Grumley died roughly three months before Robert Ferro. Ferro aimed at organizing a literary prize in his partner's honor but died himself too soon. In the end, Publishing Triangle initiated the Ferro-Grumley literary award, given to a book deemed the best LGBT fictional work of the year. The first prize was awarded in 1990 and until 2008, one prize was present for gay and another for lesbian fiction. Currently the awards are merged into one prize.
12. Another queer Italian American who has never been properly studied is Vito Russo, noted film scholar and LGBTQIAA+ activist.
13. Asking students what name they would like to be addressed by is critical because many public institutions will not allow students to legally change names while enrolled in the institution. The reasoning I have heard relates to legal issues at the state level. In any case, this means that a student who is transitioning while enrolled at the university is unable to utilize the name to which they identify.
14. For more information about this program, see https://diversityingermancurriculum.weebly.com.
15. Currently I am teaching a course titled Retro-Reading Dante: *Inferno*, and it was originally the idea of the University of Arkansas's Honors College Dean Lynda Coon. Colleagues, however, have been teaching Dante like this for a while and a Digital Humanities website exists that charts Dante in the contemporary world. Visit Arielle Saiber and Elizabeth Coggeshall (2019), Dante Today: http://research.bowdoin.edu/dante-today/. It is also worthwhile to see Elizabeth Coggeshall's "Dante and the Modern Imagination" and Guy Raffa's "Dante's Hell and Its Afterlife" syllabi under the "Teaching Resources" section.

16. For more information regarding courses on MADE IN ITALY or for materials for a course of this type, visit https://wordpressua.uark.edu/made-in-italy/.

17. See the newly founded journal *Simultanea: Journal of Italian Media and Popular Culture*, Marco Arnaudo and Andrea Ciccarelli (Indiana University).

Works Cited

Aricò, Santo L., ed. 1990. *Contemporary Women Writers in Italy: A Modern Renaissance*. Amherst: University of Massachusetts Press.

Aricò, Santo L. 1998. *Oriana Fallaci: The Woman and the Myth*. Carbondale, IL: Southern Illinois University Press.

Baraka, Amiri. 2016. *The System of Dante's Hell*. New York: Akashic Books.

Bolongaro, Eugenio. 2007a. "Leo's Passion: Suffering and the Homosexual Body in Pier Vittorio Tondelli's *Camere separate*." *Italian Studies* 62(1): 95–111.

Bolongaro, Eugenio. 2007b. "A Scandalous Intimacy: Author and Reader in Pier Vittorio Tondelli's *Camere separate*." *Italica* 84(4, Winter): 815–830.

Bolongaro, Eugenio. 2018. "Tondelli and the 1980s: Four Keywords for a Reassessment." *Quaderni d'italianistica* 39(1): 11–34.

Burns, Jennifer. 2000. "Code-breaking: The Demands of Interpretation in the Work of Pier Vittorio Tondelli." *The Italianist* 20(1): 253–273.

Capirossi, Arianna. 2017. "GelosMente—Tondelli: L'amore e la gelosia nelle 'Camere separate' di Leo e Thomas." http://www.artspecialday.com/9art/2017/05/15/gelosamente-camereseparate-tondelli/ (accessed June 10, 2019).

Cappozzo, Valerio. 2009. "Libri dei sogni e geomanzia: La loro applicazione tra Islam, medioevo romanzo e Dante." *Quaderni di Studi Indo-Mediterranei 2, Dreams and Visions in the Indo-Mediterranean World*, 206–227.

Cestaro, Gary. 2008. "Self-Shattering in a Queerer Mirror: Gaze and Gay Selfhood in Pier Vittorio Tondelli," *Modern Languages Notes* 123(1, January): 96–124.

De Lauretis, Teresa. 1991. "Queer Theory: Lesbian and Gay Sexualities." *Differences: A Journal of Feminist Cultural Studies* 3(2).

Edelman, Lee. 2004. *No Future: Queer Theory and the Death Drive*. Durham, NC: Duke University Press.

Ferme, Valerio. 1999. "The English Translation of Aleramo's *Una donna*: A Political Reinterpretation of the Sybil's Vision." *American Journal of Italian Studies* 22(60, Fall).

Ferme, Valerio. 2007. "A Home of One's Own: Illness and Writing as Metaphors of Difference in Pier Vittorio Tondelli's *Camere separate*." *Italica* 84(4): 799–814.

Fresu, Rita. 2008. "Il gender nella storia linguistica italiana (1988–2008)." *Bollettino di italianistica* 1(January-June).

Hoctel, Patrick. 1988. "A Talk with Novelist Robert Ferro." *San Francisco Sentinel*, March 25, 17.

Looney, Dennis. 2011. *Freedom Readers: The African American Reception of Dante Alighieri and the Divine Comedy*. Notre Dame, IN: University of Notre Dame Press.

Looney, Dennis, and Natalia Lusin. 2019. "Enrollments in Languages Other Than English in United States Institutions of Higher Education, Summer 2016 and Fall 2016: Final Report." https://www.mla.org/content/download/110154/2406932/2016-Enrollments-Final-Report.pdf (accessed August 1, 2019).

Luciano, Bernadette. 1996. "The Diaries of Sibilla Aleramo: Constructing Female Subjectivity." In *Italian Women Writers Form the Renaissance to the Present: Revising the Canon*, edited by Maria Ornella Marotti. University Park, PA: University of Pennsylvania Press.

Luraghi, Silvia, and Anna Olita, eds. 2006. *Linguaggio e genere*. Rome: Carocci.

Marconi, Giorgio, and Dario Trento. 1988. "Allegoric c varianti in *:riflessi* di Aldo Palazzeschi." *Quaderni di critica omosessuale* 4: 5–51.

Marconi, Giorgio and Trento, Dario. 1988, "Allegoric e varianti in:*riflessi* di Aldo Palazzeschi." *Quaderni di critica omosessuale* 4: 5–51.

Morrison, Toni. 2007. *The Bluest Eye*. New York: Vintage International.

Naylor, Gloria. 1986. *Linden Hills*. New York: Penguin Books.

Panizza, Letizia. 2011. *A History of Women's Writing in Italy*. Cambridge: Cambridge University Press.

Pispisa, Guglielmo. 2013. "Pier Vittorio Tondelli: Identità sessuale, religiosa e artistica di un cittadino d'Europa tra fraintendimenti critici e scelte personali." *Humanities* 2(1, January).

Reed, Paul. 1988. "To Find Through Fear and Horror: Author Robert Ferro Tells Why He Wrote 'Second Son.'" *Bay Area Reporter*, 45.

"Ri-leggere Aldo Palazzeschi" (2011). Presentation at Middlebury College's *La scuola italiana* as part of the visiting scholar series. Summer.

Robustelli, Cecilia. 2019. *Linee guida per l'uso del genere nel linguaggio amminiatrativo*. https://www.uniss.it/sites/default/files/documentazione/c._robustelli_linee_guida_uso_del_genere_nel_linguaggio_amministrativo.pdf (accessed November 9).

Sabatini, Alma. 1986. *Raccomandazioni per un uso non sessista della lingua italiana*. Rome: Presidenza del Consiglio dei Ministri.

Sabatini, Alma. 1987. *Il sessismo nella lingua italiana*. Rome: Presidenza del Consiglio dei Ministri.

Saiber, Arielle, and Elizabeth Coggeshall. Dante Today: http://research.bowdoin.edu/dante-today/ (accessed August 6, 2019).

Sapegno, Maria Serena, ed. 2010. *Che genere di lingua? Sessismo e potere discriminatorio delle parole*. Rome: Carocci.

Tamburri, Anthony Julian. 1990. *Of* Saltimbanchi *and* Incendiari: *Aldo Palazzeschi and Avant-Gardism in Italy*. Madison, NJ: Fairleigh Dickinson University Press.

Tamburri, Anthony Julian. 1992. "Aldo Palazzeschi's *:riflessi*: Other Reflections of Reading and Writing." *Italian Culture* 10: 115–30.

Fear and Nostalgia in Italian Studies

ROSETTA GIULIANI CAPONETTO

Because I am Somali and Italian, it will perhaps come as no surprise that, as a scholar in the field of Italian studies, my academic focus has been on Italy's colonialism in Africa and the African diaspora in Italy. What may instead come as a surprise is that I arrived at this field through German literature. Why I was initially drawn to the complexity of the German language and fascinated by its literary works is not as important a question to me as why I chose to drop my major in German literature after only two semesters at the University of Bologna. I was attracted to German because I had nothing to do with it, no memories attached to the language, no pains attached to the culture. And that is also why I left it. Should every subject we study in college touch our personal lives? Absolutely not, but our majors should touch us in a way that becomes personal to us and should give us tools for looking at culture that we can apply to other academic and personal fields of research. The German culture I came to learn about in college interested me without ever touching me or allowing me to take it outside of the classroom.

Sometimes I wonder: If just one of my professors had mentioned in class the German Jews who were able to build a new life for themselves in postwar Germany, or the African Germans who relocated to Germany from the country's colonies in Africa, or the fact that Germany had the largest community of emigrants from Turkey in all of Europe since the 1960s, and that German culture had been profoundly affected by these influences, would that have convinced me to stay?[1] Luckily for me this departure was not in vain. My failed experience as a student of German literature has made me more attentive and more sensitive to how I think of Italian studies today.

I will never forget seeing the image, at the Diversity in Italian Studies conference on January 17 and 18, 2019, organized by the John D. Calandra Italian American Institute, of an Italian-language class made up entirely of African American students at a historically Black college.[2] I found myself even more emotional in the company of scholars gathered together for this symposium as they shared their personal and professional stories as spokespeople for the renovation of a field of study whose numbers are declining precipitously. I have not stopped thinking about the appeal of Deborah Parker's question: "How can we make Italian studies more diverse?" nor about one of the solutions that she proposes—identity politics and the inclusion of minority scholars who would open, enrich, and contribute to the survival of Italian studies, thanks to the human connection that is forged when students identify with those they see before them (Parker 2019). This identification, this feeling of "I want to be like you," would stimulate "a greater demographic among students," who might want to pursue a degree or a minor in Italian studies (Parker 2018). The identity politics goes hand in hand with the motto, "Seeing is believing." If you open the professorate to a greater number of minority scholars, it will be mirrored in a greater number of students who recognize themselves in them and who will be able to imagine transforming their passion for Italian language and culture into a profession, whatever it may be, and who will each, in their time, contribute to the expansion of Italian studies.

This wishful thinking, however, would be hindered if students visit Italy and discover that their teacher's diversity, and in turn their own, is not necessarily a value in that country, as recent episodes have proved.[3] Therefore, the lesson I brought home from this symposium is that Parker's identity politics is much more complex than the simple synergy created between students and professors. It is a lifelong commitment that demands constructive discussion of what is hiding beneath the resistance to diversity. And it is this conversation that truly makes up the transformation that the scholars in this symposium promote each day with their work, with the curricula that they propose, with their research, and with their personal stories. This is their resistance to "exclusionary practices for close membership and whiter scholarly community" of which Parker spoke in her keynote address (Parker 2019). My research has moved in the same direction over the years, and in this essay I intend to look back on that journey in order to examine the sentiments of nostalgia and fear that bind Italian society. These two states of mind could be the lenses through which to understand both Italy and Italian studies, a field of study at risk if we do not shake ourselves free of a nostalgia for practices of the past and a fear of change.

In my life in Italy, I bore witness to two forms of nostalgia. The first one touches me very closely because it has to do with the story of my family, and it includes me in a historical vision of Italianness, over which I took control through my research. The second nostalgia excludes my family and me from a traditional vision of Italianness, relegating us to a category of exceptions. Today my Italianness is becoming a rule, not an exception. My family was formed in

Somalia. My Italian father, Vincenzo, was assigned to the Italian embassy in Somalia as an interpreter and translator of Arabic, and it was there he met and married my mother, Haua. After graduating with a degree in Arabic language and civilization from the University of Oriental Studies in Naples, my father worked as a translator and interpreter for the National Assembly of Somalia and the Ministry of Justice in the attorney general's office in Mogadishu. My mother was born in Belet Uen, a small Somali shepherding village. She was raised Muslim, though educated by Italian Catholic nuns from a nearby village, and worked as a staff member at the presidency of the council of ministers in Mogadishu until 1976.[4]

The gradual devastation of Somalia and the escalation of violence under Siad Barre's rule led to my family's relocation to Italy in the late 1970s. We moved to a small village in Southern Italy, where my father found a job as a high school teacher. This was the first time that I heard the expression *black Venus* in reference to my mother, though she was more often associated with the expression *Somali princess*. As children we didn't know what it meant. For a large family living on the salary of a school teacher, we felt rather flattered to be considered heirs to a princess. During the draft of my article on black Venus figures in the cinema of the 1970s,[5] I came to understand the more disturbing connotations of that expression.

Caterina Romeo (2019) dedicates sections of her book *Riscrivere la nazione* to Isabella Marincola, who explores the myth of the black Venus that she carried with her throughout her life (63). For a young girl born to an Italian father and a Somali mother and who had perfect mastery of Italian, ancient Greek, and Latin, she was held up as an example of Italy's civilizing mission in 1940s Italy (62). In her adult life, when Isabella demonstrated that her blackness exceeded the bounds of the exotic, erotic stereotype of the black Venus, her independence gained her the title of "princess," because such exceptionality in a Black woman could only be explained by a title of nobility (63).

In our youth in Italy at the end of the 1970s, it was clear that my siblings and I were perceived as different. Our parents were certain that things would change and that giving up was not an option. Indeed, the vision of the life that they imparted on us built armor around us that allowed us to shake off each comment related to our difference. That is not to say that the armor remained unscathed, because armor protects from comments, name calling, and unflattering comparisons, but regardless of its strength armor does not protect you from a profound exclusion that my siblings and I did not recognize until adulthood. Over the years our difference intensified, because difference can be forgiven as a child. As adults, everything becomes more complicated.

Luckily, things were changing around us. My family observed these changes with mixed feelings of pride and hope. By the end of the 1980s, the number of African migrants in Italy was growing, and that physical presence ignited the fear of "the Black man." *Black man* here does not mean only African migrants, but rather the transformation of the foreign Other, beyond gender and race, into a boogeyman.[6] A collective imaginary was constructed around this figure of the Other as a threat, stoked by specious arguments that describe it as a menace to the safety of Italians, to their physical well-being, and to their cultural values.

Italian society turned a blind eye and adopted a position of denial to these veiled forms of racism, which caused a state of overdramatization, which conveniently transformed the presence of foreign immigrants into a social crisis and therefore into currency on the electoral market (Avanza 2010, 134–140). Knowing this, the success in the 1990s of a political party like Lega Nord can be blamed more than anything else on the Black man alarm. The widespread sense of crisis permitted this political movement to catalyze public attention and channel widespread dissatisfaction with Italian political institutions into an exclusionist regionalism, which justified the ostracization of immigrants through the perceived duty to safeguarding the physical and cultural assets of Italians, and Northern Italians in particular (Ardizzoni 2007, 95–96; Avanza 2010, 139–141).

As proof of the fictitious nature of the Black man in 1990s Italy, one can turn to Lydia DeMatteo's (2011) beautiful discussion in her volume *L'idiota in politica* in which she sketches a portrait of the Lega leader Umberto Bossi, whom she identifies with the seemingly sarcastic moniker "idiot politician." In reality, anthropologically the word *idiot* can be interpreted in an etymological sense to indicate a person "devoted to the most irreducible autochthony and makeshift identity" (16)—one who outside of his group is awkward, clumsy, and unaware of how to behave (17). Bossi was an idiot both for having made himself the spokesperson of a political movement resistant to any change coming from outside his community and also for the skillful way he donned, when necessary, the disguise of the idiot, of the court jester (23).

Idiocy, affirms the journalist Gad Lerner, who wrote the preface to DeMatteo (2011), allowed the Lega leader to say the unthinkable and to express publicly the most violent anti-Southern and xenophobic sentiments without fearing the consequences because jesters are granted immunity (10–11). Bossi transformed Italian politics into a circus that—through "threats, *pernacchie*, and promises as shocking as they are impossible to keep"—conquered the electorate (16). In this playful game, the Black man became a choreographed element, which along with the green shirts and Celtic-inspired outfits worn at Lega rallies initially contributed to the creation of a sense of community and then was gradually embedded in the Italian imaginary as a real and imminent threat.

The feeling of nostalgia offers a vantage point through which to understand the fear of the Black man. Svetlana Boym is the author of the most influential book dedicated to nostalgia. The etymology of the word *nostalgia* embodies the desire to return home, to a space that instills safety because it is characterized by the sight of familiar presences (Boym 2001, xv). However, it is "a longing for a home that no longer exists," and for this reason nostalgia refers as much to time as to space, since it compels us to revisit a space that exists in the memory (Boym 2001, xiii, xv). Boym accentuates this deceitful nature of nostalgia, which "tends to confuse the actual home with the imaginary one" (xvi). The nostalgic memory brings to the surface a fantasy that Boym describes as a "delusionary" home (43).

Other similarly focused scholarship, including that of Sophie Gaston and Sacha Hilhorst (2018), outlines the study of nostalgia in the fields of sociology, psychology, and political theory, which describes this feeling as "a coping strategy to life events," a state of mind provoked by fear, anxiety, and uncertainty (24). The longing to reclaim the past through a nostalgic memory is one of the most effective means "to strengthen self-esteem and identity, to give meaning to an uncertain present, to reinforce bonds with symbolic others" (24). Moreover, Patricia Lorcin and William Cunningham Bissell's insightful comments underscore nostalgia as a subjective experience that strategically migrates from the realm of subjectivity to the domain of collectivity "bridging gaps and crossing boundaries between public and private spheres. . . . In the nostalgic domain, the personal is inherently political" (Lorcin 2012, 10; Bissell 2005, 216).

The nostalgia that accompanies the return of colonial memory in Italy was fundamental in understanding the meaning behind the figure of the black Venus and her personifications in contemporary Italian culture in my research.[7] Alessandro Triulzi and Ruth Iyob describe this nostalgia as mal d'Africa, Africa-ache, the nostalgic recovery of a colonial past idealized in its recollection. For these scholars the colonial memory, left dormant during the years immediately after the war in which Italian society was preoccupied with "turning the page," reemerges in moments of crisis in the form of nostalgia for the colonies. In the moments in which it returns, the colonial memory is selective, since it excludes events that cause pain and longingly recalls only reassuring facts and characters (Iyob 2005, 258–263; Truilzi 2008, 6–11). This type of nostalgia, similar to Boym's "restorative nostalgia," reclaims the past "without guilt" (Boym 2001, xiv). The black Venus is a favorite figure that colonial nostalgia brings again to the forefront in

Italy. Mal d'Africa is an example of restorative nostalgia, as it establishes a positive understanding of colonial time and is a longing rooted in colonial imagery that historically exploits representations of black femininity as a means to conceal the dark side of Italian colonialism.

The use of the moniker black Venus in reference to my mother included myself and my siblings in a sugarcoated colonial Italian history. The bottom line here is that the colonial memory recalled to the surface by the expression *black Venus* was describing us as heirs to a past of which Italians were proud, and therefore as someone who did not strike fear. However, there was another type of nostalgia that prevented us from being considered Italian, although we were citizens in every respect. This nostalgia is even more insidious, because it impeded, and still impedes, the hope of change. Indeed, this nostalgia is not only a gaze backward but also a means of manifesting the future. For Boym, it is as much a "retrospective" phenomenon as it is "prospective" (xvi). The nostalgia looks back to the past with the goal of forging the future; it wants to instill optimism, motivation, and self-confidence for the time that is coming. The nostalgic reclamation of the past, or rather the imaginary construction of the past, intends to affect the future, to influence it. This perspective creates a vicious cycle of a past reclaimed by nostalgia with the intent of controlling the future, with the goal of mitigating anxiety and instilling a sense of safety.[8]

One can understand how studies on nostalgia have piqued the interest of political analysts, who describe this state of mind as a rhetorical device used in the electoral campaigns of parties considered "populist" (Gaston and Hilhorst 33). On the role of nostalgia on the political stage, Nigel Rapport and Andrew Dawson (1998) emphasize how this feeling is today provoked by migratory flux, against which the wall of nostalgia is raised, "a longing for homes of the past that were socially homogenous, communal, safe, and secure" (Gaston and Hilhorst 29). In this characterization, nostalgia is a tool for creating and reinforcing the threads of belonging within a community that believes itself cohesive because it shares an "imagined memory"[9] and through that memory draws the confines of their group, refusing access to undesirable people (Gaston and Hilhorst 30). Ultimately, scholarship on nostalgia as a rhetorical tool in political campaigns mostly draws upon Boym when she affirms that "nostalgia knows two main narrative plots: the restoration of origins and the conspiracy theory" according to which "home is . . . forever under siege, requiring defense against the plotting enemy" (Boym 2001, 43).

Through the points of view illustrated here, one can understand better the relationship between nostalgia and fear and the interconnection that is established between past and future among communities that perceive the present as uncertain and precarious. It also becomes clear that this second nostalgia is responsible for the exclusivist vision of Italianness in which Black Italians like me, even when they are citizens, represent an exception to the rule. This restorative nostalgia must uphold the status quo in order to create optimism that is founded in the perceived safety of a community. As a consequence, the Italians who for physical and phenotypical reasons don't conform to the traditional representation of Italianness are invisible, even if they constitute, and do so more every day, the true face of contemporary Italy.

The perception of Italian society as bound by nostalgia for an imaginary Italianness and fear of the foreign boogeyman is acknowledged in the titles of several works written in the last few years, including Teresa Fiore's *Pre-occupied Spaces* (2017), Caterina Romeo's *Riscrivere la nazione* (2018), Leonardo De Franceschi's *Cittadinanza come luogo di lotta* (2018), and Áine O'Healy's (2019) *Migrant Anxieties. Italian Cinema in a Transnational Frame*. In *Re-visioning Italy. National and Global Culture* (1997), David Ward has already pinpointed the roots of the "fear of the Black man" when he asserts that the strategies of discrimination "bear not so much on the fear of difference, but the fear of equality" (91). According to Ward, immigrants are considered unwelcome guests because their cultural values are seen as irreconcilable with the norms of the majority, or *too* reconcilable, which would represent the even more pressing fear of being replaced (91). Romeo identifies a similar irony when she observes that the Italian nation space is constructed as a "white" site through the physical presence of white bodies and through the constant reiteration of whiteness presented by a presumed racial homogeneity of the Italian population (82, 87). The ban on nonwhite bodies inside the confines of Italian whiteness is never something explicitly expressed (Romeo 2018, 87). It is instead something that is left unsaid; it is implicitly accepted every time nonwhite bodies are defined as alien or "space invaders" (87, 99).

The irony, for Romeo, lies in the ways in which those who are *hyper*visible by way of their phenotypical characteristics such as skin color are rendered *in*visible because they are "out of place" in a space that is constructed as white ("a black man in Rimini or Riccione is always a black man out of place," says the writer Pap Khouma [2006]) (Romeo 2018, 88). But the greater irony is that Black Italians are held between two injustices: being condemned to invisibility by virtue of their hypervisible somatic norms within a society that defines itself as white, and being the object of suspicion because their mastery of the Italian language and the familiarity with the culture in which they were born and raised bring them into "dangerous proximity" with those who claim themselves to be "legitimate" Italians and fear being deprived of their privilege (91).

Teresa Fiore (2017) makes fear the subject of her book, adopting strategically the title *Pre-occupied Spaces* that puns with the multiple meanings of this expression—describing the fear of Italian immigrants who come to replace Italians, to take the place formerly "occupied" by Italians, and in this way transforming this space into a site that causes *pre*occupation (12). The expression is particularly effective because it contains within itself both time and space, as Fiore explains: "[S]pace hosts time"; it is understood as the point of arrival and departure that acknowledges the migratory experiences of Italians and puts them in dialogue with those of foreign immigrants in order to show the richness "of human experiences in motion" (12–13). In the third sense, Fiore's expression takes on a positive meaning and contains the hope that the reflection, the idea "of being preoccupied with space" in the sense of being engrossed in it or engaged with it, promotes another way of "being in space" (12).

In this discussion I chose to keep myself in a space pervaded by nostalgia unleashing fears of being replaced by outsiders. The risk is that whenever we exclude someone from the present, we prevent ourselves from playing a part in the future. This is true of Italian studies that will not survive if the field continues to mirror a culture that is not accepting of outsiders and if its job market continues to label scholars who diversify the field, with their personal background, their academic field of research, and innovative course offerings as exceptions rather than the rule, and therefore as not always a desirable fit for Italian studies departments. In my journey to Italian studies via my failed experience as student of German literature, I grew to believe that, over those years, I lived at the crossroads of fortunate coincidences for upholding a vision that was the result of having parents of different ethnicities who maintained their individual religions and cultures inside and outside the home; for having the best academic mentors anyone could wish for, and the most supportive community of colleagues and friends; for being hired in 2009 by a department led by professor of German Robert Weigel, in an institution located in Alabama that considered a Somali-descent scholar of Italian studies to be an asset. When I think of the future of Italian studies, I see a field that can stay relevant and maintain its place in institutions across the United States and the world if it stops relying on fortunate coincidences happening to the next generation of minority scholars.

Notes

1. On the struggle of engaging minority students in German studies, see the *New York Times* article titled "German in a Multicultural World" (Dillon 2012). On the topic of diversity in Germany, see Naika Foroutan's (2017) analysis in her extensive publication on the subject and several projects she has been engaged in over the years as head of the department of Integration Studies and Social Policy at the University of Humboldt, Berlin. Most of her talks on diversity in Germany can be found on YouTube, one in particular examines diversity and German society's "emotional distance" and is titled "How Diverse Is Germany (How Is This Diversity Perceived)?" (Foroutan 2017). Since 2017, Regine Criser and Ervin Malakaj (2019) have organized a biennial conference specifically on diversity in German studies in higher education whose CFP can be found on their website Diversity, Decolonization, and The German Curriculum. Related to the topic is also *Afro Germany*, a 2017 documentary by Jana Pareigis, Susanne Lenz-Gleissner, and Adama Ulrich (2017).

2. I refer here to Nicolino Applauso's (2019) picture of his class at Morgan State University in Baltimore. In his presentation, he raised the issue of instructional material for teaching Italian language and culture that fails to show the newest face of multiracial Italy, thus hindering the promotion of Italian studies in several academic institutions, including historically Black colleges.

3. I refer here to the article "My Very Personal Taste of Racism Abroad," by Nicole Phillip, which appeared in the *New York Times* on October 23, 2018. See also Mateo Askaripour's account "Losing Myself in Florence" included in the series "Travelling While Black" that appeared on August 15, 2018, on the online publishing platform named *Medium*.

4. My monograph *Fascist Hybridities* (Giuliani Caponetto 2015) contains a more extended version than the few memories shared here, about my family's journey from Somalia to Italy.

5. I examined the figure of the black Venus in Italian cinema in two studies, respectively, "Blaxploitation Italian Style" in *Postcolonial Italy* (Giuliani Caponetto 2012) and "Zeudi Araya e Ines Pellegrini, e il cinema di seduzione coloniale" in *Studi postcoloniali di cinema e media* (Giuliani Caponetto 2013).

6. In "Chi ha paura dell'uomo nero?" (Giuliani Caponetto 2011) I discuss the fear provoked by African migrants in 1990s Italy. In the article, I drew upon the dual meaning of the expression *l'uomo nero* that translates as *Black man* but also as boogeyman, a figure of bedtime stories, a character who appears in the night, dressed in black and ready to steal away defiant children who refuse to go to bed.

7. *Fascist Hybridities* (Giuliani Caponetto 2015) examines more thoroughly the relation between nostalgia and mal d'Africa, and here I rely on that same analysis to show the ways nostalgia is wielded to include or exclude those who are considered outsiders of the Italianness construct.

8. A team of psychologists of the University of Southampton in Great Britain arrived at similar results in the article "Nostalgia Shapes and Potentiates Future," after nostalgia was induced in an experimental group. Exposed to images, odors, and sounds that evoked their past, the subjects showed signs of contentment and optimism at the end of their sessions. Most important, the leaders of the study, Constantine Sedikides, Tim Wildschut, and Elena Stephan (2018) arrive at the conclusion that "nostalgia is a social emotion" in the sense that it imbues optimism and stimulates a feeling of community, and feeling part of the community works to increase the self-esteem of the subjects (189–191).

9. This expression by Benedict Anderson (1983), discussed in his book *Imagined Communities*, is in this context used to describe a remembered imagery, a recollection of events of the past that are prone to inaccuracy.

Works Cited

Anderson, Benedict. 1983. *Imagined Communities. Reflections of the Origin and Spread of Nationalism*. New York: Verso.

Applauso, Nicolino. 2019. "African-Americans and the Future of Italian Studies. Teaching Italian in Historically Black Colleges and Universities in the United States." Presentation at the Diversity in Italian Studies Conference, John D. Calandra Italian American Institute, New York, January 17–18.

Ardizzoni, Michela. 2007. *North/South, East/West. Mapping Italianness on Television*. Lanham, MD: Lexington Books.

Askaripour, Mateo. 2018. "Losing Myself in Florence." *Medium*, August 15. https://medium.com/s/traveling-while-black/traveling-while-black-in-florence-6555d3959e28 (accessed August 20, 2019).

Avanza, Martina. 2010. "The Northern League and Its Innocuous Xenophobia." In *Italy Today. The Sick Man of Europe*, edited by Andrea Mammone and Giuseppe Veltri, 131–142. London: Routledge.

Bissell, William Cunningham. 2005. "Engaging Colonial Nostalgia." *Cultural Anthropology* 20(2): 215–248. https://anthrosource.onlinelibrary.wiley.com/doi/pdf/10.1525/can.2005.20.2.215 (accessed March 5, 2019).

Boym, Svetlana. 2001. *The Future of Nostalgia*. New York: Basic Books.

Caponetto, Rosetta Giuliani. 2011. "Chi ha paura dell'uomo nero? L'altro nel cinema italiano degli anni novanta." In *L'altro e l'altrove nella cultura italiana*, edited by Fulvio Orsitto, 69–80. Cuneo: Nerosubianco.

Caponetto, Rosetta Giuliani. 2012. "Blaxploitation Italian Style. Exhuming and Consuming the Colonial Black Venus." In *Postcolonial Italy. Challenging National Homogeneity*, edited by Cristina Lombardi-Diop and Caterina Romeo, 176–191. New York: Palgrave Macmillan.

Caponetto, Rosetta Giuliani. 2013. "Zeudi Araya, Ines Pellegrini e il cinema italiano di seduzione colonial." In *L'Italia in Africa. Per una controstoria postcoloniale del cinema italiano*, edited by Leonardo De Franceschi, 109–124. Rome: Aracne.

Caponetto, Rosetta Giuliani. 2015. *Fascist Hybridities. Representations of Racial Mixing and Diaspora Cultures Under Mussolini*. New York: Palgrave Macmillan.

Criser, Regine, and Ervin Malakaj. *Diversity, Decolonization, and the German Curriculum*. https://diversityingermancurriculum.weebly.com/ (accessed March 1, 2019).

De Franceschi, Leonardo. 2018. *Cittadinanza come luogo di lotta. Le seconde generazioni in Italia tra cinema e serialità*. Rome: Aracne.

DeMatteo, Lydia. 2011. *L'idiota in politica. Antropologia della Lega Nord*. Bergamo: Feltrinelli.

Dillon, Sam. 2012. "German in a Multicultural World." *The New York Times*, April 13. https://www.nytimes.com/2012/04/15/education/edlife/german-in-a-multicultural-world (accessed February 1, 2019).

Fiore, Teresa. 2017. *Pre-occupied Spaces. Re-mapping Italy's Transnational Migrations and Colonial Legacies*. New York: Fordham University Press.

Forountan, Naika. 2017. "How Diverse Is Germany (How Is This Diversity Perceived)?" Interview. *Migration Matters*, October 6. https://www.youtube.com/watch?v=MyA8uVlaY8o (accessed February 10, 2019).

Gaston, Sophie, and Sacha Hilhorst. 2018. *Nostalgia as a Cultural and Political Force in Britain, France, and Germany. At Home in One's Past*. https://www.demos.co.uk/wp-content/uploads/2018/05/At-Home-in-Ones-Past-Report.pdf (accessed January 10, 2019).

Khouma, Pap. 2006. *Io venditore di elefanti*. Milan: Garzanti.

Iyob, Ruth. 2005. "From mal d'Africa to mal d'Europa." In *Italian Colonialism: Memory and Legacy*, edited by Jacqueline Andall and Derek Duncan, 255–282. Oxford: Peter Lang.

Lorcin, Patricia. 2012. *Historicizing Colonial Nostalgia*. New York: Palgrave Macmillan.

O'Healy, Áine. 2019. *Migrant Anxieties. Italian Cinema in a Transnational Frame*. Bloomington, IN: Indiana University Press.

Pareigis, Jana, Susanne Lenz-Gleissner, and Adama Ulrich. 2017. *Afro Germany*, March 29. https://www.youtube.com/watch?v=pcfPVj5qR1E (accessed August 5, 2019).

Parker, Deborah. 2018. "Race and Foreign Language." *Inside Higher Ed*, June 21. https://www.insidehighered.com/views/2018/06/21/paucity-asians-and-other-minorities-teaching-and-studying-italian-and-other-foreign (accessed November 15, 2018).

Parker, Deborah. 2019. "Diversifying Italian Studies." Presentation at Diversity in Italian Studies Conference, John D. Calandra Italian American Institute, New York, January 17–18.

Phillip, Nicole. 2018. "My Very Personal Taste of Racism in Italy." *New York Times*, October 23. https://www.nytimes.com/2018/10/23/travel/racism-travel-italy-study-abroad.html (accessed January 28, 2019).

Rapport, Nigel, and Andrew Dawson. 1998. *Migrants Identity. Perceptions of "Home" in a World in Movement*. New York: Bloomsbury.

Romeo, Caterina. 2018. *Riscrivere la nazione. La letteratura italiana postcoloniale*. Rome: Le Monnier Università.

Sedikides, Constantine, Tim Wildschut, and Elena Stephan. 2018. "Nostalgia Shapes and Potentiates the Future." In *The Social Psychology of Living Well*, edited by Joseph Forgas and Roy Baumeister. 181–200. New York: Routledge.

Triulzi, Alessandro. 2008 "Ritorni di memoria nell'Italia postcoloniale." In *L'Impero fascista: Italia e Etiopia, 1935–1941*, edited by Riccardo Bottoni, 573–598. Bologna: Il Mulino.

Ward, David. 1997. "Italy in Italy: Old Metaphors and New Racism in the 1990s." In *Re-visioning Italy. National Identity and Global Culture*, edited by Beverly Allen and Mary Russo, 81–100. Minneapolis, MN: University of Minnesota Press.

The Value of Cross-Cultural Studies

MARY ANN McDONALD CAROLAN

Ghetto, an Italian word that most likely derives from the word for foundry, *getto*, is synonymous with the notion of exclusion and marginalization. As such it embodies the antithesis of diversity. First used to identify the place of confinement for Jews in early modern Europe, *ghetto* in common parlance today describes a low-income, inner-city neighborhood. This term, which is laden with historical, social, and political connotations, may also be used to describe a nongeographic place or mental space where people become trapped. I fear that we Italianists now find ourselves confined to an academic ghetto. But are we to blame for this marginalization, as we focus narrowly on our research, our majors, our canonical authors, and neglect the possible links that connect us to the rest of our institutions and to the changing needs of our students? This essay suggests some ways to address our current situation.

THE NEED FOR CHANGE

We must reach out to wider populations if the field of Italian studies is to survive. Maintaining the status quo will not work. The latest published data from the Modern Language Association (MLA) on language enrollments, from a report titled "Enrollments in Languages Other than English in United States Institutions of Higher Education, Summer 2016 and Fall 2016: Preliminary Report" (Looney and Lusin 2018) shows a 9.2 percent drop in language enrollments in the United States. Italian has lost a startling 20 percent of its enrollments since 2013. All languages except Japanese and Korean have lost students; yet the decline for Italian is quite notable in comparison to those of other languages such as Spanish (almost 10 percent), French (11 percent), and German (7 percent). The 2018 MLA report also underscores the continuing gap between Italian enrollments in lower-level (first- and second-year) and advanced (third- and fourth-year) courses. These statistics demonstrate the difficulty of populating advanced Italian courses. Whereas one in ten students in a lower-level Italian course will enroll in advanced courses in Italian, twice as many introductory students in Spanish, French, and German will continue their studies. Those of us who seek to preserve our programs in Italian recognize the urgency of this situation; if our elective courses do not have sufficient enrollments, they will be eliminated. Without elective courses in Italian, our programs will founder. The threat is real. In an article in *The Chronicle of Higher Education* in January 2019, Dennis Looney, director of the Association of Departments of Foreign Languages, discussed the recent MLA report on language enrollments that he authored with Natalia Lusin. Looney noted that a record number of foreign-language programs have been eliminated between 2013 and 2016: Spanish, which still accounts for about half of enrollments in languages other than English, lost 118 programs, French lost 129, German lost 86, and Italian lost 56. Looney expressed fears that this "stunning" loss of language programs might continue into the future: "I don't want to call it a trend yet," he said, but "everything has really accelerated" (Johnson 2019).

THE CASE FOR CROSS-CULTURAL STUDIES

What can we do to address the alarming loss of enrollments and programs in Italian? One approach is to offer courses that engage with the peoples and lands that have contributed in the past, and those that continue to contribute today, to the development of Italian culture. We can add new courses that transcend the boundaries of Italy and, consequently, of our discipline as perhaps it has been too narrowly defined. These courses may also open up our particular ghettoes, which are typically departments of romance, modern, or world languages and literatures. Such "extramural" courses will attract a more diverse student body beyond potential majors and minors while simultaneously elevating the profile of Italian studies. Additionally, we can enrich our current courses by considering contributions from other cultures that have combined to produce Italian literature and film. These "intramural" courses represent our commitment to viewing Italy as a heterogeneous, rather than a homogenous, culture. This perspective in turn allows students to make connections across cultures in order to see the relevance of Italian studies to the larger world.

The history of the Italian peninsula supports a cross-cultural approach to our studies. Throughout the centuries, Italy has absorbed elements from diverse peoples, trading partners as well as invading forces, including the Etruscans, Normans, Arabs, Moors, Greeks, Berbers, Jews, and North Africans. Italy enjoys a strategic yet vulnerable position in the center of the very sea whose name, Mediterranean, situates it in the middle of the Earth. We typically begin our study of Italian culture in the thirteenth century in Palermo, at the court of the Holy Roman Emperor Frederick II. Son of Emperor Henry VI of the Hohenstaufen dynasty and of Constance, heiress to the Norman kings of Sicily, Frederick was the product of northern and southern Europe. He invited to his court luminaries from all over the world including mathematician, translator, and astrologist Michael Scot from England, as well as artists, poets, mathematicians, and philosophers from Spain and the Arab world. A polyglot, Frederick purportedly spoke six languages: Latin, Sicilian, Middle High German, *langue d'oïl* (the precursor of modern French), Greek, and Arabic. Known as the *stupor mundi* for his varied interests in scientific method and the natural world, as well as for his considerable military prowess, Frederick was the author of a treatise on falconry, *De Arte Venandi cum Avibus* (The Art of Hunting with Birds). Frederick II, in my mind, embodies cross-cultural studies: He was a man who appreciated the expertise of those from around the world to teach him about science, poetry, astrology, and philosophy.

Our students who choose to study Italian also embody cross-cultural exchange. As they read Italian texts, listen to Italian pop music, watch contemporary Italian films, and follow Italian haute couture, they implicitly draw comparisons with their native culture in the United States. But who are our students, and what draws them to Italian studies? They need not perfect their language skills to study abroad since many programs offer courses primarily in English rather than in the language of the country. Most are less interested in learning the language in order to read the great works of literature in the original. Current students' motivations and goals may differ from those of their professors: Captivated by the richness of Italian culture, some may wish to work abroad, while others may wish to remain in the United States to serve Italian clients or promote Italian products. For both the domestic and international options, students seek to perfect their linguistic skills. Our students are very practical. Economic factors compel them to think about how their costly education (which may also result in crushing debt) will translate into a job and ultimately into a career. We must acknowledge our students' reality and try to serve them as best we can by offering courses that are consonant with their needs. We can and should teach elective language classes aimed at refining language skills for various professions, as well as content courses on the Italian commercial and artistic success stories that constitute the Made in Italy phenomenon.

"EXTRAMURAL" COURSES

First, let us consider courses that reach larger populations at our respective colleges and universities. Italian faculty should teach courses in the honors curriculum and first-year and interdisciplinary seminars, as well those courses that satisfy general education or core requirements. Consequently, we must offer courses in English. How could we not teach the poetry of Dante, the literature of the Renaissance, or the novels of Elena Ferrante to students who cannot read these texts in the original Italian? We cannot and should not teach only in Italian.

Several years ago, my colleague Jiwei Xiao, who teaches Chinese, and I developed a course for the honors curriculum at Fairfield University, in Fairfield, Connecticut, titled East/West: China and Italy through the Ages. Designed with the parameters of interdisciplinary inquiry in mind, this course traces and critiques the artistic and literary exchange between China and Italy from the medieval period to the present day. We study the intersections of these two cultures in literature from Marco Polo (*Il milione*) to Italo Calvino (*Le città invisibili*), in paintings by Giuseppe Castiglione, in the scientific discoveries of Matteo Ricci, in the music of Giacomo Puccini's opera *Turandot*, and through various representations in film including Michelangelo Antonioni's documentary *Cina/Chung Kuo* (1972), Bernardo Bertolucci's *L'ultimo imperatore/The Last Emperor* (1987), Gianni Amelio's *La stella che non c'è /The Missing Star* (2006), and Matteo Garrone's *Gomorrah* (2008). In addition to reviewing the historical connections between China and Italy, we analyze representations of conflict and trade between the two countries in the modern period. This exploration brings us to consider the Chinese presence, and resulting tensions, in Italy today. Although the course is predicated primarily on a Western (or Italian) view of China, we emphasize critical perspectives from both sides to avoid a completely Eurocentric reading of the dialogue between these two cultures. In addition to the Orientalist perspective defined by Edward Said (1979), our students read Chinese theorists Longxi Zhang and Rey Chow. A visit to Little Italy and Chinatown in New York allowed us to examine the confluence of Italian and Chinese cultures in the United States. On that excursion we also included a trip to the exhibition of the artwork from Qianlong's eighteenth-century dynasty, The Emperor's Private Paradise: Treasures from the Forbidden City, at the Metropolitan Museum of Art. This exhibition included paintings by Jesuit lay brother Giuseppe Castiglione, whose work the Chinese emperor appreciated.

By contributing to initiatives, such as the honors program, that transcend disciplines, we reach students outside our typical constituency while increasing the visibility of Italian studies. We may cultivate interest in Italian culture in students who have never studied the language. In the course that Xiao and I developed, honors students were upperclassmen from a broad array of departments in the College of Arts and Sciences, as well as those from the Nursing, Business, and Engineering schools at the university. Our scholarship and teaching benefited from this collaborative teaching experience. Xiao (2013, 103–120) has published an article on Antonioni's documentary *Cina* and developed a new course on China and the West for the Chinese curriculum, and I am finishing a book manuscript on Italian views of China and the Chinese in film. My colleague and I were very lucky to share an interest in cinema as well as an interest in each other's fields. We were also willing to commit the time and energy necessary to develop and teach this course as a team, which is often more demanding than teaching solo.

"INTRAMURAL" COURSES

Not everyone will want to teach an entire course focused on Italy and another culture. But cross-cultural studies can be viewed as an approach toward teaching. In that vein, I would like to offer two examples of how cross-cultural studies within our current course offerings can promote more diversity of thought and hopefully expand our reach to students. Within our own curricula we can think about breaking down disciplinary walls by demonstrating to students that our field is not circumscribed by Italy's borders.

Most Italian studies programs offer courses on Dante. To read and understand the Italian poet requires knowledge of different time periods and disparate worlds. Dante calls attention to language in several ways: He writes his *Commedia* in Italian, the language of the people, but he also includes Arnaut Daniel's native Provençal language in his epic poem. Dante looks forward as well as backward; he is both innovative and philological in his approach to language. His poetic world is multifaceted; it is geographically vast and chronologically broad. Characters from his beloved Florence abound, as do figures from more exotic locales such as Cleopatra of Egypt, Semiramis of Assyria, and the poets of classical antiquity (Virgil, Horace, Lucan, Homer, Ovid). Dante refers to places he has visited and those he has not, such as Pola on the Istrian peninsula and Tikrit in today's Iraq. Mythological figures underscore the poem's insistence on imagination and fantasy. Dante did not limit himself to Italy, nor should we as we teach his poetry.

In my course on Dante I encourage students to understand not only the poem but its cultural impact in the United States. We listen as Ruth Draper, in her 1925 monologue titled "The Italian Lesson," prepares to study Dante in the original with her tutor, an Italian *signorina*. We understand the importance of Dante's poem for early twentieth-century wealthy matrons like Draper's character, but we also see the continuing importance of his text in movies such as *Bruce Almighty* (2003, directed by Tom Shadyac) or *Hannibal* (2001, directed by Ridley Scott) and in the Dante's Inferno video game, which is quite loosely (and inaccurately) derivative of the *Commedia*'s first canticle. In this seminar, students enjoy an essay assignment that requires them to identify sinners in contemporary society and assign them a place in Dante's hell.

Italian cinema offers many possibilities for cross-cultural study. For example, the distinctly Italian adaptation of the quintessentially American western, the western *all'italiana*, exemplifies the transatlantic conversation in film. In the United States, critics' use of the derogatory term *spaghetti western* reflected a disdain for the European adaptation of this most American of genres. This genre, one of the most successful in Italian cinema, produced the prototypical Italian cowboy, Django. Immortalized by Franco Nero in Sergio Corbucci's 1966 eponymous film, Django became an international phenomenon. His namesake was another icon, the jazz musician Jean Django Reinhardt who was born in 1910 while his Roma parents were traveling in Belgium. A European who mastered the quintessentially American musical genre of jazz, Django Reinhardt personified cross-cultural exchange.

With *Django Unchained* (2012), Quentin Tarantino introduces a new American Django, played by Jamie Foxx. Midway through the film, the title character encounters Amerigo Vessepi (Franco Nero); an African American meets an Italian, in white hat and gloves, who played the lead in Corbucci's *Django* (1966). Vessepi questions Django about the spelling of his name, an inside joke that points to Nero's signature role: Tarantino's playful naming of Nero's character recalls the Italian explorer Amerigo Vespucci, whose moniker graces the New World. Nero, like Vespucci before him, is a European coming from the Old World to the new. The surname *Nero* aligns him with the color of the slaves whom he owns, yet his skin, hat, and gloves suggest the opposite in this movie that is all about slavery and racism. Tarantino borrows and intensifies not only the gratuitous violence characteristic of the spaghetti western but its political motivations as well. Like Corbucci and other directors of spaghetti westerns before him who had made their leftist (Marxist) views known, with *Django Unchained* Tarantino has created a new west that addresses historic, and unfortunately persistent, problems in the United States. His new *Django* supplies a critical link for understanding the dynamic between the Old and New Worlds, Europe and America, black and white.

CONCLUSION

In this essay I have offered some possible ideas for enriching our Italian curricula from inside and outside the walls of our departments and programs. We Italianists are limited only by our imagination as to the kinds of cross-cultural materials and courses to develop. As we challenge ourselves to think broadly, we expand our students' minds, and we escape the ghetto that is the narrowly construed field of Italian to become relevant to the wider curricula at our colleges and universities. If we stay in our ghetto, we will be vulnerable to budget cuts and claims of irrelevance in the face of continuing affronts on the humanities, and on languages in particular. Emphasizing cross-cultural bonds does not dilute Italian studies. Rather it enriches and expands horizons by creating more opportunity for our students to engage in the culture to which we have dedicated our professional lives.

Works Cited

Chow, Rey. 1991. *Woman and Chinese Modernity: The Politics of Reading between West and East.* Minneapolis, MN: University of Minnesota Press.

Johnson, Steven. 2019. "Colleges Lose a 'Stunning' 651 Foreign-Language Programs in 3 Years." *The Chronicle of Higher Education,* January 22. https://www.chronicle.com/article/Colleges-Lose-a-Stunning-/245526 (accessed January 10, 2019).

Looney, Dennis, and Natalia Lusin. 2018. "Enrollments in Languages Other Than English in United States Institutions of Higher Education, Summer 2016 and Fall 2016: Preliminary Report." New York: Modern Language Association, February.

Said, Edward. 1979. *Orientalism.* New York: Vintage Books.

Xiao, Jiwei. 2013. "A Traveller's Glance." *New Left Review* January/February(79): 103–120.

Zhang, Longxi. 1988. "The Myth of the Other: China in the Eyes of the West." *Critical Inquiry* 15(1): 108–131.

Italian Studies, Queer Possibilities

JOHN CHAMPAGNE

Reading the temperature of a discipline is always difficult, as one's perspective is typically relative: It is easy to wrongly assume that one's local position is symptomatic of more global trends, particularly given the different kinds of working conditions we face (public versus private university, contingent versus permanent position, Department of Italian versus Modern Languages, undergraduate versus graduate, Italy versus abroad, and so forth). Additionally, recent critics of chrononormativity—"the use of time to organize individual human bodies toward maximum productivity" (Freeman 2010, 3)—have argued for an attentiveness to differences in temporal rhythms. The pace with which a discipline can accommodate new kinds of scholarship and local alternative classroom pedagogies is often quicker than that at which it welcomes substantive curricular reform, new faculty lines, and productive challenges provided by new faculty and their hopefully iconoclastic ideas. One of the many potential hazards of the precariousness of faculty positions today is a chilling of the atmosphere for innovation.

As someone who began his career in what was then called LGBTQ studies, whose PhD is in English, and who has a tenured position at a branch campus of a land-grant university, my perspective on diversity in Italian studies is unique; that I am contributing to this conversation at all is itself evidence of Italian studies' queer possibilities. I have been fortunate that, although my Italian remains *sempre un lavoro in corso* (always a work in progress), editors have been willing to publish my research and colleagues open to reading it, and at least one journal trusts me to review scholarship on gender/sexuality/Italy. That my entrée into Italian studies occurred as a result of a disciplinary interest in interdisciplinarity may suggest that it was the interdisciplinary nature of my scholarship—and not its queerness—that got me in the door in the first place. But perhaps it was not one or the other, but both.

I understand that, in the face of institutional pressures to fill classroom seats, *interdisciplinarità* risks diluting the appeal of courses in Italian in favor of English-language Italian courses on culture. But some excellent recent Italian scholarship in queer studies reminds us that the either/or opposition—either monodisciplinary work in Italian or interdisciplinary work in English—is false. What we still lack are institutionalized structures to foster collaboration among faculty—faculty from different institutions, faculty from different disciplines, faculty whose differing historical experiences of global inequality have shaped their understanding of what it means to work in Italian studies, and even faculty with different abilities in Italian.

While there is something emotionally and intellectually thrilling about warding off the Huns at the gate, ultimately this kind of disciplinary policing does not respond to the complex global networks of which our lives today are composed. I am not being ironic here; in the face of the daily compromises we must make in today's neoliberal university, it is emotionally gratifying to argue for maintaining standards. People today live with and speak a variety of Italians, however, and, as someone who chairs a program in Global Languages and Cultures, I have been struck by a certain divide between, for example, instructors who teach pronunciation via the phonetic alphabet and those who focus instead on how real human beings speak today, between those instructors who do not expose students to anyone's version of the target language apart from the teacher's own and those who deliberately introduce students' ears to regional and global variations. Of course, the choice is itself a false one, but several factors increasingly place pressure on the language classroom, from calls for maintaining, in the face of immigration, a mythical standard version of the national language, to instructors who resist the idea that language pedagogy should respond to the changing conditions in which languages are lived in the present and new technologies and the pedagogical opportunities to which they might give rise.

While not a teacher of Italian, I regularly teach English composition, the subfield that historically has perhaps most responded to the need to reimagine English as a discipline. The opening of the American university to second- and third-language learners made us aware both of the way structuralism's synchronic focus on *langue* rather than *parole* failed to capture the dynamism of language and of the concept of fluency as a relative one and hardly ideologically neutral. With its emphasis on cultural production that includes but is not limited to language, interdisciplinary work is poised to confront the distinctions between high and low culture (and the class biases informing those distinctions) that often underlie the teaching of one version of the target language versus another or emphasize one location's habits of pronunciation or even diction over another's: In Louisiana, for example, one can in fact "*demander* (rather than *poser*) *une question*" (Valdman 2010, 507).

But interdisciplinary work requires institutional structures of support. One that I have relied upon is the American Association for Italian Studies' (AAIS) Queer Studies Caucus, which provided me with a welcoming point of entry into Italian studies. Its organizers have worked to enact a queer politics by keeping the caucus as nonhierarchical as possible; fostering a diversity of membership in terms of gender, race, ethnicity, age, and location; imagining generously what it means to study Italian culture and language; and sponsoring not only traditional conference panels but also more democratic forms of exchange like roundtable discussions. The caucus was and remains a self-sustaining effort; it exists because a group of queers—specifically, graduate students—did the necessary labor to bring it into being. In other words, AAIS did not invite the caucus in; the caucus elbowed its way through the door. It remains largely underused by members who do not self-identify as queer. Its position is precarious. To return to this issue of different disciplinary rhythms: In English studies today, no one can get away with simply closing his/her/their eyes in the hope that queer studies goes away. My sense is that, in Italian studies, it is still possible to conduct one's intellectual life without even a bit of disciplinary guilt at one's ignorance of Italian queer work.

That is, those different rhythms should not blind us to the fact that queer Italian studies remains to some degree marginalized. To return to the caucus, following the 2018 meeting in Sorrento, AAIS members received a letter regarding the creation of a Diversity and Inclusion Committee. No members of the caucus, however, were invited to participate, and no one came to our roundtables to introduce the idea to us or seek our input. In a letter written in response, caucus members reminded AAIS leadership that "many of us in the Queer Studies Caucus have decided or have had to find our paths outside of Italian studies because of, or in conjunction with, the pervasive experience of marginalization and conservatism within the field"—again suggesting that interdisciplinary scholarship, and not Italian studies per se, has been a place where Italian queer work has been welcome ("Letter to AAIS" 2018).

An announcement of the 2019 Brown-Harvard Graduate Student Conference, Queering Italian Studies: Pensieri e pratiche italiane di sovversione culturale is puzzling in its lack of recognition of existing work. The call, for example, "aims to suggest directions for queering Italian studies"—as if such an effort is not already under way ("Queering Italian Studies" 2019). The call continues, "We wish to stimulate a debate that, in Italy, remains outside the institutional discourse." This news would presumably surprise the many intellectuals, activists, and artists who for some years now have been working in conjunction with the Centro di Ricerca's Politesse: Politiche e Teorie della Sessualità of the

Università di Verona, as well as the Centro Interuniversitario di Ricerca Queer (CIRQUE) of the Università di Pisa. It is also worth noting that the extremely fine keynote speakers chosen for the conference do not identify their own research interests as queer Italian studies and have not been active in the Queer Studies Caucus of AAIS.

I am not suggesting that their work could not be interpreted as a part of queer Italian studies. I am suggesting that choosing keynote speakers demonstrably and deservedly famous who do not, however, identify as scholars of queer Italian studies centers one body of work and risks pushing to the margins another and that such gestures are not disciplinarily innocent. The claim that queer theory remains a concern external to Italy paradoxically not only marginalizes the queer work being done there but suggests that this existing work is a foreign import, a familiar Italian attempt to adopt fashionable Americanisms or Anglicisms.

Two recent works in queer Italian studies—one in English, the other in Italian—are suggestive of the current environment and its queer possibilities. Both are self-consciously aware of their liminal status; both address issues of methodology and signal their attempt to speak across linguistic and disciplinary divides. One is written in English by a native Italian speaker currently working in Italy. One is written in Italian by a native Italian speaker currently working in the United States. Both are excellent examples of scholarship produced by young Italianists who have pursued the arduous task of remaining current in their fields—in one case, Italian cinema; in the other, Italian modern art—by engaging with both Italian language and anglophone sources.

Mauro Giori's 2017 *Homosexuality and Italian Cinema, From the Fall of Fascism to the Years of Lead* is a first-of-its-kind survey of images of male and female homosexuality in postwar film. It is much more than this, however. Among queer scholars, *queer* is often used as a verb to indicate the attempt to unsettle established categories or definitions, to blur some of the handy disciplinary distinctions we take for granted, and to deconstruct binarized notions of sexuality and gender. In his book, Giori performs a fascinating, highly effective, and convincing *queering* of the distinction between the film text and its reception. Rather than simply provide close readings of the films in question, Giori sets them in a larger discursive context, including not only their production histories and press reviews, but the discursive constructions of homosexuality "beyond" film representations: from texts that emphasize that the cinema was a place where men met for homosex or to gossip, to ultraconservative tabloid accounts of the menace of homosexuality, to competing and contradictory accounts of whether homosexuality was situational or congenital and whether it took the form of a pederastic relationship, a third sex, some combination of the two, or some other model. The *and* in the book's title is delightfully polyvocal, as Giori has authored a history of postwar cinema, a history of postwar homosexuality, and a history of cinema and postwar homosexuality.

As Giori attempts, in his introduction, to situate himself vis-à-vis queer theory and its multiple interventions in historiography, one has a sense of someone tiptoeing through a minefield. The equivocating is jarring but perhaps expected. In Italy, the stage had already been set by gay historian Giovanni Dall'Orto's dismissals of queer theory (2012; 2015). These dismissals turn on the assumptions that queer theory falsifies history by denying the existence of a transtemporal, transcultural homosexual subject and is part of a larger plot by the anglophone world to colonize the Italian gay intellectual scene.

Dall'Orto's concerns are rooted in a long-standing tension in the historiography of sexuality between those writing a continuist history emphasizing similarity and those writing histories emphasizing difference, the first associated with scholars like Dall'Orto who understand not only homosexual behavior but homosexual identity as forever existing across time and space and those who understand categories of sexual and gender identity as themselves historical—that is, bound by time and space. (I deliberately avoid referring to gender and sexuality as historical or cultural *constructions* here, as these terms risk simplifying the temporal and spatial dynamic whereby subjectivities emerge. That is, they suggest there is something *external* to sexual and gender subjectivity, something called history, that brings them into being, rather than conceiving of material history and all subjectivities as mutually constitutive.)

Even this précis is potentially reductive, as a body of scholarship called *queer unhistoricism* also takes to task histories that emphasize rupture over continuity, but on very different grounds than Dall'Orto's. Seeking "to craft a fruitful form of historical-political consciousness" (Brown 2001, 16) that "does not resort to discredited narratives of systematicity, periodicity, laws of development, or a bounded, coherent past and present" (143), such work challenges the idea of a recoverable past that can be cleanly separated from "our modern sexuality." As Dall'Orto does, it rejects the distinction between sexual acts and sexual identities—not, however, to project back into history an eternal homosexual but rather to challenge the very notion of sexual identities and the periodization of history on which the idea of a specifically modern sexual identity relies.

That Giori is aware of these polemics is signaled in his introduction when he feels compelled to add a note on methodology—something Dall'Orto, for example, feels no need to take up in his own work. In a move typical of critiques of theory, one casts one's own methodology as "a-theoretical," common sense, obvious, or self-evident. This move not only naturalizes one's own practice, it also discredits others by suggesting they are the opposite—obtuse, mannered, self-indulgent, and just plain false.

The introduction of the theme of queer theory, however, provokes, in Giori's text, a kind of semiotic trauma, evidenced in a sentence whose circuitous syntax features two subordinate clauses:

> Since, now that academic resistance to issues like those addressed in this book is slowly lessening in Italy, queer theory is becoming increasingly fashionable at the expense of historical research, it is worth adding a final note on method. (Giori 2017, 7)

The first clause suggests what I have already proposed—that, in Italy, one can no longer maintain that queer theory "remains outside the institutional discourse" ("Queering Italian Studies" 2019). The second is puzzling on several counts. First, a problem of reference: Is the author alluding to Italy, the United States, the UK, somewhere else, all the above? Second, a problem of causality: What is the relationship between these first two subordinate clauses? Has the author simply omitted the *and* that might follow the first, employing the comma instead, or is some other relationship being implied? Had the absent *and* been present, it would suggest a correlation or even causal relationship between the two, as if the Italian lessening of hostility toward queer theory has caused it to become fashionable at the expense of history. (Not coincidentally, when scholars in the United States first became interested in French theory, they were accused of doing so for reasons of fashion. *Plus ça change*.) It would also, however, render the *since* redundant (since *since* means because). Perhaps, then, this *since* is meant to take the place of the *and*. But minus this *and*, what we have are not only two propositions whose causal relations are unclear; rather, we are given two statements about queer theory, one presumably positive (the author crediting queer theory with the lessening, in Italy, of resistance to the kinds of issues his book addresses), the other presumably negative (the author opposed to the fashionableness of queer theory), and no sense of how we are to connect the two, if at all. In fact, the employment of the two commas suggests that the subordinate clause enclosed by them could be removed without substantially changing the meaning of the sentence. But should a reader choose to remove this clause, the sentence's statement in favor of queer theory—that academic resistance to it in Italy has lessened—disappears.

However ambiguous the syntax, the opposition between theory and history is a familiar if false one. For what is actually at stake is not the purportedly trivial, wasteful, and facile fashionableness of theory as opposed to the serious, productive, and labor-intensive work of history—and note the dour heteronormative assumptions operating here, the idea that being fashionable is somehow "easier" and more noble than what in Giori's book's case often amounts to scouring right-wing tabloids for their lurid accounts of homosexual scandal. Not that such a project is without value. Quite the opposite: It is contradictory to make the case for the study of popular culture with references to standards of value drawn from elite culture.

In any case, what is truly at stake is the question of what it means to write history, the same thing that is at stake in Dall'Orto's dismissals of queer theory. But the critique of continuist, teleological, historicist approaches to historiography cannot be laid at the doorstep of queer theory alone; it was suggested by Nietzsche (1988), developed by Benjamin (1968) and Foucault (1988), and followed up by historiography that confronts the unintelligibility of the past (Ginzburg 1992; White 1984), the queer unhistoricism debates in Renaissance studies (Freccero 2006; Goldberg 1992; Goldberg and Menon 2005; Halperin 2002; Traub 2013), subaltern studies postcolonial historiography (Spivak 1988), and antifoundationalist feminist historiography (Doan 2013; Scott 1993).

What immediately follows Giori's concerns regarding the fashionableness of queer theory—his statement on method—is, however, an equivocating *defense*. First, Giori assures us that, in forgoing extensive close readings of the texts he analyzes, he is *not* suggesting, as David Gauntlett has, that such readings are worthless and self-indulgent. The citation of Gauntlett is idiosyncratic, as he is not a familiar figure in queer scholarship, and Gauntlett's charge—that queer theory produces textual readings that "the author probably didn't intend and which most audiences probably won't think of" (Gauntlett 2008; cited in Giori 2017, 7)—is specious. In the United States, American New Criticism and, in Italy, Benedetto Croce, long ago questioned the attempt to stabilize the meaning of a text via reference to the author's intentions (Compagno 2012). As for offering the audience something it won't initially think of, isn't that the point?

Giori's concern, rather, is that queer close readings "have lacked—as far as Italian cinema is concerned," rigor (7). No citations are provided to support this claim, leaving us again to wonder if the author is speaking of Italian-language criticism or criticism in some other language, and what might constitute a rigorous reading is undefined. Not to mention that such rigorous readings are exactly what someone like Gauntlett trashes, since, if we are going to traffic, however problematically, in ideas about typical spectators, most audiences are not known for their critical rigor. Instead, Giori suggests that Gauntlett's lament may result from "the imbalance between the emphasis on a theory which dictates a strict agenda and the undervaluing of research, an imbalance that results in an overvaluation of subjectivity in the critical process" (Giori 2017, 7).

The idea that queer theory "dictates a strict agenda" is patently false. Arguably no "school" of criticism—if queer theory can even be called a school—is as capacious and resistant to definition as queer theory; Dall'Orto's suspicion that queer theory is an aide de camp to neocolonialist American foreign policy is precisely a critique of that capaciousness. As for the undervaluing of research versus the overvaluing of subjectivity, this is another version of the critique of critical history—that is, history that does not assume that the position of the historian as investigating subject is transparent, for example. And again, there is that unresolved question of context: Where is research undervalued and subjectivity overvalued? Italy? The United States? Somewhere else?

Following this critique, Giori then *defends* queer theory on the grounds that it has met theory's obligation to provoke new ways of thinking. This, however, is followed by the equivocation that:

> [I]n no field more than this one are summonses such as Ginzburg's to oppose history and documents to the temptation of reducing research to a rhetorical exercise . . . pivotal in order to avoid the former [theory] paralyzing the latter [history] instead of fueling it. (8)

I literally cannot follow this account of Ginzburg's summonses. Assuming that "the temptation of reducing research to a rhetorical exercise" is a bad thing, I am still not sure how this temptation—note again the moralizing—can be warded off by history and documents, nor even what it means to reduce research to a rhetorical exercise. Given the invocation of Ginzburg, I suspect that this is another version of the critique of the alleged excesses of critical history, as Ginzburg (1992) has tried to occupy a middle ground between what he perceives as an overemphasis on the intervention of the subjectivity of the historian and a crude, naïve empiricism that would deny the ways in which any historian must cope with the unintelligibility of the past, rather than pretend it doesn't exist or is the result of a massive repression of truth by power—the historian's heroic task being to set that truth free.

As for theory causing paralysis, this, too, is a very familiar charge. It has been directed at deconstruction for decades, despite the fact that this allegedly paralyzing intervention in criticism has produced an abundance of scholarship—thus the charge of being fashionable. Similarly, no historian I know of has been led by the critique of historicism to stop writing. In fact, the opposite—the queer unhistoricism debates, for example, have produced a rich and growing body of scholarship that attempts to think through with ever more rigor and subtlety our relationship and responsibilities to the past. Such work, however, has often been dismissed as "culturalist" by more traditional historians (Benadusi 2013). Where, then, is the evidence of paralysis?

Whatever concerns I have about this methodological statement, which seems above all to be the product of the author's sense of divided loyalties and the purpose of which seems to be to avoid losing readers on either side of the great divides—between anglophone queer theory and Italian gay and lesbian historiography, between native speakers of Italian and non-native-speaker Italianists, between "foreign" and "indigenous" theories—the fact that he is even engaging in this discussion demonstrates that Giori has produced a work in queer Italian studies. Giori's equivocations in fact distinguish his take on queer theory from Dall'Orto's and perhaps even Lorenzo Benadusi's, who has accused me specifically of "un eccesso di psicanalisi e decostruzionismo, combinati con il materialismo storico e la teoria *queer*" (an excess of psychoanalysis and deconstructionism, combined with historical materialism and *queer* theory) (Benadusi 2013, 167; all translations are my own).

The easiest critique of my position will be that I am "colonizing" Giori's text and have not been attentive to how the importation of the term *queer* to nonanglophone (non-U.S.?) contexts will bring unexpected results in league with American neocolonialism. I may also be subject to the charge of careerism, appropriating Italian homosexuality for personal gain. The problem with these knee-jerk critiques is that they redeploy the very model of power as sovereign that Foucault—who was not an American—demanded we reconsider. They also forget that extra-local exchanges were one of capitalism's conditions of possibility, and Marxism's critique of capitalism is also extra-local. Never mind that Mediterranean cultures have always been hybrid; that hybridity itself provides grounds for the critique of the conceit that Greece represents the "cradle" of civilization. And as Kobena Mercer (1994) reminds us, cultural exchanges do not go in one direction only; to suggest otherwise is precisely to deny the agency of the subaltern.

While the queer unhistoricist debates have sometimes been as unnecessarily polemical as Dall'Orto's claim that the idea that homosexuality is a historical construction is "*Fascisticamente* prescrittivo" (Dall'Orto 2012, emphasis in the original), some of the most interesting work being done today in queer historiography is in the interstices between historicist and unhistoricist approaches (Ferguson 2016; Doan 2013). In the interest of full disclosure, I myself have struggled to figure out what kind of history someone with my disciplinary training and location can write about Italian homoerotic art between the wars, its discomfiting ties to Fascism, and its articulation of a pederastic model of same-sex desire via recourse to sexism and Orientalism. Speaking across disciplinary divides is difficult, as is evidenced by the historian Benadusi's suggestion that I believe Pirandello's *Enrico IV* "abbia a che fare con l'intento di distruggere la mascolinità fascista, mettendo in scena il desiderio di 'deconstruct phallic subjects'" (has to do with the intent to destroy Fascist masculinity, dramatizing the desire to "deconstruct phallic subjects") (Benadusi 2013; the quoted words are my own; Champagne 2013). Nowhere in my study of representations of Fascist masculinity, characterized by Benadusi as *anglossasono*, do I ever suggest anything about anyone's *intentions* to destroy Fascist masculinity—or even deconstruct phallic subjects. As is the case with most anglophone critics of my generation, the author's intentionality is rarely even on my radar, and I am not opaque enough to suggest that Pirandello, of whose politics I am aware, would set out to destroy Fascist masculinity. But even the most rigorously historicist reading of *Enrico IV* must cope with the fact that its hero may be mad and thus not a ready-made model of Fascist virility. It is Pirandello's play—and not my fanciful reading—that deconstructs the distinction between madness and sanity: "Ah! Eh! Che rivelazione?—Sono o non sono?—Eh, via, sì, sono pazzo! *Si fa terribile* Ma allora, *perdio, inginocchiatevi! Inginocchiatevi!* [italics in the original]" (Hah! What! What revelation? Am I or am I not? Ah, right, yes, I am mad! *He becomes frightening* Well then, *for Christ's sake, kneel! Kneel!"*) (Pirandello 2011, 68). Does pretending to be mad drive Enrico crazy, and, if so, how sane was Enrico in the first place? What is truer, how one is perceived and labeled by others, or how one perceives oneself? Unless Fascism made a heroic virtue of this deconstruction—something presumably an empiricist historian like Benadusi has an obligation to prove via the citing of evidence rather than a facile dismissal of my reading—my argument stands.[1]

Raffaele Bedarida's 2018 book on Corrado Cagli's exile in the United States is another example of recent work in queer Italian studies, not only in terms of its subject matter but also its reflections on methodology and attempts to dislodge established ways of conducting scholarship. Bedarida's book is remarkable in that it is to my knowledge the very first text in Italian to openly and directly discuss the artist's bisexuality; according to Bedarida:

Cagli passa con disinvoltura dal sodalizio intellettuale che spesso sconfina nel triangolo amoroso con il poeta Libero de Libero e lo scultore Mirko Basaldella (che alla fine del 1938 sposa la sorella di Cagli, Serena) e una relazione con Elsie Reiti, con la quale parla anche di avere figli, sebbene lei sia la moglie del compositore Vittorio. (16–17)

(Cagli moved with ease from an intellectual bond that often crossed over into a love triangle with the poet Libero de Libero and the sculptor Mirko Basaldella [who at the end of 1938 married Cagli's sister Serena] and a relationship with Elsie Reiti, with whom he spoke of having children, even though she was the wife of composer Vittorio.)

Like more traditional gay and lesbian historiography that pursues a partially recoverable past, Bedarida, via a careful and extensive reading of previously unavailable archival materials, reveals something that other studies have overlooked. But he goes further, highlighting the tendency of his discipline to ignore and obfuscate. In so doing, Bedarida "queers" business as usual.

Bedarida asserts that, up until this point, Italian art criticism has been largely content to maintain Italian culture's long-standing policy—a policy that cuts across Italian history—of "Don't ask, don't tell." (Giori also mentions this strategy, titling one of his chapters "Silence"; 2017, 11–45.) Bedarida breaks this silence, first admitting that, in an earlier version of this study, his thesis, he did not even hint at Cagli's homosexuality because "seguivo la tendenza allora dominante nella pratica storico-artistica in Italia e in particolare nella letturatura su Cagli" (I followed the then dominant tendency in art historical-artistic practice in Italy and in the literature on Cagli in particular) (14–15); he then criticizes this tendency as being intellectually dishonest. This leads to a methodological statement on why a reading of Cagli's life and work must engage with the artist's homosexuality:

Il rischio da evitare è il determinismo psico-bio-graphico. L'obiettivo è individuare i livelli operativi e discorsivi attraverso cui l'omosessualità di Cagli entra a far parte del suo lavoro d'artista e della sua rilevanza storica, cercando il linguaggio più adatto per non banalizzare. (15)

(The risk to avoid is psycho-biographical determinism. The objective is to identify the operative levels and discourses by means of which Cagli's homosexuality

> joined his artistic work and its historical relevance, searching for the language most suited to avoid trivializing it.)

Given the cultural climate of the *ventennio*, which rendered impossible almost any public discourse on homosexuality, Bedarida reminds us that it is a mistake to seek "una documentazione che attesti esplicitamente la componente omosessuale nelle intenzioni dell'artista così come nella ricezione della sua opera. Bisogna inevitabilmente leggere tra le righe" (a record that explicitly attests to the homosexual component of the intention of the artist or the reception of his work. One must inevitably read between the lines) (15). Bedarida's book argues that a queer reading of Cagli's work is essential. Such a reading, however, depends precisely upon producing the kinds of "alternative" readings Gauntlett laments (cited in Giori 2017, 7). This is what it means to understand Cagli and his audience as historical and not transcendent.

One of Bedarida's queerest moves, however, is his refusal to turn Cagli into a hero. Cagli's relationship to the regime is ambiguous at best, and it is perhaps his lingering association with Fascism that has prevented him from receiving the recognition many other painters from the period, including Carlo Levi and Renato Guttuso, believed was his due. Bedarida's book is prefaced with an essay authored by perhaps the greatest living art historian of the *ventennio*, Enrico Crispolti (2018). Crispolti praises Bedarida's study but takes issue with its account of Cagli as "attivo promotore e costruttore della retorica di regime e della più esplicita propaganda Fascista" (active promotor and constructor of the rhetoric of the regime and the most explicit Fascist propaganda) (135).

Like Crispolti, I hesitate over this description of Cagli, and in my own work I challenge what Crispolti characterizes as Bedarida's "attribuire allusivamente tout court" (attributing allusively tout court) to the young Cagli the role of propagandist (2018, xv). Cagli's work is more contradictory than Bedarida's claim suggests, and its homoerotic portrayals of masculinity are often of a type specifically rejected by Fascism, too close to the classical figure of the ephebe (on this rejection, see Papa 2003, 192–193). But in its refusal to plumb the past for gay heroes and to attend to Cagli—someone whose biography resists our attempts to forge a heroic queer past of which we are the outcome—Bedarida's study is queer. His refusal to redeem Cagli disrupts "not only the progress narrative of queer history but also our sense of queer identity in the present" (Love 2007, 8).

To return to the question of uneven temporalities, a recent experience in Italy highlighted for me the complexities of engaging in research in Italian queer studies. At work on a book on Cagli and encouraged by Bedarida's study, I visited the painter's archive to discuss permission to publish images. Before granting me permission, the archivists asked to read my manuscript. I then mentioned a section of the book on Franco Muzzi, Cagli's former assistant and lover, who is still alive and was at the time of our conversation literally sitting in the next room. The section in question interpreted a photograph of the two men for the signs of intimacy it offers to those willing to look and see. One of the archivists asked me to remove this section, and when I asked why, he specifically joked that Muzzi was Sicilian.

I do not want to over-read this very local occurrence. Nonetheless, it represents a concrete instance of how heteronormative assumptions and concerns still interfere with the producing of knowledge of queer Italy. That such efforts remain, over fifty years after Cagli's death, hindered by that widely normalized practice of "Don't ask, don't tell," suggests the work ahead of us.

Notes

1. To state what is at issue here another way: "There is no necessary, unified, privileged connection between the single works of art, philosophy, and so forth created in a given historical period and the main features which, by accretion and sedimentation, are most often used in elaborating the traditional narrative about that period" (Valesio 2004: xvi).

Works Cited

Bedarida, Raffaele. 2018. *Corrado Cagli, la pittura, l'esilio, l'America (1938–1947)*. Rome: Donzelli.

Benadusi, Lorenzo. 2013. "Review of John Champagne." *Aesthetic Modernism and Masculinity in Fascist Italy. Il mestiere di storico* 2013(1): 167.

Benjamin, Walter. 1968. "Theses on the Philosophy of History." In *Illuminations*, edited by Hannah Arendt, translated by Henry Zohn, 253–264. New York: Harcourt Brace Jovanovich.

Brown, Wendy O. 2001. *Politics Out of History*. Princeton: Princeton University Press.

Champagne, John. 2013. *Aesthetic Modernism and Masculinity in Fascist Italy*. New York: Routledge.

Compagno, Dario. 2012. "Theories of Authorship and Intention in the Twentieth Century. An Overview." *Journal of Early Modern Studies* 1(1): 37–53.

Crispolti, Enrico. 2018. "Prefazione." In *Corrado Cagli*, edited by R. Bedarida, ix–xxv. Rome: Donzelli.

Dall'Orto, Giovanni. 2012. "Contro la 'queer theory.'" http://www.giovannidallorto.com/saggistoria/queer theory/queertheory.html (accessed March 21, 2019).

Dall'Orto, Giovanni. 2015. "Perché Michel Foucault sbaglia." https://www.academia.edu/20009201/Giovanni_DallOrto__Perch%C3%A9_sulla_nascita_dellomosessuale_Michel_Foucault_sbaglia (accessed March 21, 2019).

Doan, Laura. 2013. *Disturbing Practices, History, Sexuality, and Women's Experience of Modern War*. Chicago, IL: University of Chicago Press.

Ferguson, Gary. 2016. *Same-Sex Marriage in Renaissance Rome, Sexuality, Identity, and Community in Early Modern Europe*. Ithaca, NY: Cornell University Press.

Foucault, Michel. 1988. "Nietzsche/Genealogy/History." In *Language, Counter-Memory, Practice*, edited by Donald F. Bouchard, 139–164. Ithaca, NY: Cornell University Press.

Freccero, Carla. 2006. *Queer/Early/Modern*. Durham, NC: Duke University Press.

Freeman, Elizabeth. 2010. *Time Binds, Queer Temporalities, Queer Histories*. Durham, NC: Duke University Press.

Gauntlett, David. 2008. *Media, Gender, and Identity: An Introduction*. London: Routledge.

Ginzburg, Carlo. 1992. *The Cheese and the Worms: The Cosmos of a Sixteenth-Century Miller*, translated by John and Anne C. Tedeschi. Baltimore, MD: Johns Hopkins University Press.

Giori, Mauro. 2017. *Homosexuality and Italian Cinema, From the Fall of Fascism to the Years of Lead*. London: Palgrave Macmillan.

Goldberg, Jonathan. 1992. *Sodometries: Renaissance Texts, Modern Sexualities*. Redwood City, CA: Stanford University Press.

Goldberg, Jonathan, and Madhavi Menon. 2005. "Queering History." *PMLA* 120(5): 1608–1617.

Halperin, David. 2002. *How To Do the History of Homosexuality*. Chicago, IL: University of Chicago Press.

"Letter to AAIS." 2018. July 19. https://groups.google.com/forum/#!msg/aais-queer-studies-caucus/Z-D7_8hrab0/p4U8USJ4CAAJ (accessed March 22, 2019).

Love, Heather. 2007. *Feeling Backward, Loss and the Politics of Queer History*. Cambridge, MA: Harvard University Press.

Mercer, Kobena. 1994. "Black Hair/Style Politics." In *Welcome to the Jungle: New Positions in Black Cultural Studies*, 97–130. New York: Routledge.

Nietzsche, Friedrich. 1988. "On the Uses and Disadvantages of History for Life." In *Untimely Meditations*, translated by R. J. Hollingsdale, 59–123. Cambridge: Cambridge University Press.

Papa, Mauro. 2003. "La rappresentazione del corpo maschile nell'arte dell'Italia fascista." *Memoria e Ricerca* 14(September-December): 177–194.

Pirandello, Luigi. 2011. *Enrico IV*. https://www.liberliber.it/mediateca/libri/p/pirandello/enrico_iv/pdf/pirandello_enrico_iv.pdf (accessed March 21, 2019).

"Queering Italian Studies." 2019. https://conferencechiasmi.wordpress.com/ (accessed March 22, 2019).

Scott, Joan Wallach. 1993. "The Evidence of Experience." In *The Lesbian and Gay Studies Reader*, edited by Henry Abelove, Michèle Aina Barale, and David. M. Halperin, 397–415. New York: Routledge.

Spivak, Gayatri Chakravorty. 1988. "Subaltern Studies: Deconstructing Historiography." In *Selected Subaltern Studies*, edited by Ranajit Guha and Gayatri Chakravorty Spivak, 3–32. New York: Oxford University Press.

Traub, Valerie. 2013. "The New Unhistoricism in Queer Studies." *PMLA* 128(1): 21–39.

Valdman, Albert, ed. 2010. *Dictionary of Louisiana French*. Jackson, MS: University Press of Mississippi.

Valesio, Paolo. 2004. "Foreword: After *The Conquest of the Stars*." In *Italian Modernism, Italian Culture between Decadentism and Avant-Garde*, edited by Luca Somigli and Mario Moroni, ix–xxiii. Toronto: University of Toronto Press.

White, Hayden. 1984. "The Question of Narrative in Contemporary Historical Theory." *History and Theory* 23(1): 1–33.

What's So Different about "Diversity"? Reflecting (on) Plurality of Italian Experience in Teaching and Research

MARK CHU

INTRODUCTION: WHERE I'M COMING FROM AND THE INSTITUTIONAL CONTEXT

The symposium, titled Diversity in Italian Studies and held January 17 and 18, 2019, organized by Anthony Tamburri and Deborah Parker and hosted by the John D. Calandra Italian American Institute, provided a wonderful opportunity to meet students and colleagues from a wide range of backgrounds and to listen to their experiences as minorities or working with minorities as defined by the subtitle of the event: Race/Ethnicity, Gender, Sexuality, Disability, Class. The two days were emotionally charged: As I listened to the accounts of those experiences, I was, at various moments, inspired and frustrated, energized and drained, *commosso* (moved) and angered, even bemused and amused, though sadness often tinged the latter sentiment. Rather than talk about my own varied experiences in Italian studies, which I had recounted anecdotally to Deborah when she was conducting the investigation for her op-ed piece "Race and Foreign Language," I chose to talk about the efforts in my department to embed diversity into the Italian studies curriculum and into our research, and these will be the focus of my essay here. In order to provide some context, however, and not in any attempt to establish my "credentials," it may be useful initially to outline my personal background and status, which, of course, affect my perspective on diversity. I will also, subsequently, include some more personal reflections on my teaching of diversity than I had time for during the symposium.

Appointed in 1991 as lecturer in Italian at University College Cork (UCC), Ireland, I was promoted to senior lecturer in 2002 and served as head of the Department of Italian from 2004 to 2018: As a senior, tenured member of faculty, male and heterosexual, I enjoy a privileged status compared to that of many of the symposium's participants. My personal experience of being (perceived as) "different," however, is long and has often been fraught. My father and maternal grandfather were both Chinese but did not speak the same dialect, and I grew up anglophone, speaking neither my father's rural version of Shanghai-*hua* nor the Cantonese spoken by my grandfather and by the Chinese originating from Hong Kong who made up the majority of the community in 1960s and 1970s London. The other predominant cultural influence in my upbringing was Irish Catholicism, thanks to my maternal great-grandmother. In fact, in answer to the question referred to by Deborah in her article—"How did *you* get into Italian?"—it was attendance at Catholic schools in East London that afforded me the first opportunity to study Italian, as there were, at the time, sufficient numbers of children of Italian origin in my predominantly Irish and Afro-Caribbean secondary school to justify the half-time presence of an Italian government *insegnante di ruolo* (tenured teacher). The inner-city area where I grew up, which is now patchily gentrified and officially renamed and rebranded "Docklands," was then decidedly working class: In Britain, where, it has been suggested, class consciousness is still "[w]hat . . . race is to the U.S." (Wagner 2003) and in the context of Reay's (2005, 912) assertion that, "[i]n contemporary British society social class is not only etched into our culture, it is still deeply etched into our psyches," my mother's attempts to have me and my sisters speak "properly" resulted in our being singled out and victimized at school for "talking posh," while later in life and in other contexts my accent was seen as a marker of my working-class and (as they were once defined) "Chinese Cockney" origins. At passport control in Britain, more than in any other country I have lived in or traveled to, I have been annoyed and, on occasions, enraged by being repeatedly singled out for additional checks and searches that my white compatriots were not subjected to. Perhaps the most blatant and infuriating example of this was when, in December 1997, while driving off a ferry in Wales, I was the only person to be stopped, interrogated about the details and reason for my journey, and asked to produce a passport, which is not a requirement for British or Irish citizens traveling within the Common Travel Area established around the time of the foundation of the Irish state in 1922 (Citizens' Information Board 2019)—even more infuriating to have the immigration officer laugh in my face when I asked if it was not strange that I should be the only person treated in this way. I refer to this and other episodes only as a corrector to those of my white compatriots who think that racism is something that happens somewhere else—in the United States, for example—or that has emerged only recently as a corollary of the Brexit discourse.

To complicate matters further, having lived in Ireland for almost thirty years, I have an English accent that establishes an association with the historic colonizer, so that, on the odd occasion when I have been told to "go back to [my] own country," I was unsure if the exhortation had the same ethnic significance that it would have in Britain, or if it carried a different ideological meaning. In the professional context, in which I have never experienced any overt institutional racism (although I have privately witnessed and challenged anti-Semitic comments and suggestions that Europeans are more intelligent than Africans, and that I, as an Asian, am even more intelligent than the European colleague speaking), I have nevertheless frequently found myself to be the only visible minority at meetings of the Academic Council. When, at one such meeting in 2016, I pointed this out while speaking in opposition to the university's decision to name a building after scientist James Watson, despite his well-documented racist views, I was informally and cordially but nevertheless firmly reminded after the meeting by two colleagues originally from Northern Ireland, at least one of whom was in favor of the name, that I did not have a monopoly on understanding discrimination.[1]

To give the institutional context to my discussion of diversity in Italian at UCC, the university announced the establishment of an Equality, Diversity & Inclusion (EDI) Unit only on March 8, 2017, albeit building on the work of its equality committee and an earlier Higher Education Equality Unit. The EDI Unit's first director was appointed to the role in January 2018. The EDI Unit recently carried out student and staff equality surveys and invited Kalwant Bhopal of the University of Birmingham (England) to give a presentation on a University and College Union sponsored report co-authored with Clare Pitkin (Bhopal and Pitkin 2018). This latter event provided the opportunity for a discussion, also in the Irish context, of the report's recommendations and more generally about race- and ethnicity-related issues, including white bias in the curriculum.

Bhopal and Pitkin's report on the U.K. context highlights a "lack of representation of BME [Black and minority ethnic] staff at all levels, but particularly at senior levels (both for academic and professional staff)" as well as a BME attainment gap among students (2018, 4). The Irish situation is perhaps more extreme, given its different colonial experience and the historical prevalence of emigration over immigration. Consequently, Ireland has a less well-developed discourse regarding diversity, and my institution might be perceived as coming late to the diversity debate.[2] There are, of course, internal questions of diversity in Ireland, not least those associated with the country's imperfect bilingualism (Mac Giolla Chríost 2012) or the contested status of Irish Travelers as an ethnic group (Hayes 2006), but if the institution has been slow off the mark, there is now a climate in which diversity issues are being discussed broadly and appearing high on the institutional agenda, through, for example, the designation of UCC as a University of Sanctuary and the creation of Sanctuary Scholarships (UCC 2019c), and the establishment of the UCC Rainbow Alliance-Allies

Scheme (UCC 2019d). University College Cork has signed onto the Athena SWAN Charter, established by the U.K. Equality Challenge Unit in 2005 "to encourage and recognise commitment to advancing the careers of women," initially in science, technology, engineering, math, and medicine in higher education and research, but extended in 2015 "to recognise work undertaken in arts, humanities, social sciences, business, and law, and in professional and support roles, and for trans staff and students" (Advance HE 2019): The charter was launched in Ireland in early 2015, and UCC received its Bronze Award in April 2016.[3] In any case, as our EDI website points out, "Equality, Diversity and Inclusion have been a core focus of teaching, research, and policy activity for a wide range of UCC staff and students for decades" (UCC 2019b), and it is precisely this kind of normalization of diversity in our teaching and research that I will discuss in the body of this essay.

A look at the staff list of the Department of Italian, UCC, shows a certain level of diversity and, indeed, equality, though this has not been achieved by design:[4] In terms of the tenured staff, we have two senior lecturers, one male and one female (with Silvia Ross having taken over the headship of the department in September 2018), and one male lecturer, Daragh O'Connell, as well as two female College Language Teachers (CLTs), M. Gabriella Caponi and Louise Sheehan, and one male CLT, Donald O'Driscoll. Of our as-yet nontenured lecturers, Chiara Giuliani is full time, while Marco Amici is part time. The research of Silvia Ross and Chiara Giuliani, along with my own research interests, includes questions of gender, migration, and identity. Not untypically, our currently part-time administrator, Aisling O'Leary, is female.

To complete the picture of the institutional context, I should outline the structure of what has traditionally been our main degree, the BA Joint Honours. This involves a four-subject first year, with students taking fifteen European Credit Transfer System credits in each subject: Subsequently, students choose two of the four subjects and take thirty credits in each in both the second and third years.[5] In each year, students of Italian take a ten-credit language module and choose the remaining credits from our offerings of five-credit culture and specialist language modules. Students in the four-year BA (International) spend the third year at a host institution abroad before returning to UCC to complete their degree; in the second year, they take an interdepartmental module, LL2108 (UCC 2019e), coordinated by Silvia Ross, of the Department of Italian, the aim of which is "to develop awareness and understanding of key themes and concepts underlying the societal and cultural impact of internationalisation and globalisation in world perspective" and in which, importantly, students are encouraged to reflect on their own privileged status when crossing borders. Like this course, some of the specifically Italian modules, which can be found by looking at the UCC (2019f) online *Book of Modules*, reflect diversity in their titles, but this has not always been the case, and I will now proceed to outline how we have arrived at the current situation.

FIRST STEPS: THE QUESTION OF GENDER

Toward the end of the 1990s our department decided to diversify a curriculum that had long focused on a male canon, despite the majority of the student body being female.[6] The first step was through the introduction of an optional module within our major program dedicated to "Italian Women Writers" (IT3307) and involving the study of twentieth-century prose and poetry: Conscious of the fact that such a title risked confining women writers to a marginal space, it was nevertheless felt that their near absence from the curriculum at the time justified the establishment of a dedicated space. The use of broad titles of this kind is determined in part by the bureaucratic structures of our institution, which require the listing of available modules for the coming academic year at a very early stage and before approval of research leave. "Italian Women Writers" has been taught by different faculty members over the years, and graduate students have at times taught the course as backfill for faculty on maternity leave or secondment to other roles. Teaching and research on questions of diversity feed into each other: For example, in the context of this course, Silvia Ross has taught on Elena Gianini Belotti's *Adagio un poco mosso*, and she has also published on the author's challenges to societal constraints on and discrimination against older women (Ross 2007; 2017).

Engagement with women writers and female perspectives is even more evident in the thesis topics of doctoral candidates. One such example is Claire Buckley's 2017 thesis, "Wild Woman: Representations of Female 'Deviance' in Modern and Contemporary Italian Fiction," supervised by Silvia Ross. In her study, Buckley engages with Gianna Manzini's *Tempo innamorato* (1928) and Margaret Mazzantini's *Non ti muovere* (2002), comparing the representation of "the ugly woman" in these works with Iginio Ugo Tarchetti's well-known treatment of them in *Fosca* (1869); in a chapter on "the prostitute," she analyzes Armanda Guiducci's *Due donne da buttare* (1976), as well as *La romana* (1947) and *La straniera* (1999), by male writers Alberto Moravia and Younis Tawfik; and in her discussion of "the woman terrorist," she explores Anna Laura Braghetti's *Il prigioniero* (1998), Antonella Tavassa La Greca's *La guerra di Nora* (2003), and Marco De Franchi's *La carne e il sangue* (2008). As can be seen, the emphasis here is not solely on "women writers," but rather on the investigation of a topic that foregrounds women from a range of perspectives.

A similar approach is taken by Nicoletta Mandolini in her 2018 thesis on "Il femminicidio raccontato. Il discorso narrativo italiano sulla violenza letale di genere tra giornalismo e letteratura," again supervised by Silvia Ross and funded by the Irish Research Council (previously the Irish Research Council for the Humanities and Social Sciences, or IRCHSS). Gianluca Cinelli, who won both a President's Scholarship and an Arts Faculty PhD Scholarship (2006; Ross), was encouraged to include a female perspective in his study, "Memoria, storia e soggettività. Un'analisi ermeneutica delle opere autobiografiche di Primo Levi, Nuto Revelli, Rosetta Loy e Mario Rigoni Stern." Women writers and challenges to the male canon are the focus of the research of the following doctoral graduates/candidates: Serena Todesco, "L'isola delle madri assenti: Tracce di presenza femminile nella narrativa storica siciliana contemporanea (1990–2007)" (2012; supervisor Mark Chu)[7]; Alessia Risi, "Azione destabilizzante e impegno politico: Le figure femminili tra il giallo e il nero italiani dal 1980 a oggi (2013; IRCHSS funded; Chu); Mafalda Barbuto, "La migrazione nella scrittura femminile contemporanea: Identità, oralità, multilingualismo, multiculturalismo" (ongoing; Ross); Annette Feeney, "Rappresentazioni delle malattie mentali nella scrittura femminile moderna e contemporanea" (ongoing; Ross). Mariangela Sanese's ongoing doctoral research, "Alexandria in Between. Tropes of Emotional Involvement and Displacement in the Egyptian City-Space of Giuseppe Ungaretti, F.T. Marinetti, and Fausta Cialente" (Ross), again places men and women writers alongside each other in its study of place and adopts postcolonial theory. An earlier dissertation by Nuala Quinton for an MA by Research, "The Controlling Eye: The Female as Object of the Male Gaze in Selected Texts by Alberto Moravia" (1995; Chu) reinterprets a canonical male author through feminist methodology. While these research projects are on modern and contemporary writers, reflecting the primary areas of expertise of the supervisors, Martina Viscardi's IRC-funded study, "Italian Vistas: Mobilities, Texts and Intertexts of Nineteenth-Century Italian and Anglophone Women Travel Writers" (ongoing), is linked to Ross's interest in travel writing, while David Bowe's IRC-funded Postdoctoral Research Fellowship (2018–2020), mentored by Daragh O'Connell, explores "Writing Women's Voices at the Origins of Italian Literary Culture."

FROM INTRODUCING INTERSECTIONALITY TO FOREGROUNDING DIVERSITY

The inclusion of women writers is an obvious way of introducing diversity into the curriculum. At the same time, we have integrated other elements of our research interests to provide a picture of how gender and other interlocking power dynamics combine to marginalize other groups in Italian society.

Courses previously taught by colleagues now retired addressed the Italian Jewish experience, for example, through the inclusion of Bassani's *Il giardino dei Finzi-Contini*, in a course on the modern Italian novel and the module IT2304, "Primo Levi: The Survivor and His Works." Silvia Ross, on "inheriting" the latter, chose to extend the scope of the module, changing the title to "Primo Levi: The Survivor and His Works in the Context of the Holocaust," which allowed her to include Lia Levi's account of her childhood experience of the Racial Laws, *Una bambina e basta*, as well as works by Elena Gianini Belotti and Giuseppe Pederiali, which also feature in Ross's (2003) research.

	Program	
WEEK 1	Introduction to the course: The Risorgimento, 1	MC/CG/DOC
WEEK 2	The Risorgimento, 2	CG
WEEK 3	Themes and Moods in Italian Art, 1870–1910	MC
WEEK 4	Futurism	SR
WEEK 5	Italy and the First World War	MC
WEEK 6	Fascism: Life under the Regime	MC
WEEK 7	Women under Fascism: Motherhood and Propaganda	SR
WEEK 8	Fascism: the Racial Laws and the Holocaust	SR
WEEK 9	World War II in Film	SR
WEEK 10	Essay Writing Workshop	DOC
WEEK 11	World War II in Literature	MC
WEEK 12	*Donne resistenti*	CG
WEEK 13	The Cold War	MC
WEEK 14	The Risorgimento Revisited, 1	DOC
WEEK 15	The Risorgimento Revisited, 2	DOC
WEEK 16	*Il miraculo economico*: the Oppression of the Worker	MC
WEEK 17	*Il sessantotto*	MC
WEEK 18	*Gli anni di piombo*	CG
WEEK 19	*Le donne*: The Women's Movement in the 1970s and 1980s	NM
WEEK 20	*La mafia*, 1	DOC
WEEK 21	*La mafia*, 2	DOC
WEEK 22	Immigration and the Media	MC
WEEK 23	Immigrant Voices	CG
WEEK 24	Examination/Commentary Writing Workshop	DOC

FIGURE 1: ITI201 Syllabus, 2017–2018

Our team-taught first-year culture module IT1201, "Post-Unification Italian Culture and Society," is a text-based survey of Italian culture and key historical moments from 1860 to the present day and, through the study of art, poetry, narrative, music, film, and historical documents, addresses intertwining themes such as class, gender, sexuality, ethnicity, poverty, labor, colonialism, and emigration and immigration. The module was first introduced in 1998–1999, and its teaching team was awarded a President's Award for Excellence in Teaching in 2001–2002 on the basis of a course portfolio and observation of our teaching. Figure 1 shows the syllabus in a typical year (2017–2018) and also gives an idea of how the structure allows us to adapt the syllabus according to research or maternity leave, as is the case with Silvia Ross's research leave in the second semester of the year in question: Topics and/or texts used can be changed within the chronological structure that we have used on most occasions, with a couple of years of experimentation with individual staff members teaching in thematic blocks.

In IT2102, "The Language of the Italian Media," formerly a compulsory module for all second-year students spending their third year in Italy, we examine the language of the political and economic institutions but also look at sexist discourse and discourse on immigration through the lens of critical discourse analysis. Gender and immigration are also regularly included in the team-taught IT2310, "Issues in Contemporary Italian Society through Film and Documentaries," while even the apparently canonical IT2306, "Italo Calvino and the Interpretation of Reality," allows the introduction of discussion of themes such as poverty, class, and the environment. Similarly, the question of the representation of alterity is normalized in modules such as IT2309, "Italian Crime Narratives," reflecting the research of graduate students such as Alessia Risi, referred to above and who taught the module on two occasions, and my own work on authors such as Lucarelli (2001) and Camilleri (2011a–c). Synergy between research on diversity in the department and undergraduate teaching can be found in Chiara Giuliani's module, IT3317, "Cinematic Representations of the 'anni di piombo,'" which resonates with Claire Buckley's work on representations of female terrorists referred to above. The research project of another of our IRC-funded Postdoctoral Fellows, Martina Piperno, also mentored by Daragh O'Connell—"The Other (in) Italy: Survival and Legacy of the Italics (1800–2000)"—directly addresses the question of alterity and, within the context of a module like IT3312, "Italian Contributions to European Culture," allows for the representing of classics, such as Leopardi, argued for by Dennis Looney in his contribution to the Calandra symposium Diversity in Italian Studies. Even in

IT3310, "Futurism: Word and Image," the question of diversity is referenced through discussion of the misogyny of the Futurists.

In addition to our established courses on Primo Levi and on women writers, in recent years we have added modules in which the canon is further challenged and questions of diversity are foregrounded. Chiara Giuliani's module IT2311, "New Italians: Race, Identity, and Memory in Contemporary Literature," is one such example and draws directly on her research in this area. Silvia Ross's module IT3315, "Italian Foodways: Culture, History, Identity," adopts a critical approach to a topic traditionally associated with women but also allows discussion of other forms of diversity through the inclusion of texts such as Igiaba Scego's "Salsicce." A final mention should be made of our team-taught contribution to the MA in languages and cultures in the School of Languages, Literatures, and Cultures: IT6214, "City, Region, and Nation in Italian Literature and Film," directly addresses questions of identity, referring to Italy's tradition of internal diversity.

CONCLUDING REFLECTIONS

These reflections on how diversity manifests itself in the teaching and research in our department are not intended to signal "virtuous" practice or, even less, to claim any primacy in the area. In this respect, I would point to other colleagues' concerted efforts to expand the curriculum of Italian studies to include a more outward-looking approach: A good starting place for an investigation of the topic is Charles Burdett's (2018) policy paper. I hope instead to have provided a modest example of how "diversity" can be normalized within an Italian studies curriculum that aims to expose students to both canonical and noncanonical texts and, in both cases, to do so through what bell hooks describes as the "mutually illuminating interplay of anticolonial, critical, and feminist pedagogies" (10). As the debate around decolonizing the curriculum and the university in general develops (Muldoon 2019), I hope to have illustrated how it is possible to question biases in the curriculum that reinscribe systems of domination, such as racism and sexism, and to reflect a plurality of experiences in what we teach and research.

With regard to my own current research project on contemporary Italian representations of the Chinese, I would admit that it is not something that I would have considered undertaking when I began my doctoral studies in 1982, as I would have been concerned at that time that I would have been *bollato* as having too limited a perspective (in any case, the texts I am examining all date from after 2000). Nor is it a topic that I would have been methodologically equipped to address before my work on the textual construction of identity in Sicilian literature. Postcolonial methodologies have now become mainstream in Italian studies, and

I hope, too, that an environment exists in the discipline that would not discourage younger academics from embarking on research topics that reflect diversity in either their content or their perspective.

Finally, I would like to say that, perhaps inevitably, given the deep personal investment that each of us has in the issues that arose during the symposium, we will probably on occasion disagree on our approach and methodologies and perhaps even offend each other's sensibilities, for, as we agreed during the two days in New York, we cannot put ourselves in each other's shoes. I would like to commend Deborah Parker and Anthony Tamburri, however, for their initiative in opening up a space in which we can learn through the sharing of our own plurality of experience and a range of opinions on diversity can be discussed in a robust and constructive manner.

Notes

1. Coincidentally, the Cork-based *Irish Examiner* carried a story on the second day of our symposium, announcing that UCC was to revoke the naming of the building after Watson (O'Neill 2018).
2. Index Mundi (2018) estimates the following ethnic and religious breakdown of the population of Ireland in 2016. Ethnic groups: Irish 82.2%, Irish Travelers 0.7%, other white 9.5%, Asian 2.1%, black 1.4%, other 1.5%, unspecified 2.6%; Religions: Roman Catholic 78.3%, Church of Ireland 2.7%, other Christian 1.6%, Orthodox 1.3%, Muslim 1.3%, other 2.4%, none 9.8%, unspecified 2.6%.
3. Again by coincidence, while attending the Calandra symposium, I received email notification of a seminar on February 1, 2019, organized by UCC's School of Applied Social Studies, in which Ruth Pearce of the University of Leeds, U.K., engaged in a critical discussion with Chris Williams, head of UCC's College of Arts, Celtic Studies and Social Sciences (CACSSS), on the topic of "Doing gender equality: The contradictions of Athena SWAN." Bhopal and Henderson (2019) "highlight a significant risk that gender and race inequalities become conflated in current equalities work" in universities in the U.K. and argue that "as a consequence of a logic of efficiency that drives Higher Education Institutions (HEIs) to combine gender and race equalities work, and the privileging within this combination of gender, HEIs can publicly work towards equality and inclusion in general terms, without having to confront uncomfortable and deeply embedded practices that perpetuate White privilege in the academy" (Abstract).
4. I refer here only to gender, omitting the more personal questions of ethnicity and sexuality.
5. Within the BA, students can also choose to split their credits 50/10 (Single Honours) or 40/20 (Major). Italian is also taught in the BComm (International), which also involves fifteen credits of Italian in the first year and twenty-five credits in second and fourth years, with the third year spent studying business subjects in Italy. Another important degree program is the recently established four-year BA (World Languages), of which I am program director.
6. One notable exception within the male-dominated canon was former colleague Catherine O'Brien's (1996) teaching and research on Italian women poets.
7. This project is also linked to teaching in our module IT3314, "Imagined Histories: The Historical Novel in Italian."

Works Cited

Advance HE (previously Equality Challenge Unit). 2019. *Athena SWAN Charter*. https://www.ecu.ac.uk/equality-charters/athena-swan/ (accessed July 12, 2019).

Bhopal, Kalwant, and Holly Henderson. 2019. "Competing inequalities: Gender versus race in higher education institutions in the UK." *Educational Review*, August 1. https://doi.org/10.1080/00131911.2019.1642305 (accessed August 8, 2019).

Bhopal, Kalwant, and Clare Pitkin. 2018. *Investigating Higher Education Institutions and Their Views on the Race Equality Charter*. University and College Union. https://ucu.org.uk/HEIs-and-the-Race-Equality-Charter (accessed January 7, 2019).

Burdett, Charles. 2018. "Moving from a National to a Transnational Curriculum: The Case of Italian Studies." Policy paper. *Multilingualism: Empowering Individuals, Transforming Societies*. http://www.meits.org/policy-papers/paper/moving-from-a-national-to-a-transnational-curriculum-the-case-of-italian-st (accessed February 6, 2019).

Chu, Mark. 2001. "*Giallo sarai tu!* Hegemonic Representations and Limits of Heteroglossia in Carlo Lucarelli." *Spunti e ricerche* 16 (*Il giallo*): 45–58.

Chu, Mark. 2011a. "Crime and the South." In *Italian Crime Fiction*, edited by Giuliana Pieri, 89–114. Cardiff: University of Wales Press.

Chu, Mark. 2011b. "Impegno da vendere: Società e politica nella serie del commissario Montalbano di Andrea Camilleri." In *Specchi di realtà: Narrativa e società*, edited by Roberto Bertoni, 67–80. Dublin and Turin: TCD-Trauben.

Chu, Mark. 2011c. "L'etica del potere: Sciascia e i suoi eredi giallisti." *Todomodo. Rivista internazionale di studi sciasciani* (*Journal of Sciascia Studies*) I: 43–54.

Citizens' Information Board. 2019. *Common Travel Area between Ireland and the United Kingdom*. https://www.citizensinformation.ie/en/moving_country/moving_abroad/freedom_of_movement_within_the_eu/common_travel_area_between_ireland_and_the_uk.html (accessed July 12, 2019).

Hayes, Michael. 2006. *Irish Travellers: Representations and Realities*. Dublin: Liffey Press.

hooks, bell. 1994. *Teaching to Transgress*. New York: Routledge.

Index Mundi. 2018. "Ireland Demographics Profile 2018." https://www.indexmundi.com/ireland/demographics_profile.html (accessed January 7, 2019).

Mac Giolla Chríost, Diarmait. 2012. "A Question of National Identity or Minority Rights? The Changing Status of the Irish Language in Ireland since 1922." *Nations and Nationalism* 18(3): 398–416.

Muldoon, James. 2019. "Academics: It's Time to Get Behind Decolonising the Curriculum." *The Guardian*, March 20, 2019. https://www.theguardian.com/education/2019/mar/20/academics-its-time-to-get-behind-decolonising-the-curriculum (accessed July 3, 2019).

O'Brien, Catherine. 1996. *Italian Women Poets*. Dublin: Irish Academic Press.

O'Neill, Kevin. 2018. "UCC to Review Building Name in Light of Comments on Race by Nobel Scientist James Watson." *Irish Examiner*, January 18. https://www.irishexaminer.com/breakingnews/ireland/ucc-to-review-building-name-in-light-of-comments-on-race-by-nobel-scientist-james-watson-898499.html (accessed January 18, 2019).

Reay, Diane. 2005. "Beyond Consciousness? The Psychic Landscape of Social Class." *Sociology* 39(5): 911–928.

Ross, Silvia. 2003. "Remembering Betrayal: The Roman Ghetto's *Pantera Nera* (Black Panther) in Elena Gianini Belotti and Giuseppe Pederiali." In *Cultural Memory: Essays on European Literature and History*, edited by Edric Caldicott and Anne Fuchs, 391–406. Berne: Peter Lang.

Ross, Silvia. 2007. "Subverting Stereotypes of Aging in Elena Gianini Belotti's *Adagio un poco mosso*." *Italica* 84(2–3): 422–437.

Ross. Silvia. 2017. "The Space of the Older Woman in Elena Gianini Belotti's Fiction." In *Women and the Public Sphere in Modern and Contemporary Italy. Essays for Sharon Wood*, edited by Simona Storchi and Marina Spunta, 121–133. Leicester: Troubadour.

University College Cork. 2019a. "People." Department of Italian. https://www.ucc.ie/en/italian/people/ (accessed July 26, 2019).

University College Cork. 2019b. "About the EDI Unit." Equality, Diversity & Inclusion Unit/Comhionannas, Éagsúlacht agus Ionchuimsitheacht. https://www.ucc.ie/en/edi/about/ (accessed January 7, 2019).

University College Cork. 2019c. "University of Sanctuary." Equality, Diversity & Inclusion Unit/Comhionannas, Éagsúlacht agus Ionchuimsitheacht. https://www.ucc.ie/en/edi/universityofsanctuary/ (accessed January 7, 2019).

University College Cork. 2019d. "UCC Rainbow Alliance-Allies Scheme." LGBT Staff. https://www.ucc.ie/en/lgbtstaff/rainbowalliance/ (accessed July 7, 2019).

University College Cork. 2019e. "Crossing Borders: Cultures and Societies." LL2108. Module description. https://www.ucc.ie/admin/registrar/archive/20162017/modules/descriptions/LL.html#LL2108 (accessed July 7, 2019).

University College Cork. 2019f. *Book of Modules*. https://www.ucc.ie/admin/registrar/modules/ (accessed July 7, 2019).

Wagner, Thomas. 2003. "Class Consciousness: Despite Social Changes, Britain's Class Traditions Still a Part of Life." *Tribune* (Welland, Ontario), June 23, B9.

Race and Ethnicity in Italian Film Studies

SHELLEEN GREENE

I begin this essay with a discussion of a scene from Federico Fellini's *Nights of Cabiria* from 1957, starring his wife, Giuletta Masina, in the title role. The scene is from the first night episode in the film, when Cabiria, a prostitute, is picked up by the actor Alberto Lazzari (played by Amedeo Nazzari), and he takes her to the Piccadilly, a Roman nightclub. There they see an "exotic" dance performed by two Black women. The performance lasts for no longer than a couple of minutes, and we are quickly taken back to the main storyline between Cabiria and Alberto. I wanted to begin with this scene because, for me, it was my first entrée into my research and scholarship in the Italian cinema. Having seen this scene repeatedly, I wanted to find out more about these women and their presence in the film. However, at the time, I found no extensive discussion of this scene from the film and little to no studies of race or racial representation in Italian cinema. (See discussion on this scene by Àine O'Healy [2009].) So, I began with a question of absence—an absence in the scholarship that I felt I wanted to address. As a consequence, in my dissertation prospectus, I wrote that I wanted to conduct a study on the presence of African subjects in the films of Federico Fellini. By the time I finished my dissertation, I had not written one word on the work of Federico Fellini. The director was too large and looming of a figure in the Italian cinema, and his films aren't often discussed in relation to race.

I would like to introduce some brief discussion points on the question of diversity in the field of Italian film and media studies and Italian visual cultural studies, where I've produced the majority of my research and scholarship. This conference on Diversity in Italian Studies, held at the John Calandra Italian American Institute on January 17 and 18, 2019, returns me to a question that I (and many of the conference presenters) have heard throughout my career: "Why Italy?" or "Why Italian cinema?" It's a question that I often attempt to evade as it returns me to the anecdotal or personal narrative. Like many at the Calandra diversity conference, I am not of Italian descent, nor did I come to Italian film studies through a traditional Italian studies undergraduate or graduate program. I might say I can't speak directly, or as directly, to the question of diversifying

Italian studies proper. I have always studied the Italian cinema at disciplinary margins and began by posing questions that eventually became an intervention of sorts. If I wanted to study the representation of African-descent subjects in the Italian film, how does one begin? What are my sources? Where are my archives? What are my theoretical and methodological frameworks? U.S. film studies has an extensive body of scholarship on race and representation, due to various histories of the Atlantic slave trade, New World colonialism, chattel slavery, immigration, identity politics, and systemic institutional racism. However, in approaching the Italian national context with different histories of colonialism and of racial hierarchies, I could not simply apply the same methodologies to this area. So, my approach was to draw upon scholarship in both Italian American and Italian studies.

Rather than respond to the "Why Italian cinema?" with a "Why not?" I often trace my interest in Italian film studies to my introduction to postcolonial theory. I began my research in the early 2000s as a graduate student in the PhD program in visual studies at the University of California, Irvine—a program that itself was challenging traditional disciplinary boundaries between art history and film and media studies. Irvine also had a robust Critical Theory Institute, which hosted among other scholars Homi Bhabha and Gayatri Spivak. Postcolonial theory and critical theories of race were my starting point for the Italian cinema. This was occurring at a time when postcolonial theory was making its way into Italian studies. Also during that period, I was influenced by new scholarship on Italian colonialism, such as Karen Pinkus's (1995) *Bodily Regimes: Italian Advertising under Fascism* and later Patricia Palumbo's (2003) edited volume *A Place under the Sun: Africa in Italian Colonial Culture from Post-Unification to the Present*. Another significant moment was finding Vetri Nathan's (2010) "Mimic Nation—Mimic Men: Contextualizing Italy's Migration Culture through Bhabha," in which Nathan uses Bhabha's concept of mimicry to examine racial ambivalence in the Italian national context.

There was a substantial body of English-language scholarship on Italian cinema, indebted to the foundational work of both Peter Bondanella (1983) and Millicent Marcus (1986). Their studies were framed around Italian neorealism, and almost thirty years later, the work of Alan O'Leary and Catherine O'Rawe (2011) allowed us to think beyond the parameters of Italian neorealism and the "great" Italian auteurs. However, for me one of the most important texts was "Ways of Looking in Black and White: Female Spectatorship and the Miscegenational Body in *Sotto la croce del sud*," by Robin Pickering-Iazzi (2002, 194–222). Pickering-Iazzi used bell hooks to examine Fascist colonial cinema, and at the time, I didn't know that was possible.

However, to examine race and racial hierarchies, I actually began by reading Italian American and Italian diaspora studies. Jennifer Guglielmo and Salvatore Salerno's (2003) edited volume *Are Italians White? How Race Is Made in America* provided a framework to think about race and racial hierarchies in the Italian diaspora, especially through the lens of whiteness studies. Pasquale Verdicchio's (1997) work in *Bound by Distance: Rethinking Nationalism through the Italian Diaspora* and his (2005) translation of Antonio Gramsci's *The Southern Question* also offered a starting point to begin an intervention into Italian cinema studies.

For a while I was thinking of doing a project on Italian American and African American cinema, working with the well-known Italian American auteurs, in particular, Martin Scorsese, as well as the films of Spike Lee, both of which addressed race relations between Italian and African Americans. However, I grew up in Queens, New York, in the era of tensions (and ongoing tensions) between Italian Americans and African Americans. I was in elementary school when Michael Griffith, a young man who had immigrated from Trinidad, the same country from which my parents emigrated to the United States in the early 1970s, was beaten and chased to his death in Howard Beach, Queens.[1] I mention this only because growing up in this environment and thinking later about my academic trajectory, I don't know if I saw myself as an African American woman, or an African American of Caribbean descent, becoming or calling myself an Italian American scholar or Italian Americanist.

But still there was a question of the archive. I was looking for films and I quickly found out that searching for Italian films on or about the African diaspora was challenging. I had been studying Italian and after seeing all I could in the United States, I made my first research trip to Italy in 2004, believing I'd walk into the archives and just ask for the films, go back to the United States, and write my dissertation. In the days prior to YouTube, you went to archives and asked for films. I was given typed lists of archival holdings at the National Film Archives in Rome. The LUCE Institute was beginning to digitize its collection of newsreels. I made phone calls to find where the Pier Paolo Pasolini archive was located and was sent to Bologna and then eventually made my way to Turin, to the Archive of the Resistance, where they had a film exhibition on *L'Africa in Italia*, documenting films about or arising from Italian colonialism in Africa from the silent-film to the Fascist era. This archive also had VHS tapes, recorded from RAI television, of films featuring John Kitzmiller (1913–1965), the U.S. Army engineer turned actor who played the African American GI in such films as *To Live in Peace* (1947), *Tombolo* (1947), *Black Paradise* (1947), and *Without Pity* (1948). This work and these travels formed the foundation of what eventually became a project on mixed-race subjects, or the representation of African Italian subjects, in Italian films. I argued that the representation of mixed-race identity could serve as a means of examining constructions of racial and national identities in the Italian cinema; that, in fact, rather than positing a homogeneous Italian racial identity, one could find the construction and circulation of racial discourses in the Italian cinema (Greene 2012).

I finished my dissertation and entered the job market, placing myself within film and media studies, with an emphasis in Italian cinema. I've produced work primarily in film and media studies, but I've spent the majority of my career in a department of visual arts. Broadly, I examine race, gender, and sexuality in the Italian postcolonial imaginary; immigration and the Italian border crisis; and theories of postnationalism. I've presented my work at the South Atlantic Modern Language Association, the Modern Language Association, the American Association of Italian Studies, the Italian American Studies Association, the Society for Cinema and Media Studies, the Neal-Marshall Black Culture Center at Indiana University, and within African American and African diaspora studies conferences. One of my first presentations, back in 2011, was at the Calandra Institute, on the occasion of the publication of Grace Russo Bullaro's (2010) edited volume *From Terroni to Extracomunitario: New Manifestations of Racism in Contemporary Italian Cinema*. I've had to, for various reasons, place greater emphasis on my research and scholarship than on finding a disciplinary "home." I've found places to meet and collaborate with other scholars, one of which is the Queer Studies Caucus of the American Association of Italian Studies, organized by Julia Heim, Sole Anatrone, and S.A. Smythe (2018). I'm particularly interested in the field's expansion into Black Mediterranean studies, as part of a larger Black European studies.

I recently changed institutions and am now working within a cinema and media studies program, where I taught my first graduate seminar on Italian cinema and the African diaspora. I had the opportunity to work with the Department of Italian on a symposium, Italy and the Geopolitics of Migration, which brought together filmmakers Medhin Paolos, an Eritrean Italian multimedia artist and second-generation activist, with sociologist and filmmaker Andrea Segre, writer Ubah Cristina Ali Farah, and theorists Áine O'Healy, Alessandra Di Maio, and Alessandro Dal Lago. I think it's important to introduce new students to these scholars and artists because the work we do is not only about expanding a field, but it's also activism and remembering that we are talking about lived realities. Italy has been and remains a significant site for the current movement of non-Western migrants into countries within the European Union. Like those of many

Western European countries, Italy's government is led by populist and far-right political parties with anti-immigrant policies that have abandoned migrants in the Mediterranean and made migrant rescues illegal.[2] While the political situation grows more urgent in the face of the necropolitics of Italy's current government, an activist second generation speaks to changing demographics of the nation, undermining the myth of racial homogeneity, which was always a fiction. In terms of media production, while birthright citizenship has yet to be realized, second-generation cultural producers are challenging the narratives of migrancy and cultural homogeneity within the country.[3]

What is now referred to as the "cinema of migration" has an almost thirty-year history as established by recent book-length studies including Vetri Nathan's (2017) *Marvelous Bodies: Italy's New Migrant Cinema* and Áine O'Healy's (2019) *Migrant Anxieties: Italian Cinema in a Transnational Frame*. New frameworks, including postcolonial, queer, and critical race theories, have also allowed for a re-evaluation of the Italian national cinema, providing new theoretical approaches, which allow for expanded analysis of Italian silent historical epics, the cinema of the Fascist era, neorealist cinema, as well as the Italian art cinema of the 1950s and 1960s. In my own work, I continue to explore racial discourses in the Italian cinema and recently returned to Federico Fellini to identify the trajectories of postcolonial and racial discourse throughout his oeuvre.[4] In light of these new analytical directions, Italian cinema is truly a *global* cinema, constantly renewed by a greater diversity of scholars who challenge and reconsider the traditional parameters of a national cinema.

Notes

1. On December 20, 1986, Griffith was driving with three other Black men, Cedric Sandiford, Timothy Grimes, and Curtis Sylvester, when their car broke down on Cross Bay Boulevard in Howard Beach, Queens. After attempting to get assistance for their stalled vehicle, Griffith, Sandiford, and Grimes entered New Park Pizzeria at around 12:30 am. There they were called racial epithets and beaten by a group of armed White men. After repeated attempts to escape the beatings, Griffith ran into the Shore Parkway and was hit by car. Three men were convicted of second-degree manslaughter and first-degree assault: Jon Lester (British national), Jason Ladone, and Scott Kern.

2. I refer to the current Italian government, led by Giuseppe Conte, and controlled by the Five Star Movement (M5S) and the League (formerly the Northern League). Under Minister of the Interior and Deputy Prime Minister Matteo Salvini, the Italian government has denied entry into Italian-controlled waters to migrant rescue ships and fined or imprisoned Italians who attempt rescues at sea.

3. See, among many others, Medhin Paolos, *Asmarina* (2015); Fred Kwornu, *18 ius soli* (2011) and *Blaxploitalian: 100 Years of Blackness in the Italian Cinema* (2016); and Leonardo De Franceschi, *La cittadinanza come luogo di lotta. Le seconde generazioni in Italia fra cinema e serialità* (2018). Netflix has planned to

produce *Zero* (2020), the first series focused upon the black Italian experience, featuring writer Antonio Dikele Distefano, an Italian of Angolan descent.

4. See Millicent Marcus's chapter (2001) on *Ginger e Fred* (1986) in *After Fellini: National Cinema in the Postmodern Age*. See Shelleen Greene (in press).

Works Cited

Bondanella, Peter. 1983. *Italian Cinema: From Neorealism to Present.* New York: Continuum.

Bullaro, Grace Russo, ed. 2010. *From Terroni to Extracomunitario: New Manifestations of Racism in Contemporary Italian Cinema.* Leicester, U.K.: Troubador 2010.

Gramsci, Antonio. 2005 [1926]. *The Southern Question,* translated by Pasquale Verdicchio. Montreal: Guernica.

Greene, Shelleen. 2012. *Equivocal Subjects—between Italy and Africa: Constructions of Racial and National Identity in the Italian Cinema.* New York: Bloomsbury.

Greene, Shelleen. In press. "Racial Difference and the Postcolonial Imaginary in the Films of Federico Fellini." In *Wiley Companion to Federico Fellini*, edited by Frank Burke and Marguerite Waller. Hoboken, NJ: John Wiley & Sons, Inc.

Guglielmo, Jennifer, and Salvatore Salerno, eds. 2003. *Are Italians White? How Race Is Made in America.* New York: Routledge.

Marcus, Millicent. 1986. *Italian Film in the Light of Neorealism.* Princeton, NJ: Princeton University Press.

Marcus, Millicent. 2002. *After Fellini: National Cinema in the Postmodern Age.* 181–198, Baltimore, MD: Johns Hopkins University Press.

Nathan, Vetri. 2010. "Mimic Nation—Mimic Men: Contextualizing Italy's Migration Culture through Bhabha." In *National Belongings: Hybridity in Italian Colonial and Postcolonial Cultures,* edited by Jacqueline Andall and Derek Duncan, 41–62, New York: Peter Lang.

Nathan, Vetri. 2017. *Marvelous Bodies: Italy's New Migrant Cinema.* Fort Wayne, IN: Purdue University Press.

O'Healy, Àine. 2009. "[Non] è una somala": Deconstructing African Femininity in Italian Film. *The Italianist* 29: 175–198.

O'Healy, Àine. 2019. *Migrant Anxieties: Italian Cinema in a Transnational Frame.* Bloomington, IN: Indiana University Press.

O'Leary, Alan, and Catherine O'Rawe. 2011. "I padre e i maestri: Genre, Auteurs, and Absences in Italian Film Studies." *Journal of Modern Italian Studies,* 16(1): 107–128.

Palumbo, Patricia, ed. 2003. *A Place under the Sun: Africa in Italian Colonial Culture from Post-Unification to the Present.* Berkeley, CA: University of California Press.

Pickering-Iazzi, Robin. 2002. "Ways of Looking in Black and White: Female Spectatorship and the Miscege-National Body in *Sotto la croce del sud*." In *Re-viewing Fascism: Italian Cinema, 1922–1943*, edited by Jacqueline Reich and Piero Garofalo, 194–222. Bloomington, IN: Indiana University Press.

Pinkus, Karen. 1995. *Bodily Regimes: Italian Advertising under Fascism.* Minneapolis, MN: University of Minnesota Press.

Smythe, S. A. 2018. "The Black Mediterranean and the Politics of Imagination." *Middle East Report* 286(Spring): 3–9.

Verdicchio, Pasquale. 1997. *Bound by Distance: Rethinking Nationalism through the Italian Diaspora.* Madison, NJ: Fairleigh Dickinson University Press.

Roma: arte, cultura, identità: Diversity and Study Abroad

KRISTI GRIMES

Intercultural competence and proficiency in a second language are essential to the liberal-arts–based curriculum of Saint Joseph's University in Philadelphia.[1] In accordance with the university's mission, the General Education Program (GEP) provides students with "the broad knowledge, essential skills, appreciation of diversity, and ethically informed perspective needed by those who would aspire to be 'men and women for others'" ("General Education Program" 2019–2020). One of the six GEP learning outcomes centers on diversity and simultaneously promotes an international dimension to education: "Students will engage respectfully, in a local and global context, with diverse human beliefs, abilities, experiences, identities, or cultures" ("General Education Program" 2019–2020).

Study abroad can be transformative for students as well as for educators. St. Joseph's Center for International Programs organizes faculty-led study tours, including a four-week program based in Rome. Three classes are typically offered; one is conducted in Italian. I began teaching the Italian course in 2017 and followed the established itinerary. While the course was a success overall, I observed some students behaving more often as consumers than as learners, dedicating out-of-class time to dining, shopping, and taking selfies for a social media grand tour.[2] According to statistics reported by the U.S. Department of State, during academic year 2015–2016 "a total of 325,339 U.S. students studied abroad for academic credit."[3] The benefits of study abroad are frequently highlighted and include introducing learners to new cultures and customs while expanding and enriching their worldviews, developing their capacities for empathy, and increasing global awareness. Beyond academic and personal benefits, the professional advantages of living and learning abroad can impact future success. While away from home, students develop critical competencies, including increased adaptability and abilities to interact with peoples of diverse backgrounds. Such skills may translate to increased versatility in a rapidly changing professional landscape.

Because a purposeful and rigorous study-abroad experience prepares students for leadership in an increasingly interdependent world, research emphasizes the important role of language study and immersion.[4] For example, the report from the Association of Departments of English and the Association of Departments of Foreign Languages (ADFL) on best practices maintains "it is of utmost importance to ensure that second language acquisition be integrated meaningfully into students' study abroad experience" (74).[5] Some programs, however, are not as immersive or as language intensive as we might wish.[6] Participation does not automatically result in increased competencies. Many students complete coursework in English, while others pass the majority of their time within an English-speaking cohort and do not use the second language outside the classroom. Despite residing in the host culture, these students remain at a distance, observing the culture from the outside and using the language in sporadic consumer transactions while sampling local cuisine and purchasing souvenirs. These factors render meaningful interactions with the target culture infrequent or difficult. In order to internationalize undergraduate education and to support the goals of developing intercultural or global competencies, language educators must advocate for the importance of language study.

During my first year teaching in St. Joseph's Rome Summer Program, a student asked me where to find local businesses owned by "real" Italians, thereby igniting a vigorous conversation about Italian identities. I listened intently as my students debated the meaning of being Italian and was struck by the fact that, despite Italy's history and the reality visible in their daily interactions, *italianità* (being Italian) seemed broadly understood as singular (even though, as a group, we had considered that the word *identità* is both singular and plural) and correspondent with being White and/or Catholic. Who is a "real" Italian is a complex question that predates the Risorgimento period and is reflected in the famous line attributed to Massimo D'Azeglio: "L'Italia è fatta, gl'italiani sono ancora da farsi" (Italy has been made, Italians are yet to be made) (my translation). Historically, national identity has often been viewed as constructed in opposition to another country or group of people.[7] And, yet, identities are evolving and can be expressed in dynamic and complex ways. Bhabha (1994) has described the ways in which national identity vacillates between the historical past—the product of a dominant narrative that includes some and excludes others—and the present—a performative identity that remakes itself each time it is expressed.[8] A process of identification and ambivalence in which identities are not fixed exists at the center of the colonialist power structure.[9]

The impromptu conversation about Italian identities presented a challenge as well as an opportunity, and ultimately it inspired me to overhaul the course. Through research and trial and error, I found that focusing on diversity can help students engage in purposeful ways with the cultures and identities of Rome. I changed the course title to "*Roma: arte, cultura, identità*" and updated the content in order to focus on dynamic and expanding Italian identities. Diversity-intensive courses are part of the curriculum at St. Joseph's University. Such courses support the Jesuit mission of the university and aim to help students scrutinize "assumptions about identity and difference" ("Curricula" 2019–2020). Furthermore, these courses "analyze the construction and maintenance of social categories such as race, class, religion, sexual orientation, gender, age, and ability as well as the material, political, economic, social, and ethical consequences of these identities" ("Curricula" 2019–2020). Following are the learning objectives for diversity courses.

> Students will:
>
> Scrutinize their assumptions about identity and difference
>
> Examine issues of subordination and privilege in their own and others' lives
>
> Understand the complex, dynamic, and dialectical nature of culture and the political, historical, and economic conditions that shape it
>
> Investigate patterns of oppression and resistance among particular cultural groups
>
> Develop understandings about the experiences and contributions (political, social, economic, etc.) of particular cultural communities that have been systematically marginalized
>
> Develop an awareness of their roles as potential activists for social justice and agents for social change. ("Diversity, Globalization, and Non-Western Area Studies Courses Submission Guidelines" 2019)

Course proposals and syllabi must adhere to specific criteria and undergo a rigorous certification process.[10] Below are the benchmarks for the approval of diversity courses.

- Diversity should permeate the course. It should not be a single unit in the class but be taught throughout the course.
- Diversity courses analyze the construction and maintenance of social categories such as race, class, religion, sexual orientation, gender, age,

ability, and culture as well as the material, political, economic, social, and ethical consequences of these identities.

- In order for diversity to be taught effectively, it would be useful to establish a common vocabulary within the course so that diversity is interpreted in a systematic, rigorous, empirically grounded, and/or theoretically driven way.
- Each diversity course employs theoretical frameworks that provide sustained analytical inquiry. Each course emphasizes the ways in which social categories overlap and interact to produce multiple identities and attends to the complex consequences of these intersections.
- A course should create an inclusive and challenging atmosphere. Where possible it should foster dialogue that is open and conducive to a diverse and inclusive learning environment. This will in turn enable students to break out of their comfort zones and openly discuss sensitive issues. The syllabus should demonstrate how this will be accomplished through classroom discussion, readings, assignments, guest lecturers, and so forth. ("Diversity, Globalization, and Non-Western Area Studies Courses Submission Guidelines" 2019)

My use of the term *diversity* aligns with the description provided above as well as with the call for papers for the symposium Diversity in Italian Studies held at the John D. Calandra Italian American Institute in January 2019: "The binomial of race/ethnicity is just one of the issues pertinent to the notion of 'diversity' in Italian studies. Gender, sexuality, and class are also among significant concerns within Italian studies." In the context of study abroad, diversity applies to curricular content, expanding the diversity of students who go abroad (including, but not limited to, nonwhite students and the LGBTQIA+ community), and the variety of destinations to which students are sent. Additionally, diversity may apply to particular academic majors and concentrations or to student populations that do not participate as frequently as others (e.g., student athletes or first-generation students). For programs in which the majority of courses is taught in English, diversity extends to classes conducted in the second language (or the primary language of the host country).

One of the most impactful changes I made involved predeparture activities, which were designed to help students increase awareness of their own values and sociocultural identities and to invest in their personal learning. Guided assignments can help shape the way in which learners approach the experience and lay the groundwork for meaningful engagement with host cultures. Readings contained essential vocabulary and provided a theoretical background on the topics of postcolonial theory, cultural studies, and migration studies.[11] Additionally, I created a unit on cinema focusing on divergent Roman cultures.[12]

Prior to departure it is essential to build a strong community of learners. Group meetings allow program leaders to measure student objectives. During these sessions, students identified program expectations and set personal learning goals. The literature shows that students hold different levels of desire for integration as well as different goals for language learning. Wenger's (1998) concept of mutual engagement emphasizes the ways in which community members can support each other while negotiating meaning in a new environment. Investment and accountability are critical to personal success and to the success of the entire group. ADFL's best-practices report urges educators to "ensure that students receive extensive predeparture advising to prepare them for the challenging experience of living and studying abroad and reentry advising to help them understand and integrate their experience abroad on their return home" (73). A step beyond advising and mentoring involves the creation of predeparture and reentry courses "possibly team-taught with faculty members from other disciplines that engage the theories and practices of cross- and intercultural transitions."[13]

While in Rome students significantly improved communication skills. In comparing and contrasting similarities and differences between American cultures and those of the Italian-speaking world, students scrutinized their assumptions about difference. Through site visits and discussions on Italian history, art, film, and works by and about multiethnic and migrant artists living in Rome, students explored dynamic and expanding Italian identities.[14] Studying the experiences of Rome-based multiethnic artists and writers (e.g., Amir Issaa, Kossi Kombla-Ebri, and Igiaba Scego) allowed us to explore intersections among a diversity of cultures within one city. Guest speakers and excursions provided opportunities for deepening our analyses. Exploring the intersection of art and identity allowed for the introduction of topics on race and gender. I aimed to incorporate community activities. For example, after learning about Amir Issaa, we attended one of his performances. Additionally, we visited publishing companies and centers that promote multicultural education.

Task-based activities helped students acquire practical skills. As students increased communication skills in Italian, they engaged with diverse beliefs, abilities, cultures, and identities, thereby increasing their intercultural competence. Throughout the course, students maintained a daily journal in which they recorded perceptions about their experiences, observations about their cross-cultural challenges, successes, and failures. I asked them to pay attention to the ways in which language, identity, Otherness, subordination, and resistance coexist in the works we studied. The journal also included notes, summaries, and reflections on guest lectures and site visits as well as a vocabulary journal.

In order to contextualize our analyses and discussions and to take advantage of Rome as our classroom, I made significant changes to the itinerary. Whenever possible I took students to less-crowded monuments and museums, such as the Museo Centrale del Risorgimento. During our visit we discussed the ways in which Rome has long been a meeting place of diverse peoples, languages, and traditions. Because the contemporary situation of migration to Italy can be considered against the backdrop of Italy's diasporas, we discussed diversity from a historic perspective. For more than 150 years, Italy's historical narrative has been defined by emigration. Many art objects held at the museum, including a painting on display of the 1849 battle on the hill of Gianicolo, feature the participation of *garibaldini* of color.[15] Indeed, it is possible to overemphasize a perceived whiteness in Roman museums. For example, the white Greek and Roman sculptures at the Vatican were originally painted in vibrant colors, and many depict people of color. Margaret Talbot has recently observed that assumptions about race and aesthetics have suppressed this truth.[16]

I mentioned earlier that St. Joseph's Rome Summer Program is comprised of three courses, two of which are conducted in English. Because we participate in several excursions as a large group, when unable to change the itinerary, I modified the approach. For example, our three-day excursion to Florence focused on connections between the Renaissance and the present day. As a link to our study of multiethnic artists, I created a unit titled Race and the Renaissance: Refining Perceptions, which highlights the African presence in the long sixteenth century (circa 1450–1640). An excellent resource is the catalog for a ground-breaking 2013 exhibition held at the Walters Art Museum in collaboration with the Princeton University Art Museum. *Revealing the African Presence in Renaissance Europe* (Spicer 2012) featured works of art drawn from the Walters, major museums in the United States and Europe, and private collections.[17] The show examined the fascination with, and desire for, knowledge and power that characterized European responses to Africa during the early modern era.

During this period newly established trade routes linked Africa and Europe, and Africans entered Europe with increased frequency and in greater numbers: as pilgrims, as members of delegations sent by African rulers, and as slaves. In evaluating the vigorous relationship between Europe and Africa during the Renaissance, artworks provide evidence of the varied perceptions that developed on account of increased contact between the two continents, which also stimulated the development of ideas about race, identity, and cultural difference. Because this topic has only recently received scholarly attention, we participated in the developing academic discourse. We explored visual representations of Africans in the form of portraits, oil paintings, frescoes, and other documents produced in early modern Italy. This approach allowed us to view art-historical developments as part of a dynamic cross-cultural engagement as well as to frame our understanding of early modern visual traditions in a more inclusive manner. Two examples of artworks we studied were Benozzo Gozzoli's fifteenth-century fresco (held at the Palazzo Medici Ricciardi) displaying the procession of the Magi and Angelo Bronzino's portrait of Alessandro de' Medici (in oil on tin, painted between 1555 and 1565 and held at the Uffizi Galleries). Making connections with Pontormo's 1534–1535 portrait of the same subject at the Philadelphia Museum of Art made an ideal re-entry activity and allowed us to continue our consideration of color and social class in Renaissance Italy.[18]

Educators and program leaders must help students play an active role in their study-abroad experience. Students should engage with the host culture as active contributors and should not be like conventional tourists who experience or consume the culture. To conclude I outline strategies for an action plan designed to help program leaders make study abroad as inclusive and impactful as possible. The following recommendations are based on the Diversity Abroad Network's Access, Inclusion, and Diversity Roadmap assessment. The website contains a wealth of useful information and examples.[19]

STATS AND DATA: ASSESS THE CURRENT STATE OF DIVERSITY AND INCLUSION

Make data-driven assessments and decisions. It is essential to begin by obtaining as much data as possible in order to understand the profiles of the population that is going abroad. Assessing student participation in study abroad will help identify areas of success and areas that need development.

SET COLLABORATIVE GOALS AND CREATE A STRATEGY

Not all institutions have a specific strategy for diversity and inclusion in study-abroad programs. Collaborate with study-abroad and diversity offices, student life, fellowships offices, the athletics department, and other related areas to create a plan with goals and approaches to recruiting, supporting, and retaining students throughout the study-abroad experience.

ADVISING AND PROFESSIONAL DEVELOPMENT

The training and support that staff receive are important for diversifying the students going abroad as well as for developing inclusive programming and establishing advising, mentoring, and support systems.

MARKETING AND RECRUITMENT

Develop messaging to make study abroad more attractive and inclusive of all students.

SCHOLARSHIPS AND FUNDING

Funding is a key barrier to accessing study abroad. In addition to finding and promoting scholarships, review systems that can be put into place to make study abroad more affordable. ADFL's best-practices report notes: Development officers should seek out donors interested in funding scholarships and endowments that target study-abroad goals. . . . Whenever possible, students' financial aid (institutional, state, federal, etc.) should be portable. Websites can be useful to students, but institutions should make assistance available to students locally for determining appropriate sources of financial aid for study abroad. (74)

PROVIDE SUPPORT PRIOR TO DEPARTURE, WHILE ABROAD, AND UPON RE-ENTRY

Advising and mentoring are critical. Support should not end when students leave campus. Consider creating predeparture and re-entry courses.

Notes

1. For frameworks and definitions of intercultural and/or global competence, see https://www.actfl.org/news/position-statements/global-competence-position-statement (accessed March 29, 2019) and https://www.teachingenglish.org.uk/article/intercultural-communicative-competence (accessed March 29, 2019).
2. On study-abroad and consumerist views of education, see Goldoni (2013, 363–364).
3. The top ten destinations for U.S. students studying abroad in academic year 2015/2016: United Kingdom, Italy, Spain, France, Germany, China, Ireland, Australia, Costa Rica, and Japan. Italy was the top non-English-speaking destination. See https://studyabroad.state.gov/value-study-abroad/study-abroad-data (accessed March 28, 2019).
4. See, in particular, Byram and Feng (2006) and DuFon and Churchill (2006).
5. Studies on best practices include Thomas (2009) and Schulze (2016).

6. See, in particular, Goldoni's (2013) study on immersion and study abroad.
7. On the role of migrant literature within the construction of Italian national identity and national literature, see Orton (2012).
8. "Deprived of that unmediated visibility of historicism—'looking to the legitimacy of past generations as supplying cultural autonomy'—the nation turns from being the symbol of modernity into becoming the symptom of an ethnography of the 'contemporary' within modern culture. Such a shift in perspective emerges from an acknowledgement of the nation's interrupted address articulated in the tension between signifying the people as an a priori historical presence, a pedagogical object; and the people constructed in the performance of narrative, its enunciatory 'present' marked in the repetition and pulsation of the national sign" (Bhabha 1994, 147).
9. The colonized may take on characteristics of the colonizers' identities, while the colonizers may assume features of the colonized: "[T]he very place of identification, caught in the tension of demand and desire, is a space of splitting. The fantasy of the native is precisely to occupy the master's place while keeping his place in the slave's avenging anger. 'Black skin, white masks' is not a neat division; it is a doubling, dissembling image of being in at least two places at once that makes it impossible for the devalued, insatiable évolué (an abandonment neurotic, Fanon claims) to accept the colonizer's invitation to identity: 'You're a doctor, a writer, a student, you're different, you're one of us.' It is precisely in that ambivalent use of 'different'—to be different from those that are different makes you the same—that the Unconscious speaks of the form of the otherness, the tethered shadow of deferral and displacement. It is not the colonialist Self or the colonized Other, but the disturbing distance in-between that constitutes the figure of colonial otherness—the white man's artifice inscribed on the black man's body. It is in relation to this impossible object that the liminal problem of colonial identity and its vicissitudes emerges." Finally, the question of identification is never the affirmation of a pregiven identity, never a self-fulfilling prophecy—it is always the production of an image of identity and the transformation of the subject in assuming that image. The demand of identification—that is, to be for an Other—entails the representation of the subject in the differentiating order of otherness. Identification, as we inferred from the preceding illustrations, is always the return of an image of identity that bears the mark of splitting in the Other place from which it comes (Bhabba 1994, 64).
10. For information about certification policies visit https://sites.sju.edu/geprog/gep-certification/.
11. Students read excerpts from the following: Parati (2005, 2012, 2017), Gore (2005), Kinginger (2010), Norton (2000), Ogden (2007), Orton (2012), and Talburt and Stewart (1999).
12. Students selected two films from a list that included *Cuori Puri* (Roberto De Paolis, 2017), *Le fate ignoranti* (Ferzan Özpetek, 2001), *La finestra di fronte* (Ferzan Özpetek, 2003), *Aulò* (Simone Brioni, 2012), *La quarta via* (Simone Brioni, 2012), *Terra di transito* (Paolo Martini, 2014), *Scialla!* (Francesco Bruni, 2011), *Se Dio vuole* (Edoardo Maria Falcone, 2015), *Non essere cattivo* (Claudio Cagliari, 2015), *Lo chiamavano Jeeg Robot* (Gabriele Mainetti, 2016), *Perfetti sconosciuti* (Paolo Genovese, 2016), and *Gente di Roma* (Ettore Scola, 2003). As a postviewing task, students read critical essays, including Brioni's (2013) "Migrant Stories and Italian Colonialism," and then answered questions and wrote reflection essays.
13. See ADFL report (73). For examples from a variety of institutions, see "Internationalizing Undergraduate Education" (73).
14. A number of excellent scholarly and pedagogical resources are available and include: Graziella Parati's *Migrant writers and urban space in Italy: proximities and affect in literature and film* (2017) and *Migration Italy: the art of talking back in a destination culture* (2005), and Vetri Nathan's *Marvelous Bodies* (2017). *Migrazioni contemporanee: Testi e contesti* by Di Filippo and Di Florio (2017) features literature and in-depth interviews with migrant writers, including Christiana De Caldas Brito, Ubax Christina Ali Farah, Gabriella Ghermandi, Gëzim Hajdari, Kossi Kombla-Ebri, Ron Kubati, Amara Lakhous, Salah Methnani, Ingy Mubiayi, Igiaba Scego and Laila Wadia.
15. Artist: B. Petraglia, *Un fatto d'arme della Repubblica Romana del 1849 sul Gianicolo*, 1853, oil on canvas, part of the permanent collection of the Museo Centrale del Risorgimento, Rome.
16. See, e.g., Talbot's (2018) essay.
17. Additional resources include Earle and Lowe (2005) and Northrup (2009).
18. In addition to the unit Race and the Renaissance: Refining Perceptions, we discussed the representation of women in the Early Modern Period. Readings included Cropper (2001), Langdon (2006), Martines (1974), and Simons (1992).

19. See http://www.insightintodiversity.com/11-steps-to-diversifying-study-abroad/. Useful websites on this topic include: Diversity Abroad Network's Access, Inclusion, and Diversity roadmap (https://www.diversityabroad.com/); the Institute of International Education (https://www.iie.org/); the Forum on Education abroad (www.forumea.org); and Insight into Diversity's action plan (http://www.insightintodiversity.com/11-steps-to-diversifying-study-abroad/).

Works Cited

Bhabha, Homi K. 1994. *The Location of Culture*. London: Routledge.

Brioni, Simone. 2013. "Migrant Stories and Italian Colonialism: A Report on Two Documentaries." *The Italianist* 33(2): 321–324.

Byram, Michael, and Anwei Feng. 2006. *Living and Studying Abroad: Research and Practice*. Clevedon, U.K.: Multilingual Matters.

Cropper, Elizabeth. 2001. "Life on the Edge: Artemisia Gentileschi, Famous Woman Painter."

"Curricula." 2010–2020. St. Joseph's University online academic catalogue. https://academiccatalog.sju.edu/curricula/#overlaytext (accessed April 2, 2019).

Di Filippo, Giusy, and Martina Di Florio. 2017. *Migrazioni contemporanee: Testi e contesti*. New York: Farinelli.

"Diversity, Globalization, and Non-Western Area Studies Courses Submission Guidelines." 2019. St. Joseph's University General Education Program. https://sites.sju.edu/geprog/files/2017/07/d-g-nw-CITF-criteria.pdf (accessed March 28, 2019).

DuFon, Margaret A., and Eton E. Churchill. 2006. *Language Learners in Study Abroad Contexts*. Buffalo, NY: Multilingual Matters.

Earle, T. F., and K. J. P. Lowe, eds. 2005. *Black Africans in Renaissance Europe*. Florence: Herzog.

"General Education Program." 2019–2020. St. Joseph's University online General Education Program requirements. https://sites.sju.edu/geprog/ (accessed March 29, 2019).

Goldoni, Federica. 2013. "Students' Immersion Experiences in Study Abroad." *Foreign Language Annals* 46(3): 59–376.

Gore, Joan Elias. 2005. *Dominant Beliefs and Alternative Voices: Discourse, Belief, and Gender in American Study Abroad*. New York: Routledge.

Kinginger, Celeste. 2010. "American Students Abroad: Negotiation of Difference?" *Language Teaching* 44: 216–227.

Langdon, Gabrielle. 2006. *Medici Women: Portraits of Power, Love and Betrayal from the Court of Duke Cosimo I*. Toronto: University of Toronto Press.

Mann, Judith, and Keith Christiansen, eds. 2001. *Orazio and Artemisia Gentileschi*, 263–280. New Haven, CT: Yale University Press.

Martines, Lauro. 1974. "A Way of Looking at Women in Renaissance Florence." *Journal of Medieval and Renaissance Studies* 4:15–28.

Nathan, Vetri. 2017. *Marvelous Bodies: Italy's New Migrant Cinema*. West Lafayette, IN: Purdue University Press.

Northrup, David. 2009. *Africa's Discovery of Europe 1450–1850*, 2nd ed. Oxford: Oxford University Press.

Norton, Bonny. 2000. *Identity and Language Learning: Gender, Ethnicity and Educational Change*. New York: Longman.

Ogden, Anthony. 2007. "The View from the Veranda: Understanding Today's Colonial Students." *Frontiers: The Interdisciplinary Journal of Study Abroad* 15: 2–20.

Orton, Marie. 2012. "Writing the Nation: Migration Literature and National Identity." *Italian Culture* 30(1): 21–37.

Parati, Graziella. 2005. *Migration Italy: The Art of Talking Back in a Destination Culture*. Toronto: University of Toronto Press.

Parati, Graziella. 2017. *Migrant Writers and Urban Space in Italy: Proximities and Affect in Literature and Film*. Cham, Switzerland: Palgrave Macmillan.

Parati, Graziella, ed. 2012. *New Perspectives in Italian Cultural Studies: Definitions, Theory, and Accented Practices.* Madison, NJ: Fairleigh Dickinson University Press.

Schulze, Whitney L. 2016. *Best Practices for Increasing Diversity in Study Abroad: A Manual for Small Private Co-Ed Universities in the United States.* Master's Projects and Capstones 347. https://repository.usfca.edu/capstone/347 (accessed May 7, 2019).

Simons, Patricia. 1992. "Women in Frames: The Gaze, the Eye, the Profile in Renaissance Portraiture." In *Expanding Discourse: Feminism and Art History,* edited by Norma Broude and Mary D. Garrard, 39–57. New York: Harper Collins.

Spicer, Joaneth. 2012. *Revealing the African Presence in Renaissance Europe.* Baltimore, MD: The Walters Art Museum.

Talbot, Margaret. 2018. "The Myth of Whiteness in Classical Sculpture." *The New Yorker,* October 29. https://www.newyorker.com/magazine/2018/10/29/the-myth-of-whiteness-in-classical-sculpture (accessed March 28, 2019).

Talburt, Susan, and Melissa A. Stewart. 1999. What's the Subject of Study Abroad? Race, Gender, and "Living Culture." *Modern Language Journal* 83: 163–175.

Thomas, Downing A. 2009. "Best Practices in Study Abroad: A Primer for Chairs of Departments of Foreign Languages." *The Chair's Reference: Special Joint Issue: ADE Bulletin and ADFL Bulletin* Winter-Spring: 72–76.

Wenger, Etienne. 1998. *Communities of Practice: Learning, Meaning and Identity.* Cambridge: Cambridge University Press.

"Un uom nasce a la riva de l'Indo": Expanding the Field of Medieval Italian Studies

AKASH KUMAR

When Dante meets the eagle of justice in *Paradiso* 19, it quotes him asking a remarkably pointed question: If a man born on the banks of the Indus river where Christ is not read nor written about, but he is virtuous in all ways, where is the justice that condemns him?: "Ov'è questa giustizia che lo condanna? / ov'è la colpa sua se ei non crede?" (Where is this justice then that would condemn him? / Where is his sin if he does not believe?) (*Paradiso* 19.77–78, Mandelbaum trans.). The heavenly answer that Dante receives amounts to a Job-like brush-off: Who are you to ask such a question? Who are you to judge events a thousand miles away from where you are? But the question lingers in the air and indeed finds further force later on in the canto with the radical statement that an Ethiopian might well shame those Christians who go around shouting "Christ, Christ" and be saved himself when they are not. There is still more heterodoxy to be had with the surprise appearance of Ripheus, the saved Trojan in *Paradiso* 20, who necessarily draws our attention back to the problem of exclusion that Virgil so poignantly embodies in the *Commedia*.

But the specific mention of the man born on the bank of the Indus has long held special meaning for me. My father was born not far from the Indus, perhaps some hundred miles away in a small village in the district of Sargodha in what is now Pakistan. In drawing together the personal and the scholarly, I take as a model Alberto Manguel's 2015 book *Curiosity*. Launching on an extended reading of Dante's poem and meditating on his own personal life experience, Manguel fuses together a remarkable array of sources that range from the literary to the philosophical and span the globe in a display of what might appeal to a broadly conceived twenty-first-century readership. In laying out his claim for the value of what he does, Manguel writes: "And yet, one might be able to justify such an exercise by suggesting that every reading is, in the end, less a reflection or translation of the original text than a portrait of the reader, a confession, an act of self-revelation and self-discovery" (Manguel 2015, 8). I propose to balance self-revelation and a historicizing approach to the *Commedia* that grounds it in the Italian literary tradition of the thirteenth and fourteenth centuries, its reception across time and space by readers of many stripes, and attention to a global Middle Ages that might serve to highlight and emphasize certain aspects of Dante's poetic practice.

In *Culture and Imperialism*, Edward Said took issue with the birth of the field of comparative literature as "epistemologically organized as a sort of hierarchy, with Europe and its Latin Christian literatures at its center and top" and drew particular attention to the "supreme importance" of Dante to Auerbach, Curtius, Vossler, and Spitzer (Said 1993, 45). Yet he found hope in the resistance mounted by writers and scholars of the formerly colonized world who "have imposed their diverse histories on, have mapped their local geographies in, the great canonical texts of the European center" (Said 1993, 53). Just as Dennis Looney found a "countertrend" in the manner in which Dante was being used for "anti-imperial" purposes by African American writers, I think we can privilege both whatever forms of reception consider Dante a text of resistance and the kind of reader response that is based not in imposing diverse histories but in being attuned to the global and radical implications present in the text itself (Looney 2011, 6).

The evocation of a man born on the banks of the Indus is a moment that resonates in a profound way across the full span of the *Commedia*. If Limbo and our deep affection for Virgilio as guide and parental figure call into question the justice of exclusion along temporal lines, *Paradiso* 19 forces us to apply nuance to our questioning of exclusion so as to accommodate the contemporary world beyond European borders. In other words, we find in this poignant question a capacious revaluation of excellence that includes not just the classical past but also the wider world of a lived global existence.

There has of course been sustained scholarly and pedagogical attention on this notion, but it merits still more. Brenda Deen Schildgen makes the compelling argument that Dante's attention to the world beyond Italy and the borders of Christendom allows him to more incisively critique his own world. Of *Paradiso* 19 and the Indus, she writes: "Dante uses the boundaries of the Christian lands to raise questions about God's justice, for the question about salvation outside of Christianity is, in fact, a human, rational challenge to received beliefs" (Schildgen 2002, 93). Though she goes on to characterize this moment as falling in line with an orthodox position, other scholars, such as Teodolinda Barolini, see this as an "extraordinary challenge to orthodoxy" in line with Dante's sympathy for the Other (Barolini 2011, 191). Such work shows how we might draw attention to the diversity that is deeply encoded within canonical voices and the new insights it might produce.

Italian scholar Francesco Benozzo in 2013 published the satirical pamphlet *Appello all'UNESCO per liberare Dante dai dantisti* (Appeal to UNESCO to liberate Dante from Dante scholars). While lamenting the defanging of Dante by philologists and professional Dante scholars, he also makes some notable exceptions of Dante readers who have looked at the poem in a more open fashion. One such exception is Ananda Coomaraswamy. Coomaraswamy, a scholar of art who was very influential in bringing Indian art into circulation in the Western world in the early part of the twentieth century, turned regularly to Dante in his attempts to make connections between Eastern and Western thought.

As a representative example, a 1936 article that he published in *Speculum* titled "Two Passages in Dante's *Paradiso*" makes the case that certain obscure fragments, such as *Paradiso* 27.136–138, are made more readily accessible by a turn to the Vedic tradition. A *terzina* (tercet) still considered, in the words of Anna Maria Chiavacci Leonardi's commentary, "di difficile comprensione" (of difficult comprehension), it describes the daughter of the sun whose white skin turns dark as part of the gradual effect of corruption due to greed. Coomaraswamy first turns to Meister Eckhart as an intertext (an oft-cited reference in his scholarship of the soul's union with God that is likened to the sun swallowing up the dawn), and then to the Hindu mythological tradition that offers up sources that consider Dawn as the Sun's daughter instead of its sister. Here is his conclusion:

> We think it has been shown that the references of an exponent of orthodox Christian principles, writing at the end of and as it were resuming all the doctrine of the Middle Ages can actually be clarified by a comparison with those scriptures that were current half the world away and three millenniums earlier in time. (Coomaraswamy 1936, 338)

Coomaraswamy's conclusion moves in the direction of a universal language of religion. While I would quibble, once again, with the notion of Dante as exclusively an exponent of Christian orthodoxy, his comparative move of widening the scope of interpretation has much to offer still. What is half a world away might well clarify and sharpen, or at the very least ask us to consider alternative possibilities and new paradigms of interpretation.

Indeed, in thinking about Indian readers of Dante, we might also highlight the importance of Dante to the poets of the Bengali Renaissance of the nineteenth century, voices like Rabindranath Tagore, the first non-European to win the Nobel

Prize in literature, and Michael Madhusudan Dutta. This importance, as Schildgen has made clear, was along political, cultural, and spiritual lines:

> Many saw Dante as a model to follow: a poet who gave birth to a new poetry and a revived (or new) language in which to express it; a political figure whose literary activity was his means to uphold a moral vision of political life in which justice was the core; and an ethical and religious visionary who strove to restore Christianity to its pristine origins. (2012, 326)

These connections are palpable and create a continuity that expands the scope of what we consider to be medieval studies or Dante studies. That Michael Madhusudan Dutta sent a sonnet to the king of Italy in 1865 on the occasion of the sixth centenary of Dante's birth makes for a vital global connection that goes beyond the more general understanding of his importation of the sonnet form into Bengali poetry. This sort of reception serves to broaden and diversify our perspective of medieval Italian and specifically of Dante's work. Moreover, as G.S. Sahota's (2018) recent reading of Dutta's neo-epic sensibilities makes clear, this is not an imposing of the sort of poetic imperialism that makes for a Third World subservience to a dominant Western cultural form. Instead, he shows that in the simultaneous retelling of Indian and Western epic motifs "both are mutually transformed in subversive ways, revealing the embedded potentialities of a liberal and perhaps even postliberal conception of imperial space" (184).

We might go further in this regard through the perspective of a global Middle Ages. As Geraldine Heng and Lynn Ramey (2014) make clear, this does not require renouncing fields of national literature for the global, but rather enhancing them: "For those of us trained in particular national literatures, languages, and histories, the investigation of globalities yields rewarding glimpses into how the national and global interlock, in literature, and in history" (392). With this in mind, we might think further about the culture around that pointed reference in *Paradiso* 19 to a man born on the banks of the Indus River.

The concept of spices offers a network of connections both literary and personal. In a version of the late thirteenth-century *volgarizzamento Fatti di Cesare*, a Tuscan translation of a French compilation of Lucan, Suetonius, Sallust, and Caesar, there is an expression of Roman lament that even foreign invasion would be better than the suffering that has come about because of the civil war. The men exclaim, "[V]engano contra noi quelli di Media e d'Asia che mangiano cardamo in companaggio" (Let those of Media and Asia who eat cardamom with their bread come against us instead) (*Fatti di Cesare* 2.1, all translations mine unless otherwise noted). It is a mode of essentializing, of course, to characterize all those across the wide span of land from ancient Persia to Asia as those who eat cardamom. For a reader of Dante, there is an almost automatic association with *Paradiso* 17.58–60 and the bitter bread of exile. In my own case, there is an almost visceral connection to my childhood and the constant presence of cardamom seeds in my father's pockets that he would regularly chew.

In the case of a spice like cardamom, medieval Italian textual traces are a little hard to come by. Cloves, on the other hand, allow for a vital perspective of connectivity to emerge. We have the historical current of Marco Polo's *Il milione*, which goes to southern and western India as well as the islands of the Indian Ocean and which consists not of orientalizing fantasy but rather a kind of sociological and mercantile perspective that defies its categorization as a travel narrative. Sharon Kinoshita refers to the work as a "textual witness" to the world of transcontinental travel, trade, and communication made possible by the so-called *pax mongolica* (Kinoshita 2016, 102).

Cloves come up in the world of Marco Polo in Jiandu (in present-day Sichuan province) and on the islands of Java and Nicobar. They are referenced as an exported commodity in the description of Malabar and Gujarat. The Malabar description in particular makes clear how materials flow, with merchants importing what is not otherwise found in the kingdom and participating in a global trading network:

> They bring cloth of gold and cloth of silk, *sendal*, gold, silver, cloves, spikenard, and other spices they don't have and they trade these things for the merchandise of this country. Know that ships come here from many places—that is, from the great province of Mangi—and the merchants take things to several areas; but things going to Aden are subsequently taken to Alexandria. (Marco Polo 2016, 174, Kinoshita trans.)

The extent of this network is made clear both by the catalog of goods as well as by the emphasis on "many places," but that last point of geographical specificity, from Malabar to Aden to Alexandria, makes clear the Red Sea route that will bring such goods into the Venetian mercantile orbit.

All this can be considered as highly compelling background to inform our reading of citations like the mention of cloves in Cielo d'Alcamo's *contrasto* and Dante's *Inferno* 29. In the *contrasto*, the woman's beauty is commodified by way of reference not just to "garofani" in an abstract sense as a highly prized spice but in a specific economic mode of weight and price: "Molti so' li garofani, ma non che salma 'nd'ài; / bella, non dispregiàmi s'avanti non m'assai" (You have many cloves, but not enough to make a full measure; / beautiful one, don't cast me aside until you've tried me) ("Rosa fresca aulentissima" 91–92). This woman may have many desirable qualities (in this case cloves), but their gathered weight does not rise to the level of a *salma*. According to Margherita Beretta, most recent editor of the *contrasto*, this was a widely used measure in medieval Sicily and amounted to the very large quantity of 300 liters (Di Girolamo 2008, 543).

By the time we come to Guittone d'Arezzo's sonnets "Ahi, chera—donna" and "Non già me greve fa d'amor la salma," the term *salma* appears to have lost its highly specific quantitative value but is still being used to quantify love and desire in some concrete sense of a weight or burden. When we come to Dante's singular usage of the term in *Paradiso* 32, it has risen in significance to stand for Christ's desire to bear the burden of our human flesh ("carcar si volse de la nostra salma," *Paradiso* 32.114). Through the perspective of the lyric history of a term like *salma*, we can see how Dante refigures language so that a commonplace measurement can assume the role of representing all that we are as human beings. This says much about the poetry of the *Commedia* that creates new vernacular meaning by elevating the quotidian. But more than that, by opening the *Commedia* out to the world of spice trade and history evoked in Cielo d'Alcamo's poem, we might find even greater meaning in Dante's embrace of a term like *salma* as one that asks us to look toward the interconnected world beyond European borders.

"Garofano," on the other hand, remains an incredibly potent marker for luxury culture in the *Commedia* such that Dante uses the spice as a symbol of the material excesses of the Sienese *brigata spendericcia* in *Inferno* 29. Dante attributes to Niccolò de' Salimbeni the custom of using cloves to flavor meat and in so doing "isolates a key feature of the male social club, namely its devotion to extravagant eating and 'la cucina'" (Barolini 2012, 11).

As Paul Freedman makes clear, cloves were less common than other spices like pepper, ginger, and saffron, but more prestigious and valuable (Freedman 2008, 22). This valuing persists well into the fifteenth century when, Freedman recounts, "Venetians were able to sell cloves for 72 percent more than they had paid for them in the Levant" (Freedman 2008, 115). What such focus on material and economic history brings forth is of course an emphasis on the vital connections between India and medieval Italy. And such perspective yet again evokes a powerful personal connection. My paternal grandfather, as a refugee forced to flee from the newly created nation of Pakistan in 1947, became a spice merchant, first selling on the streets and eventually opening a shop in the north Indian village of Dibai. Along with the constant presence of cardamom seeds that my father would chew on, there was also the occasional presence of cloves as a particular remedy for a toothache.

I would submit that these kinds of personal connections forged with medieval texts have the potential to create a transformative pedagogy. When I filled in for a colleague teaching a course on Marco Polo, I recounted the story of my father's cardamom chewing and my unexpected discovery of the descriptive phrase of the *Fatti di Cesare* that claimed those of Media and Asia eat their bread with cardamom. We spoke about stereotypes and essentializing language that might nonetheless offer a contemporary reader in the global twenty-first century an opportunity to connect, to find a place in a cultural tradition and history that is not their own.

It is in this spirit that I would like to turn to a fourteenth-century Indian contemporary of Dante. The lifespan of Delhi poet Amīr Khusraw (1253–1325) aligns neatly with Dante's (1265–1321). An important poet of the Delhi sultanate, and an incredibly prolific one at that, he turned his attention to matters as varied as astrology, social history, mysticism, politics, linguistics, and beyond, signaling an affinity with the poet of the *Commedia*. My intention is not to argue for any specific influence or direct connection between the two poets, but rather to suggest a more expansive approach to the century in which Dante lived.

I am particularly taken with Khusraw's insistent lyric hybridity: his necessary adoption of Farsi as the language of high culture and court poetry in the sultanate, but also his apparent continued writing in Hindavi, an Indian language that brought together Farsi, Arabic, Turkish, and the local Indian vernacular. His mixing of cultures at the level of vernacular literary production serves as an important paradigm for a pluralistic view of Indian culture with regard to religious and cultural interactions of the age. Sunil Sharma points out that Khusraw's Hindavi corpus is based in oral tradition and has likely been contaminated over the centuries to include inauthentic compositions, but the fact remains that the poet himself wrote of "his pride in primarily being a poet in his mother tongue" (Sharma 2005, 78). One of his most famous couplets forcefully asserts his poetic identity as based in his vernacular work: "I am a parrot of India if you ask me candidly / Ask me in Hindavi so that I can answer you correctly" (78). Through this perspective, I believe we can be drawn closer to certain radical features of Dante's poetic output. I'd like to emphasize not just select moments of the *Commedia*, but to take up a holistic approach to Dante's oeuvre that stretches across his lyric poetry.

Such a focus on vernacular mixing resonates with Dante's thoughts on language as found in his incomplete treatise on vernacular eloquence, *De vulgari eloquentia*. In an expression most telling of his exilic status, he writes, "Nos autem, cui mundus est patria velut piscibus equor" (To me, however, the whole world is a homeland, as the ocean is for fish) (*De vulgari eloquentia* 1.6, Botterill [1996] trans.). And he proceeds to make clear that he does not believe Florentine to be the most perfect or beautiful vernacular, but rather that there are many people and places ("nationes et gentes") that have more pleasant and useful ("delectabiliori atque utiliori") languages than that of Italians ("latinos").

This is a single point in a larger though incomplete whole of Dante's search for the illustrious vernacular in this text, but it does open up to a wider horizon of his thoughts on languages beyond Florence and how their pleasure and utility might serve to craft a new kind of poetic idiom. To that end, we might consider Dante's lyric experiments in translation. I will focus first on Dante's importing of the form of the sestina as part of his sequence of poems known as the *rime petrose*, stony rhymes that evoke a harsh wintry world mirroring the poet's erotic frustration in the face of his lady's stony resolve. And then I will move on to consider Dante's *canzone trilingue*, a poetic composition that combines French, Latin, and Italian to make new music.

The transition from Arnaut Daniel's (2015) Occitan sestina "Lo ferm voler" to Dante's sestina "Al poco giorno" is, at first glance, a simple one: Dante adopts the strict metrical principle of *retrogradatio cruciata*, and the similarities extend even in sound with respect to the chosen rhyme words. But there are telling differences to consider as well.

In a larger sense, this act of translation to create new poetry is reminiscent of Giacomo da Lentini "translating" Folquet de Marselha, so that the Occitan *canso* "A vos midontc" becomes the Italian *canzone* "Madonna dir vo voglio." Where Giacomo altered Folquet's content to emphasize logical coherence and to further implicate the natural world, Dante alters Arnaut's form to create a hybrid poetic, one that melds Occitan and Italian in sound and in substance. In this regard, it is a continuation of the process of vernacular innovation that necessarily has a hybrid quality to it. As Gianfranco Folena put it in complicating the model of the arch-poet who singlehandedly initiates a new poetic tradition, the reality is not *in principio fuit poeta* (in the beginning, there was a poet) but rather *in principio fuit interpres* (in the beginning, there was an interpreter) (Folena 1994, 3).

In this key of interpreting and commingling, "Al poco giorno" immediately stands out from its Occitan predecessor: From the very first line, there is a shift from Arnaut's octosyllable "Lo ferm voler qu'el cor m'intra" to what Marianne Shapiro (1980) has called "the leisurely expanses of Italianate hendecasyllable," so from "Lo ferm voler qu'el cor m'intra" we get "Al poco giorno e al gran cerchio d'ombra." A minor point, perhaps, but the result is an expanded poem and an adaptation of form that speaks as loudly as the transition in language from Occitan to Italian.

The initial sound, however, continues to resonate: *m'intra* becomes *d'ombra*, allowing a distinct aural trace to remain as a connecting thread between the two poems. Indeed, focusing our attention more broadly on Arnaut's rhyme words, we can see how *ongla / oncle* (rhyme words 2 and 5, almost homonyms) along with *cambra* (6) seem to combine in Dante's first rhyme word *ombra*. So too does Arnaut's *verga* (rhyme word 4) undergo an ever so subtle transformation to become Dante's *verde*, while remaining in the same position of the initial set. The lilt of *colli* also sounds faintly like *ongla* and *oncle*. And, of course, Arnaut's very first rhyme word *intra* bears a vestigial relation to the all-important *petra* (which is rhyme word 5 in "Al poco giorno") and a dominating sound throughout the sequence of the *petrose*.

These lexical and aural similarities indicate just what a hybrid sound emerges in Dante's crafting of his sestina, as Occitan and Italian elements combine to create new music. At the level of content, too, these shifts in the rhyme words play an important part in demonstrating the poetic hybridity at work. Arnaut's rhyme words are of a decidedly interior sort, explicitly so in the case of: *intra* (enters, 1), *arma* (soul, 3), and *cambra* (room, 6). Even *oncle* (uncle, 5) speaks to the domestic and familiar.

In "Al poco giorno," however, the emphasis is decidedly placed on the natural world and its perceptible qualities. Indeed, the only apparent sense of the personal and internal that we get at the level of rhyme words is in *donna* (6). For all of the other words, *ombra* (shadow), *colli* (hills), *l'erba* (grass), *verde* (green), *petra* (stone), even at first glance, there appears a correlate in the natural world, and an explicit sense of natural processes and seasonal change (in *ombra* and *verde*) that are so essential to the poetry of the *petrose*.

This is not to say that Dante completely departs from his Occitan predecessor here. Indeed, in *ongla* (nail) and *verga* (rod), we find the sort of violence that resonates greatly with the visceral poetry of the *petrose*. Though more of a sublimated key here in "Al poco giorno," such violence finds full voice in "Così nel mio parlar," the poem in which the crystalline artifice of the *petrose* shatters to give way to imaginings of revenge and consummation. And Arnaut too experiments with the poetics of winter and seasonal change in the opening *cobla* of the *canso* "En breu brizara 'l temps braus" and in "L'aura amara." But strictly at the level of one sestina feeding into another, there is a sense in which Dante expands the field, just as he moved from an octosyllable to hendecasyllable, he moves from uncles and chambers to the wintry world at large.

The dominant aesthetic allure of the sestina is of course its six alternating rhyme words that circle one another according to the principle of *retrogradatio cruciata*. From one modified use of this principle to create a hybrid form of a sestina in a new language, I want to shift to another, less regarded one: the *canzone trilingue* "Ai faus ris pour quoi trai aves." It is a shock worth registering to come across an incipit in Dante's poetry that is not in Italian at all, not unlike the feeling that we have in coming to the first verse of *Inferno* 7: "Pape Satan, pape satan aleppe," or the beginning of *Inferno* 34: "Vexilla regis prodeunt inferni." We can immediately see how the languages French, Latin, and Italian alternate from one line to another, still more, how they only rhyme with one another: So the first French line rhymes with the fifth, Latin with Latin in lines 2 and 4, Italian with Italian in lines 3, 6, and 7.

There is precedent for this polyglot poetry, notably in the Occitan tradition of a *descort*, where different languages are used to highlight the disharmony of the lover's lament. Perhaps the most notable example of this is Raimbaut de Vaqueiras's poem "Eras quan vey verdeyar" where the poet shifts through no fewer than five languages, from Occitan to Italian to French to Gascon to Portuguese/Galician. But Raimbaut does not use multiple languages within a single strophe; they are kept apart, disparate cultural spheres, until the end of the *descort* with alternating lines in a tornada. Moreover, he stages the linguistic confusion as a venomous response to being jilted in love: His lady loves him no more, so he writes that he will make a discord in sound and language.

We might well call "Ai faus ris" a *discordo*, for it fits in line with an Occitan understanding of the generic category. But Dante complicates that notion in his congedo that begins, "Chanson, or puez aler par tout le monde" (Song, now you may go through all the world) (line 40). He names it a *canzone*—albeit in French—and thus asks us to reconsider what we think we know about poetic genre.

In fact, at the level of rhyme, the meter of this *canzone* replicates others in Dante's lyric corpus, like "Voi ch'intendendo 'l terzo ciel movete." The difference, of course, lies in the insistence on plurilingualism that picks up on the Occitan *descort*; but more than that, in the way that the languages alternate, the form of the sestina is implicated as well. We owe the fundamental observation that the alternating of languages follows a carefully established scheme to Furio Brugnolo (Brugnolo 1978). What emerges is an understanding that the principle of *retrogradatio cruciata* dictates the way that the languages move from strophe to strophe. And thus, we have a contamination of genre: The *descort*, sestina, and *canzone* all have voice in this trilingual composition.

At the level of content, too, we find a return to the language of the *petrose*. The last line of the first stanza: "ne' gia' mai tocca di fioretto il verde" (nor does he ever touch the green of the little flower) (line 13) takes us back "Al poco giorno," with *verde* as a privileged sestina rhyme word. More compelling still is the "fioretto," picking up on Dante's precious use of "fioretti" (little flowers) in *Al poco giorno* as well as another of the *petrose*, *Io son venuto*. Gianfranco Contini calls it "una parola ben dantesca" (a truly Dantean word), and it is a word writ large across the fabric of the *Commedia* (used once in *Inferno* 2, twice at the top *Purgatorio*, and for a final time in *Paradiso* 30). But Dante is alone in the tradition of thirteenth-century Italian poetry, as far as I have been able to determine, in using the word at all. It is usage that binds Dante's sestina and *canzone trilingue* together with the strongest possible tie; it speaks to their shared language of hybridity, their polyglot and composite nature.

There are other thematic ties to the poetry of the *petrose*, like the accusation of the lady's "cuor di ghiaccio," her heart of ice, but perhaps most significant is the potentially grounding historicity of the verse in the congedo "ut gravis mea spina / si saccia per lo mondo" (so that my troubling spine / is known through all the world) (lines 42–43). The only other place that *spina* is used in Dante's lyric poetry is in "Io son venuto," but in this case it perhaps takes on the double meaning of referring not to any old thorn in the poet's side, but to the Malaspina family with whom Dante stayed during his post-exilic time in Lunigiana.

In this light, the unmoored language and play with hybrid forms of discord take on a different aspect: We are situated a decade after the *petrose*, if we are to buy into the astronomical periphrasis of "Io son venuto" that dates to December 1296, and far away from the linguistic unity of Florence. But the fragmentation of exile is nonetheless a polyglot harmony: French and Latin bow to the Italian meter, and we end the *canzone trilingue* with the definitive thud of two Italian lines.

We can find many such instances of hybrid language across the full range of the *Commedia*. In *Inferno* 7, we meet Plutus, the Greek god of wealth turned into a fearsome guardian of the fourth circle of hell. The canto begins with a pastiche of Greek and Hebrew: "Pape Satán, pape Satán aleppe / cominciò Pluto con la voce chioccia" (Pape Satan, pape Satan aleppe / so Plutus, with his grating voice, began) (*Inferno* 7.1–2).

While interpreted by many modern commentators as a nonsensical utterance, it seemed far more clear to Dante's early readers that he was working with the

Greek *papai* as an expression of surprise and the Hebrew *aleph* as an expression of pain. We can see in the rounding out of the tercet that the description of Virgil as "e quel savio gentil che tutto seppe" (the gentle sage, aware of everything), merges the Italian-Hebrew *aleppe* with knowledge itself, in the verb *seppe*, to know.

The babble of Nimrod in *Inferno* 31 is of course deliberately nonsensical, as Dante stages an encounter with the mythical builder of the tower of Babel to dwell upon the loss of shared language. But it is also an experiment in sound and confusion that is based in received language: "Raphél maì amèche zabì almi / cominciò a gridar la fiera bocca, / cui non si convenia più dolci salmi (Raphél maì amèche zabì almi began to bellow that brute mouth, for which / no sweeter psalm would be appropriate) (*Inferno* 31.67–69).

It may be nonsensical and harsh sounding, but Dante seems to be playing on what Hebrew he can gather from Jerome's Vulgate. More to the point, the rhyming of *almi* with the sweet psalms ("dolci salmi") draws our attention to the contrast created between originary babble and the debatable "sweetness" of translated poetry. As Dante (1995) writes in his incomplete philosophical treatise *Convivio* of the Psalms, "essi furono trasmutati d'ebreo in greco e di greco in latino, e ne la prima trasmutazione tutta quella dolcezza venne meno" (they were translated from Hebrew into Greek, and from Greek into Latin, and in the first translation all their sweetness was lost) (*Convivio* 1.7.15).

The experience of vernacular otherness in the *Commedia* is not just one of harshness. As a correlative to the Greek-Hebrew hybrid of *Inferno* 7, *Paradiso* 7 begins with a *terzina* that fuses Hebrew and Latin to create a new kind of sacred music: "Osanna, sanctus Deus sabaòth / superillustrans claritate tua / felices ignes horum malacòth" (Hosanna, holy God of the hosts / who illuminates from above with your light / the happy flames of this kingdom) (*Paradiso* 7.1–3). That the speaker of these words is the Eastern Roman Emperor Justinian makes for still more compelling case with respect to Dante's attention to these issues of cultural and linguistic mingling.

But far and away the most significant and sustained experiment in vernacular alterity in the poetry of the *Commedia* is Arnaut Daniel's speech in Occitan at the end of *Purgatorio* 26. Arnaut is introduced to us by Guido Guinizzelli, Dante's acknowledged poetic father, as the "miglior fabbro / del parlar materno (the best artisan of the mother tongue), a verse that remains familiar to many as T.S. Eliot's dedication to Ezra Pound in the 1925 edition of *The Waste Land*.

I had occasion to review a recent translation of *Purgatorio*, and one of the issues I took with it was the injection of a possessive into this compliment, so that the line became "best craftsman of *our* mother tongue." But Arnaut's mother tongue is not Dante's. His words are not Tuscan but Occitan. This translation made no distinction between the verses of the rest of the canto translated from Italian and those words of Arnaut translated from his own mother tongue. Such a lack of distinction results in an imposed monolingualism that masks Dante's embrace of vernacular diversity. Indeed, while Arnaut speaks in his own language, it still falls into the cadence of the meter of *terza rima*. And much like the *canzone trilingue*, this canto closes with a return to Dante's Florentine in the very last line.

The California artist Sandow Birk's translation of Dante into a twenty-first-century American urban vernacular not only captures this point of hybridity but accentuates it all the more. On the visual plane, Birk's Arnaut is no court poet but a taco-stand line cook. This provocative move asks us to lend greater attention to Dante's poetic style as embracing all levels of language, from the sublime and sweet to the harsh and filthy. And perhaps Birk is reflecting the ambiguity of this gesture of linguistic inclusion. It is true that Arnaut is the only non-Italian character afforded the opportunity to speak his own language, but the style of this Occitan is not that of Arnaut's notoriously obscure *trobar clus*; it is simple and pleading—in fact by the terms of the lyric tradition, it puts Dante's character in the position of the beloved lady being entreated by the poet.

But Birk and his fellow Californian Marcus Sanders (2005a,b) go still further in their telling choice to render Arnaut's Occitan speech into Spanish that stands apart from their slang renderings of Dante's Italian. This appropriately highlights Dante's radical poetic move and provides an incisive way to extend Dante's reflections on languages in a diverse ecosystem of cultural production to the here and now. Birk and Sanders reflect the bold heterodoxy of this poetry, seeing it both as a product of its own moment and one that can and should be "translated" to the vernacular ecosystem of twenty-first-century America.

Birk's provocations are still more enhanced and globalized in his *Paradiso* illustrations. Not content to simply continue on his act of *translatio* that renders the scenes of the poem as contemporary encounters in an American urban setting, Birk takes on the task of translating some of the most Christian imagery of *Paradiso* and opening it out to a wider global expanse. So, the cross of the heaven of Mars becomes the elegant open architecture of the Williamsburg Bridge. The "M" and eagle of the heaven of justice become the inescapable neon golden arches of the McDonald's of Times Square and Tokyo—for Birk's Paradise is a global city. In a sign of things to come in his artistic trajectory, a preview of his 2009 *American Quran*, the Celestial Rose becomes the Kaaba in Mecca.

And the vision of Mary of *Paradiso* 32 becomes a vision of the Hindu goddess of music and knowledge Sarasvati. This urbane goddess with a cell phone and bottled water continues Birk's interest in critiquing American consumer culture, for which he also finds ample inspiration in Dante's discomfort with the new mercantile and banking culture that was transforming his city, to say nothing of the economic excesses of the Church that so raised his hackles. Birk also resists Dante's text in his free artistic adaptations. Emblematic of his resistance in this image is his inability to accept what Jorge Luis Borges called "the most moving lines literature has achieved" when Dante turns to his beloved Beatrice and instead finds that she has been cruelly substituted with the old man St. Bernard (Borges 1999, 302). Birk's illustration still has Beatrice present at Dante's side.

But his provocative transformation of Mary into Sarasvati also resonates with that lingering question of the justice of exclusion on the banks of the Indus river. Such provocation pushes us still further in formulating new approaches to reading Dante; it also draws our critical gaze most forcefully to the radical voices within this cultural milieu, ones that I want to make sure ring far and wide in our stormy present.

Works Cited

Alighieri, Dante. 1991. *Commedia*, Anna Maria Chiavacci Leonardi, ed. Milan: Mondadori.

Alighieri, Dante. 1994. *La Commedia secondo l'antica vulgate*, edited by Giorgio Petrocchi, Florence: Le Lettere.

Alighieri, Dante. 1995. *Convivio*, edited by Franca Brambilla Ageno, Florence: Le Lettere.

Arnaut Daniel. 2015. *Canzoni*, edited by Maurizio Perugi. Florence: SISMEL.

Barolini, Teodolinda. 2011. "Dante's Sympathy for the Other, or the Non-Stereotyping Imagination: Sexual and Racialized Others in the *Commedia*." *Critica del testo* 14(1): 177–204.

Barolini, Teodolinda. 2012. "Sociology of the *Brigata*: Gendered Groups in Dante, Forese, Folgore, Boccaccio—From *Guido i' vorrei* to Griselda." *Italian Studies* 67(1): 4–22.

Benozzo, Francesco. 2013. *Appello all'UNESCO per liberare Dante dai dantisti*. Alessandria: Edizioni dell'Orso.

Birk, Sandow, and Marcus Sanders. 2005a. *Dante's Paradiso*. San Francisco: Chronicle Books.

Birk, Sandow, and Marcus Sanders. 2005b. *Dante's Purgatorio*. San Francisco: Chronicle Books.

Borges, Jorge Luis. 1999. *Selected Non-Fictions*, edited by Eliot Weinberger. New York: Penguin Books.

Botterill, Steven, ed. and trans. 1996. *Dante: De vulgari eloquentia*. Cambridge: Cambridge University Press.

Brugnolo, Furio. 1978. "Note sulla canzone trilingue 'Aï faus ris' attribuita a Dante." In *Retorica e critica letteraria*, edited by Ezio Raimondi. Bologna: Il Mulino.

Coomaraswamy, Ananda. 1936. "Two Passages in Dante's *Paradiso*." *Speculum* 11(3): 327–338.

Di Giroloamo, Costanzo, ed. 2008. *I poeti della scuola siciliana*, Vol. 2. Milan: Mondadori.

Folena, Gianfranco. 1994. *Volgarizzare e tradurre*. Turin: Einaudi.

Freedman, Paul. 2008. *Out of the East: Spices and the Medieval Imagination*. New Haven, CT: Yale University Press.

Heng, Geraldine, and Lynn Ramey. 2014. "Early Globalities, Global Literatures: Introducing a Special Issue on the Global Middle Ages." *Literature Compass* 11(7): 389–394.

Kinoshita, Sharon. 2016. "The Painter, the Warrior, and the Sultan: The World of Marco Polo in Three Portraits." *The Medieval Globe* 2(1): 101–128.

Looney, Dennis. 2011. *Freedom Readers: The African American Reception of Dante Alighieri and the Divine Comedy*. Notre Dame: University of Notre Dame Press.

Manguel, Alberto. 2015. *Curiosity*. New Haven, CT: Yale University Press.

Marco Polo. 2016. *The Description of the World*, translated by Sharon Kinoshita. Indianapolis, IN: Hackett.

Sahota, G. S. 2018. *Late Colonial Sublime: Neo-Epics and the End of Romanticism*. Evanston, IL: Northwestern University Press.

Said, Edward. 1994. *Culture and Imperialism*. New York: Vintage Books.

Schildgen, Brenda Deen. 2002. *Dante and the Orient*. Urbana, IL: University of Illinois Press.

Schildgen, Brenda Deen. 2012. "Dante and the Bengali Renaissance." In *Dante in the Long Nineteenth Century: Nationality, Identity, and Appropriation*, edited by Aida Audeh and Nick Havely. Oxford: Oxford University Press.

Shapiro, Marianne. 1980. *Hieroglyph of Time: The Petrarchan Sestina*. Minneapolis, MN: University of Minnesota Press.

A Voice from the Margins: Reflections of a Sister Outsider on Her Voyage to Italy and through Italian Studies

KENYSE LYONS

> We have been socialized to respect fear more than our own needs for language and definition, and while we wait in silence for that final luxury of fearlessness, the weight of that silence will choke us.
> —AUDRE LORDE, *Sister Outsider*

> What would you expect to find when the muzzle that has silenced the voices of black men [and women] is removed? That they would thunder your praise? When these heads that our fathers [and mothers] have forced to the very ground are risen, do you expect to read adoration in their eyes?
> —JEAN-PAUL SARTRE, *Black Orpheus*

> I had tried in different ways over the years to fit. I thought I could discipline my body and later my manners to take up less room. I was fine with that, but I learned that even I had limits when—in my pursuit of the life of the mind—my thinking was deemed too thick.
> —TRESSIE MCMILLAN COTTOM, *Thick and Other Essays*

BREAKING THE SILENCE

I had the privilege of being one of the forty graduate students and scholars of color contacted by Deborah Parker in the spring of 2018 as she researched the foundations of her opinion piece "Race and Foreign Languages," published on the Inside Higher Ed website in July 2018. Grateful for the opportunity to tell my story to an empathetic and interested listener, I readily shared with her the tale of the intersectional, identity-based stress and trauma I experienced while pursuing an academic career in Italian studies. My willingness to divulge, however, greatly diminished the moment she asked if she could publish aspects of my story in the body of her piece. The echoes of the adage used by Vittorio De Sica to synthesize the sentiment behind Giulio Andreotti's critique of the filmmaker's brand of neo-realism, "*i panni sporchi si lavano in famiglia*" (dirty laundry is washed in the family), rang loudly in my ears as I contemplated my response. The din of its discordant bell reverberated so deafeningly in my mind that I only agreed for her to publicly disclose my experience on the condition that whatever elements she included be shrouded behind the veil of anonymity.

Why was I so unwilling to speak up publicly? Social psychologists would say that it is because I inhabit an intersectional social location that has been well-trained to remain silent about their experiences of racial trauma and the race-based stress that exacerbates it.[1] In their article William Ming Liu et al. (2019) maintain that "people of color learn explicitly through racism, microaggressions, and racial trauma about their positionality and how to accommodate White people's needs, status, and emotions" (143–144). Cognizant of the reality that "the status for White people may be different from what it is for people of color," members of diverse social groups engage in overly accommodating behaviors that are more amenable to whites in an effort to interrupt (or counteract) the threat of exclusion, both actual and perceived. In other words, "minorities" learn to take care of members of the racial "majority's" feelings to better access the resources that would enable those of "diverse" backgrounds to survive and thrive in the world.

Silence is just one strategy often used by social minorities to accommodate the needs, status, and emotions of the members of the majority.[2] It is a practice that is anchored in the belief that by remaining silent they can keep from triggering the cognitive discomfort and the irrational, discriminatory responses rooted in "White people's racial fragility." Theorized by Robin DiAngelo (2018), a diversity educator and antiracism scholar of Italian American heritage herself, the concept of white fragility refers to a broad set of deeply entrenched forms of response enacted by those who do not see themselves as racialized when they are encouraged to listen to the ways in which racially marginalized peoples experience their racialized existence. White fragility, in other words, is a socially conditioned set of responses to the cognitive dissonance that comes when the beliefs/assumptions about race of those with racial privilege are identified and challenged. These responses range from the coerced assimilation of the racialized social subject to the racialized subject's outright exclusion, whether this alienation is intentional or unconscious. Use of the strategy of silence can be reinforced in the minds of "people of color" by hearing of the adverse professional and personal consequences of other individuals in the wake of speaking up and out against the discrimination they experienced. In addition to highlighting injustice, the circulation of these stories paradoxically works to prevent others from speaking up about the identity-based trauma/stress they inevitably suffer at the hands of often well-meaning but also occasionally malicious colleagues and teachers. By staying quiet about their experiences, students of diverse social backgrounds believe they can stay professionally safe. The strategy of silence, however, can stifle minorities in ways that cause considerable psychological and spiritual distress as well as erode both their self-image and sense self-efficacy. Staying quiet about racial trauma/stress, then, does not in reality protect people of color but instead facilitates their "internaliz[ation of] stereotypes and demeaning ideological systems [intended to exclude them]"; the accommodation of white fragility, then, is a practice that requires "the forfeiture of [minorities'] psychological and emotional welfare" (Liu et al. 2019, 144). It is a form of psychological self-abuse that prevents those of "diverse backgrounds" from self-actualizing as an autonomous and self-determining social subject. Giving away the keys to their personal power ultimately decreases diverse people's physical and mental health outcomes as well as their professional, economic, social, and political well-being (Chae et al. 2015). The origins of my silence, too, were rooted in an illusory belief that it would protect me. I thought it would shield me against the psychological and physical exhaustion resulting from the profound "lack of recognition, empathy, and responsivity" that I experienced when sharing my struggles with colleagues (Welz 2014, 423). I also believed that, by refusing to speak up, I could refrain from appearing ungrateful to the White way-makers who opened up a world of opportunities to me when admitted into their graduate programs and prestigious institutions that were historically closed to me by law. The primary reason I stayed quiet, however, was my belief that it would enable me to avoid the professional consequences I believed awaited me in the wake of my talking openly about the covert racism/racialized microaggressions I experienced at the hands of those who did not see themselves as racialized and inhabited a postracial fantasy world.

Now, almost a year—and what seems like a lifetime of experiences—since the publication of Deborah Parker's (2018) article, I have another opportunity to share my identity-based experiences as an Italianist in training who happens to not fit into the social categories typically associated with the profession. This time, I am determined to—in the strong tradition of my African American ancestors— "have my say."[3] My change in attitude is due to my more profound understanding of how the silence I believed would professionally save me only worked to protect and perpetuate the very identity-based power dynamics that served to alienate from my peers in particular and the field of Italian studies more broadly. The shift in my perception of the utility of my silence is also rooted in the rejection of my internalization of those stereotypes and demeaning ideologies at the heart of antiblack, hegemonic white supremacy. I am no longer interested in continuing to be complicit in my own victimization as a result of my, to use the words of Audre Lorde, repeated disavowal of "the tyrannies of others in an erroneous attempt to make them my own until I sicken and die from them still in silence" (Lorde 2007, 41). In doing so, part of me seeks to save the discipline I love (perhaps unrequitedly) from an extinction rooted in its conservatism. Signs of these dire consequences can already be glimpsed in the form of dwindling of class sizes rooted in students' perceptions of Italian culture's irrelevance to both their experience and contemporary world as well as in the erosion of institutional support and the program closures that inevitably come when universities see no market for a product deemed "boutique" (to use the language of business infecting all academic, administrative endeavors). The primary motivator for breaking my silence, however, is a desire to heal the wounds torn open by the trauma of my experience and to counteract the dehumanizing consequences of the discipline's often unconscious elaboration of the discriminatory, identity-based practices. Such practices, and the institutional supports that allow them to work, are responsible for the infinitesimal number of "social" minorities teaching, studying, and getting graduate degrees in Italian as well as for the drastic reduction in the quality of work/life for those minority scholars who currently participate in the field.[4] In speaking out, I hope, perhaps foolishly, to prevent students and scholars of diverse backgrounds presently pursuing careers in Italian studies from experiencing the unnecessary personal anguish and professional adversity I did. These students, as Kimberly Truong and Samuel Museus argue, are especially vulnerable to the trauma and stress associated with identity-based practices of exclusion as a result of the systems of "dominance, power, and privilege based on their [identity]-group designations," their small numbers and high visibility, as well as "the power dynamics that exist between faculty and students" (Truong and Museus 2012, 227). The un/conscious forms of racism and racialization through which these systems operate include, but are not limited to "isolation, identity intersectionality, differential support, and investment, low expectations combined with high standards, funding differences, exploitation, neglect, devaluing of research, microaggressions, second-hand trauma, and the violation of institutional and federal policies" (237). By speaking up and out about my experiences with the race-based trauma and stress that kept me from achieving my goal of an academic career, I seek to dispel the myth that silence can save you from professional ruin; it only serves to sever you from the academy and defer your career aspirations. Instead of relying on the strategy of silence, I want those seen as social minorities (not just understood in terms of race, but also gender, ethnicity, sexuality, class, ability) who are inspired to pursue the profession to refuse to suffer in silence and find solace in speaking their own truth. I also want to encourage them to actively seek resources, develop strategies, and cultivate relationships that empower them to persist along the entire trajectory of the doctoral/junior faculty pathway so that they not only survive but instead thrive.

A WORD ABOUT FORM

Speaking my truth and having my say requires an uncomfortable, though necessary, amount of the self-revelation that is often shied away from in professional circles for some strange reason. To that end, I utilize aspects of a mode of writing widely associated with the critical self-awareness and radical self-disclosure I need to share my story—the personal essay. Though considered by some to be passé, for Black women the personal essay is, as Tressie McMillan Cottom, the author of *Thick and Other Essays*, remind us, a

> contested point of entry [for Black women] into a low-margin form of public discourse where [they] could at least appeal to the politics of White feminist inclusion for nominal representation. [Black women write] personal essays because as far as authoritative voices go, the self [is] the only subject men and White people would cede to us. (Cottom 2019, 22–23)

See also Tolentino (2017) and Bennet (2015).
Black women make use of the personal essay because they

> find that no amount of pathos, logos, or ethos includes them in the civic sphere of public discourse and persuasion. [Black women] do not have enough authority, as judged by the audiences and gatekeepers who decide to whom we should listen, to speak on much of anything. (Cottom 2019, 22)

More than self-referential navel-gazing expressly written for consumption by others then, the personal essay—when used by members of socially marginalized groups—serves as "the only point of [public] access for telling the creative stories of empirical realities" (Cottom 2019, 18). By using the mode of the personal essay, I not only open up a space to tell my own story. I, like so many other Black women, use it to engage in a highly political discourse that empowers me to reclaim a position of authority and intellectual legitimacy that other people's perception of my cultural inadequacy—and my silent acceptance of this—denied. By claiming a space in the very academic discourse from which I perceive myself as having been excluded for reasons that are not my own, I seek to shape it in ways that are more inclusive.

In addition to adopting Cottom's understanding of the personal essay to "have my say," I also embrace the strategy of thick description that she utilizes to bring the experiences she writes about to life. A concept rooted in the thick ethnography of sociology, thick description is a "detailed description of [an aspect] of social life" that affords readers belonging to one culture a "proxy experience for living in another culture" (Gomm and Hammersley 2001). In other words, thick description is a discursive mode that enables those who do not share cultural backgrounds "to engage with [the] richness [of another way of life], pick up the threads, and do what [its] members do—which is to generate new meanings from the same cultural repertoire" (Gomm and Hammersley 2001). When combined with the mode of the personal essay, Cottom maintains, thick description opens up a space for members of socially marginalized people where they can interrogate their individual social location in a way that allows for the "exploration of what our selves say about our society." It is a practice that requires the sharing of "parts of [themselves], [their] history and [their] identity to make social theory concrete" (Cottom 2019, 27). I also utilize the strategy of thick description for stylistic reasons insofar as I believe it provides me with the freedom to communicate my ideas—and the ways they present themselves to me—without having to accommodate the language strategies, modes of communication, and frameworks of communication and interpretation that are more palatable to majority social groups. Thick description, then, frees me from having to reduce the complexity of my ideas (what Cottom calls "thick thinking") or try to make it "adapt to the dominant culture's actual or perceived communication and discourse style" (Endo 2015, 209).

MY VOYAGE TO ITALY

My journey to and through Italy begins, as in the case of a great many other Americans, with a love story. The object of my desire, however, was not an individual but rather the very Italian experience/culture itself. My first taste of the *Bel Paese* and its "sweet life" came in the fall of 1997 when I took my first Italian-language class at the University of Maryland. I have always been interested in international relations and the mediation of cultural difference in ways that reduce conflict and promote individual social, political, and economic well-being, hence my focus on postcommunist democratization efforts in the Slavic world. There was, however, something about the welcoming and supportive community of Italians and other *appassionati d'Italia* that I found in the university's Jimenez Hall that made me feel more at home than other languages I have studied. I could not then, nor even now, put my finger on the exact origins of this feeling of belongingness. It is possible that my love of Italy was rooted in the same small urgings of the sacred spirit of that encouraged me to choose a young Italian girl, Maria Goretti, as my patron saint during my Holy Confirmation two years prior. It could also have potentially been anchored in my ties to the tradition of

Black American folks who felt they found increased individual and social "freedom" in Europe or the long line of Black intellectuals such as Mary Church Terrell, Ralph Ellison, James Baldwin, and Tone Cade Bambara who studied and lived in Italy. Whatever it was that led me to Italy continued to sustain me as my passionate Italian love affair turned into a mystical marriage that ultimately powered a deepening desire to study all things Italian for as long as I could—to infinity and beyond, starting with the PhD.

I had always planned on applying to and graduating from a doctoral program in political science, so my decision to pursue a doctoral degree in Italian studies came as a surprise to me. It now makes perfect sense given the reality that I increasingly became dissatisfied with the quantitative tools developed by social science to support the worldwide creation of political cultures rooted in Americanist (and imperialist) definitions of democratization and the rule of law. My study of Italy enabled me to begin to explore what I felt were more qualitative and inclusion-oriented approaches to the analysis of cultural difference as well as the modalities that support sustainable individual and collective development. The humanities-based study of a culture for whom interdisciplinary thinking, cultural regeneration, and political engagement were highly valued seemed like the perfect way to do so. Upon entry into a master's program, I dove deep into the exploration of the Italian cultural perspective with the help of an equally curious and open-minded professor, Stefania Lucamante, who helped me to uncover, experience, and—more important—value another way of seeing and being in the world. With her guidance and support, I decided to pursue a career in which the exploration and mediation of cultural boundaries, along with an ability to facilitate the capacity for others to do the same, was at the center. With the encouragement of Professor Lucamante, I applied to two PhD programs and was ecstatic when I was admitted to both and even more grateful to have received full funding from one of them.

CLOSE ENCOUNTERS OF THE MONSTROUS KIND: CAUGHT BETWEEN THE ROCK OF RACIAL CONTRACTS AND THE HARD PLACE OF COLONIAL LOGIC

When I began my doctoral studies in Italian in the fall of 2005, I felt like Dante's *navicella* that, after leaving the shores of hell, readily lifted its veils "per correre miglior acque" as it made its way toward Paradise via the slopes of Purgatory. By the time I graduated seven years later, the little boat of my psyche was so battered and bruised that I felt as if it had more in common with padron 'Ntoni's boat, *I Malavoglia*, than Alighieri's *navicella*. I am the promise of a generation of

African Americans who viewed education as the primary means of overcoming the harmful effects of Jim Crow on both individual and collective well-being. Access to a PhD (and education more broadly), I believed, would provide me more access to increased social mobility as well as a more sustainable means of developing my community. It was this belief that enabled me to persist in the face of the challenges that are the subject of this essay as well as to navigate the emotional storms and treacherous waters anchored in the cultural clashes I experienced throughout my doctoral studies. Symbolizing the economic aspirations of a struggling Sicilian family very similar to my own, *I Malavoglia* was broken violently apart as punishment for having transgressed the unseen laws of positivism structuring the late nineteenth-century Italian social order. One hundred and thirty years later, I too felt as if my mind had been destroyed for having breached the defenses erected by the same positivistic laws regulating embodied social difference. The decimation of the *navicella* of my mind, I thought at the time of my graduation, was the direct result of my audacious hopes for social mobility at the heart of my specifically Black (and decidedly American) culture but denied to me by the Italian one that I loved. Like padron 'Ntoni, whose delusions of economic grandeur blinded him to the "realities" of his voyage to economic self-determination, my illusory dream for a career in Italian studies had prevented me from seeing the potential dangers awaiting me along my path. That lack of vision left me emotionally wounded and psychologically traumatized.

What exactly were the unforeseen Scylla and Charybdis haunting my journey? They were the gender- and race-based social contracts—and more specifically the discursive practices through which they manifested themselves—structurally designed, though individually unintended, to keep me in my place and out of the social locations and professional spaces deemed by the powers that be as not being for me. Though it first presented itself in the guise of the necessary acculturation that comes with entering into a cultural matrix that is not your own, I encountered a certain degree of cultural imperialism/colonialism in the field of Italian studies. These were dynamics of which I was not aware until the clash of the titans of acculturation and colonial colonization created an obstacle along the pathway of my academic and professional journey. While the concept of acculturation is characterized by the processes of indoctrination designed to integrate newcomers into an existing cultural framework, the latter is defined by the systematic subordination of one conceptual framework or cultural identity to another through assimilation, marginalization, or separation. The line separating acculturation from cultural colonization is a fuzzy one. More often than not, the difference between the two is subjective, rooted in the extent to which the cultural newcomer perceives themselves as having to deny (or give up) integral aspects of their existing ways of being in the world to be accepted by the new culture.

There is—at least in my opinion—a select group of Italianists who—even if unbeknownst to them—carry out their scholarship and teaching from what I can only describe as a "civilizing mission," appearing as if they want to save the Americans they encounter from their own barbarity through the spread of Italian civilization. An even smaller group of scholars, however, has no interest in integrating themselves within the American academy beyond their department or field of inquiry's threshold, invested instead in creating Italian-only colonial enclaves. For this small, yet powerful few, *italianità* is not just the discipline's focus and field of study but rather its preferred way of being in, perceiving, and thinking about the world. It is a privileged form of being to which non-Italian scholars are strongly encouraged to aspire and acquiesce if they are deemed to be "culturally adequate" and therefore worthy of becoming a full member of the Italian studies field.

Consenting to such norms of cultural colonialism/imperialism is something that I think all Americans in this discipline, regardless of their category of social identity, erroneously believe they must do to be granted access and opportunities. The reasons we think we have to be other than we are and the means through which we fit ourselves into acceptable molds of Italian identity, as defined by the discipline, vary. For those of us who, in addition to our Americanness, also inhabit racial categories other than White and gender categories other than male, the work of proving ourselves to be culturally adequate for entry into the Italian studies field is in direct proportion to the number of identities we have to "overcome" and disproportionate to our White, male, heterosexual, elite, able-bodied American colleagues. In other words, in addition to navigating the tacit cultural contracts shaping cultural interaction, minorities must also navigate the identity-based social agreements that work to influence their experience in the academy as well as in the Italian studies field. In my case it was select aspects of the intersectional racial contracts rooted in Italy's colonial legacy and contemporary experience with African migration.

First theorized by Charles W. Mills in the book of the same name, racial contracts are a peculiar construct that, "though based on the social contract tradition that has been central to Western political theory, is not a contract between everybody ('we the people'), but between just the people who count, the people who really are people ('we the White people')" (Mills 1997, 128). Rather than existing as a material and legally binding contract written at one time and signed by consenting parties, a racial contract is a historical discursive reality in which

Europeans became "the lords of humankind" through a series of acts including but not limited to:

> papal bulls and other theological pronouncements; European discussions about colonialism, "discovery," and international law; pacts, treaties, and legal decisions; academic and popular debates about the humanity of nonwhites; the establishment of formalized legal structures of differential treatment; and the routinization of informal illegal or quasi-legal practices effectively sanctioned by the complicity of silence and government failure to intervene and punish perpetrators—which collectively can be seen, not just metaphorically but close to literally, as its conceptual, juridical, and normative equivalent. (Mills 1997, 306)

The function of the racial contract is to establish "a racial polity, a racial state, and a racial juridical system, where the status of whites and non-whites is clearly demarcated, whether by law or custom" (Mills 1997, 261) with the purpose of "promoting the differential privileging of the whites as a group with respect to the nonwhites as a group, the exploitation of their bodies, land, and resources, and the denial of equal socioeconomic opportunities to them" (229). While not all Whites sign this racial contract, all Whites are expected to consent to its terms and conditions rooted in the maintenance of the racial order since they always directly benefit from said contract whether they want to or not. When they fulfill the terms of the agreement, individual Whites are granted the privileges of freedom, equality, and self-determination; when they do not, they are punished. Nonwhites, on the other hand, are always and forever "biologically destined never to penetrate the normative rights ceiling established for them below white persons" (301). In other words, they are denied the capacity to self-define, self-determine, or self-actualize, and any effort to do so will be subject to punishment through a death of many kinds whether physical, social, psychological, spiritual, economic, or social.

The uniquely Italian and highly gendered modern racial contract and its associated set of stereotypes shaping my experiences as a budding scholar that I failed to acknowledge (though to which I was still held accountable) is historically entrenched. Its origins are rooted in sixteenth-century texts like Leo Africanus's nine-volume *Descrizione dell'Italia* and were reelaborated in the nineteenth century through books like Cesare Lombroso's *Criminal Woman*. The conditions of the contract as defined between the Renaissance and positivism were consolidated during Fascism via the colonial practices of *madismo* and *madamento*, promoted in popular culture in songs like "La faccetta nera" as well as through laws promulgated by Italian colonial administration (e.g., the Ordinamento organico per l'Eritrea e la Somalia, Sanzioni sui rapporti di indole coniugale con cittadini e sudditi, Sanzioni penali per la difesa del prestigio di razza di fronte ai native dell'Africa italiana). These and other texts represent Black women as an always and ever-ready source of deviant sexual pleasures for White Italian men as well as a domestic stand-in for (White) Italian women (see Caponetto 2012 and Coppola and Sabelli 2012). Let us not forget the Italian academy's contribution to Italy's racist and sexist conceptualizations of Black women such as those of Lidio Cipriani (1935), a signatory to the *Manifesto della Razza*, whose work supported the idea of Africans—and Black women in particular—as intellectually inferior and downright intellectually deficient (Strazza 2012). When it is boiled down to its essence, then, Italy's racial contract with Black people not only posits them as the very antithesis of White personhood but also explicitly cites them as a source of reinforcement for Italian White men and women's feeling of cultural dominance, intellectual advantage, moral preeminence, and racial superiority.

No ancient relic to be denied via Italy's strategic amnesia as it relates to its colonial past, the historically elaborated racial contract described above continues to be developed in contemporary immigration law as well as media practices. It is in the media, as scholars such as Áine O'Healy (2009) and Rosetta Giuliani Caponetto (2012) attest, that historical tropes are "recycled, re-presented and given new life . . . [helping] to articulate the construction and reception of black (and white) bodies in the contemporary Italian context" (O'Healy 2009, 179). One need only look toward the contemporary practices—and representations of these —of Italian male exploitation (motivated for reasons that differ from that of white immigrant women) of female West African sex workers and the objectification/fetishization (in ways quite different than their White counterparts) of the Black female figure on Italian television. To be a female of African ancestry in Italy (and, for that matter, America) continues to mean being perceived as a Jezebel—all body, but no mind. The concept of African femininity (to borrow O'Healy's term) does not leave space for the idea that women of African ancestry can be serious scholars of Italy and Italian culture.

The foreboding signs of the colonial logic and intersectional racial contracts that defined my experiences as both a graduate student and budding scholar appeared on my horizon shortly after I arrived on the campus of my doctoral institution.[5] They came in the form of the stereotypes, or those uncritically elaborated and culturally conditioned cognitive shortcuts shaping our interaction with the outside world, that developed in my interaction with colleagues and teachers.

These evolutionary-based, culturally conditioned, and incredibly lazy ways of thinking about those who are different from us are more than a set of internal cognitive categories for processing the external world. Stereotypes, as Homi Bhabha correctly argues, are a discursive form of social power and "a [fetishistic] apparatus that turns on the recognition and disavowal of racial/cultural/historical differences" (Bhabha 2004, 100). As "false representations of reality" stereotypes work through simplification that allows for the arresting and fixation "of representation that, in denying the play of difference (which the negation through the Other permits), constitutes a problem for the representation of the subject in significations of psychic and social relations" (106–107). In these relations, those who are stereotyped are always either/or and never both/and and remain:

> fixed in a consciousness of the body as a solely negating activity or as a new kind of man, a new genus. What is denied the colonial subject, both as colonizer and colonized, is that form of negation which gives access to the recognition of difference. It is that possibility of difference and circulation which would liberate the signifier of skin/culture from the fixations of racial typology, the analytics of blood, ideologies of racial and cultural dominance or degeneration. "Wherever he goes," Fanon despairs, "the Negro remains a Negro"– his race becomes the ineradicable sign of negative difference in colonial discourses. For the stereotype impedes the circulation and articulation of the signifier of "race" as anything other than its fixity as racism. We always already know that blacks are licentious, Asiatics duplicitous. (Bhabha 2004, 108)

The stereotypes we use to frame and fix Others are embedded in the foundations of social institutions (like the academy) and enacted/recycled through its members (particularly those who have not yet confronted how race conditions their thinking). The structural recycling of culturally codified stereotypes, for Bhabha, is the compulsory setting up of a set of "a discursive form of racial and cultural opposition in terms of which colonial power is exercised" (112). This power gives rise to discriminatory forms of governability through which the stereotyped are "imprisoned in a circle of interpretation" and constrained by the social categories to which they are assigned as well as the privileges or lack of opportunities associated with these—such as educational access. The imprisonment of the diverse peoples in this cycle of interpretation and social categorizations "doesn't [always] depend on willful intent" (DiAngelo 2018, xiii). The actors and agents through which stereotypes rooted in colonial logic and intersectional racial contracts work often are not fully conscious of their tacit acceptance and uncritical elaboration of the terms of these oppressive practices—that is, unless they actively work to extricate themselves from their modalities—an act that is quite rare.

The first stereotype rooted in the Italian racial contract with Black women (the idea that blackness, femininity, and *italianità* are mutually exclusive) that I encountered was not so well hidden beyond the façade of the new moniker I was received shortly after I arrived: *la perla nera*. A potentially un/conscious racialization with echoes of *faccetta nera*, my new name stripped me of my personhood, cleaving my mind and spirit from my body. No longer Kenyse, as the black pearl I was just an exoticized, but nevertheless useful, black body whose presence could temporarily proxy, but never equate, the discipline's most privileged form, that is, heterosexual, economically elite, able-bodied, and always White male of European descent. Along with my new name came pats on the head in class when giving an answer thought of as cute (read: banal) and the expectation of my cleaning up after departmental lectures with the other female students. Other instances of this stereotype operating during my graduate studies include the times colleagues told me that Black people have nothing to do with Italy, marveled at my strength as they could never be in this field if they were Black, and shared their belief that I was not really Black because I was studying Italian. They also include the times when my all-male cohort excluded me from study groups and community-building opportunities, when the ethnic White guards at Sterling Library refused my entry into it because, in their opinion, I did not deserve to be there, and people in Italy who barred me entry into public spaces because they thought I was a prostitute.

The most destructive stereotype I encountered during my studies showed up in the form of a trusted professor's claim—unsupported by any textual analysis of my writing—that language would be my "Achilles heel." On its surface, their pronouncement would seem to be anchored in the best of intentions. In other words, when compared to the work of the more experienced, older, and White scholars whose work we read in class, how I expressed and communicated my worldview vis-à-vis Italy, whether in my language or Italian, was found wanting. The pronouncement that language would be my weakness and my inevitable downfall loses its innocuousness when situated within the situation's optics as well as the cultural contexts and power dynamics shaping the interaction of its actors. A White older male professor telling a much younger woman of color and scholar in training that they must conform to a way of using language and thought (whether in English or Italian) in ways deemed more palatable to their narrow cultural tastes is problematic. It is only when contextualized in its full social context that a profound—even if unconscious—lack of sensitivity to the specifically American racial context framing the student's strategies of interpretation can be seen. My teacher's pronouncement failed to acknowledge as real the existence of an interpretive framework that would cause me to perceive their protestations about my language skills—which had never been a problem until the PhD—as a devaluation, marginalization, and outright rejection of the thought processes and modes of cognition they mirror. The negativity of their unsubstantiated critique was also exacerbated by the power dynamics between us. As an inexperienced student of a much more mature scholar, it was hard for me to not see their comment as anything other than fact. When viewed from my "inferior" vantage point, it becomes apparent how I could go on to believe that I had to give up my mode of communicating and develop methods of linguistic expression and structures of thought that fit "the dominant culture's actual or perceived communication and discourse style" (Endo 2015, 209). To do otherwise was to risk the foreclosure of access to opportunities and privileges. It was a manipulative strategy that I then could not put my finger on, but for which I now have a term for identifying: *linguicism*.

A term coined by linguistic anthropologist Tove Skutnabb-Kangas,

> linguicism is akin to the other negative isms: racism, classism, sexism. Linguicism can be defined as ideologies and structures which are used to legitimate, effectuate and reproduce an unequal division of power and resources (both material and non-material) between groups which are defined based on language (on the basis of their mother tongues). (Skutnabb-Kangas 1989, 41)

This practice of "conscious or unconscious biases directed toward speakers whose primary dialects or languages are not aligned [common definitions of standard language forms]" manifests itself through a spectrum of practices ranging from the un/conscious stigmatizing of a speaker's use of their native language to other aspects of speech including accent, vocabulary size, grammar, modality, syntax, and style (Endo 2015, 208). Linguicism is not unique to my department but is instead embedded in the cultural fabric of both Italy and America as well as the very structure of the academy and Italian studies discipline. In these and other educational settings, as Rachel Endo argues in her essay, linguicism often results from a teacher's inability to "understand the needs of learners from assumed or real 'non-dominant' background" rooted in the belief that "language use in the classroom was not negotiable because "standard" [language forms] was the only acceptable option" (Endo 2015, 207). These beliefs are anchored in a set of "attitudes influenced by racially coded and rigid attitudes about what constitutes proper forms of communication in academic as well as non-academic setting" (208). More often than not, these attitudes are predicated on an over-reliance on "normative linguistic expressions [associated] with affluent and middle-class Whites," and such "intersections between language and race in academic settings illustrate powerful patterns of dominance, exclusion, and uneven expectations" (208 and 209). These expectations, Endo goes on to argue, have "clear implications for how educational and long-term opportunities are denied or distributed to learners from diverse backgrounds" (208). Linguicism often leads to "inequitable learning opportunities" because of how learners' social categories "consciously or unconsciously shape how a teacher views an individual's academic potential [therefore] impacting how and what [they] teach" as well as which learners do or not get attended to (208). Teachers, then, have a unique power to give life to or speak death over the intellectual lives of their students as a result of the authority of their perspective and the tendency of their students to trust their opinions more than their own, especially when these teachers act as the gatekeepers to educational opportunity. What they may have intended to help only works in the minds of diverse students to continually alert them to the fact that they are not enough and therefore do not belong academically as a result of their social difference. It is a dynamic whose stakes are incredibly high for racial minorities who are strongly encouraged to learn the dominant language to the detriment of their own. At the heart of the racialized linguistic discrimination students of diverse backgrounds experience is a set of dynamics that can best be understood, I believe, through the lens of the theories of Frantz Fanon.

In his seminal work *Black Skin, White Masks*, the Caribbean anticolonial scholar alerts us to the reality that language and worldview/ideology are inextricably linked when he writes "a man who possesses a language possesses as an indirect consequence, the world expressed and implied by this language" (Fanon 1967, 2). It is a worldview that is expressed via the nut and bolt mechanics of grammar, syntax, and morphology operate, as well as other aspects including expressions, vocabulary, and phrases: "[T]o speak [this language] means being able to use a certain syntax and possessing the morphology of such and such a language, but it [also] means above all assuming a culture and bearing the weight of a civilization" (1–2). "The more the colonized has assimilated the cultural values of the metropolis," Fanon writes, "the more he will have escaped the bush. The more he rejects his blackness and the bush, the whiter [less black] he will become" (2–3). To this I would add that the less black and whiter he (she, or they) become, the more socially acceptable (and culturally adequate) the colonized believes themselves to be and are perceived to have become. Language is an important site of this dynamic. Fanon argues that "all colonized people—in other words, people in whom an inferiority complex has taken root, whose local cultural originality has been committed to the grave—position themselves [and are positioned by the social structure] in relation to the civilizing language" (2). Mastery of the colonial language is one of the principal ways through which colonized subjects are encouraged to distance themselves from their culturally abject status (blackness) and become closer to whiteness and, thus, prove their adequacy. It is an idea that is made patently clear in the first chapter of *Black Skin, White Masks* when its author writes of a man who, when entering into the metropole, locked "himself in his room and read for hours—desperately working on his diction" and always on "the lookout for the slightest reaction of others [to their language performance], listening to himself speak and not trusting his own tongue" (5). He does so under the impression that the more he assimilates the colonial language, "the whiter he gets—i.e., the closer he becomes a true human being (1). To be judged as human means to receive all the benefits that come as being seen as such.

Like the colonial subject in Fanon's text, I too set about trying to prove my cultural adequacy—and intelligence—through language in the hopes of being seen as bright and belonging. I read my teacher's critique of my writing as evidence of my inferiority and constant reminders of the idea that I could never equally participate in the Italian world. To not make use of linguistic expressions that would mark me as "impoverished, derivative, less than, and fundamentally abject," I began to actively participate in my oppression and to reflect the very structures of your alienation. Whether it concerned my writing style, the use of the wrong preposition when speaking in a language that was not yet my own, using terminology associated with ideas that did not fit within other people's worldview, or the length of time I needed to process other people's words and produce my own, it felt to me as if every aspect of my communicative abilities were under fire—no matter how much I self-censored. I watched every word—and the thought they reflected/embodied—said for fear that it would be found unacceptable to the ears of the those who held—or at least I thought at the time—my academic/professional future in their hands. I thought I could overcome my alienation through my use of language and go on to be seen as equal to the "native" inhabitants of my new cultural milieu. No matter how much I tried to perfect my use of language, it did not erase the linguistic embodiment of the blackness that others saw as a limit. Embodiment, as Fanon maintains, always frames Black people's linguistic performance and limits its significance. Even when I spoke/wrote correctly the surprise expressed by others at my "eloquence" and command of the language also worked to remind me of my difference vis-à-vis the dissonance created by a "white" voice emanating from a black body. I could not win for trying. Why did I work so hard? I so desperately wanted to be approved of so that I would not lose out on opportunities that others in my department had.

The more I tried to prove my language use to be anything but "broken" and more like that of my White and native Italian-speaking counterparts, the more alienated I became from my ideas and their expression—and my psychological well-being—more stunted. My professor's proclamation, then, ultimately went on to become a self-fulfilling prophecy through the power of those twin psychological forces known as stereotype threat and confirmation bias. According to the American Psychological Association (2006), "group stereotypes can threaten how students evaluate themselves, which then alters academic identity and intellectual performance. This social-psychological predicament can, researchers believe, beset members of any group about whom negative stereotypes exist." In other words, stereotype threat is the unique set of psychological responses social minorities utilize to manipulate or reframe perceptions of their relationship to the existing social stereotypes that creates a decline in our academic motivation and performance. Confirmation bias, on the other hand, is the tendency our minds have to seek proof of (and go about recreating) what we already believe to be true about ourselves and our world. The writing workshops suggested by a trusted professor had planted the seed that I could not correctly communicate in any language (even my own) as a result of my linguistic expression and thought-forms not fitting what they thought academic writing/scholarship in the field of Italian studies should look like. The workshops also provided fertile soil in which the fruit of this seed could flourish. They gave me ample opportunities to see my lack of cognitive abilities and communicative competencies as accurate or adequate. It did so in two key ways. The workshops did so on the one hand by not adhering to what I now know to be best practices in current pedagogical approaches to the intentional development of minority students' writing skills.

On the other hand, the workshops lacked a clear definition of what constituted "good" academic writing as well as well-delineated set of processes and procedures designed to bring my written language expression up to standard. The mysterious ambiguity that lay at the foundation of my teacher's special "writing" workshops created a dynamic in which I was led to disavow my intelligence as a result of less than stellar writing abilities and continuously be on the lookout for proof of my inadequacy to meet a standard that was never really clear. Quite a Sisyphean task. If I overlooked any element of my deficiency as an Italianist and an academic, my hypercritical professor would be sure to point it out to me to remind me of the reality that, when it came down to it, Black and Italian were two distinct—and rigid—categories of being. Inevitably whatever words I utilized were always found wanting—and not just because they did not measure up to someone else's standard. They were found wanting because they were not my own, but a poor reflection of who I thought I had to be not just in order fit in, be seen, understood . . . and inevitably, considered enough.

The "helpful" words I heard during my writing workshops turned—by my third year—into what I read as an outright shunning that came as a punishment for having failed to get my language—and my Blackness—in line. My teacher's state of silence in my regard only further spiraled me into the psychological and performance peril associated with stereotype threat discussed earlier as well as the race-based stress that Liu and co-workers reminds us is a "reasonable expected outcomes of an acculturative process that racializes people of color as 'other,' in a world where the norms of White supremacy reign supreme" (Liu et al. 2019, 144).[6] By the time I submitted the first draft of my dissertation—which explored postwar Italian cinema's remediation of photography and photographic discourse—my ability to communicate my thoughts, even in my first language, was so distorted and the words/ideas I expressed so contorted that I was told to get checked out for a learning disability. If it was not for the patience of Millicent Marcus, my dissertation supervisor, and Michelle Nearon (the graduate school's associate dean for diversity who would not let me quit even though I wanted to), I would have never completed, submitted, or successfully passed the dissertation. When I graduated in 2012, I became the first African American to earn a PhD at my institution and one of the only 1.3 percent of Black people in the United States, according to the National Science Foundation's (2012) *Survey of Earned Doctorates*, to obtain an advanced graduate degree in foreign languages.[7] I finally had the diploma in hand and a place in history. What I did not have was peace of mind.

MAKING SENSE OF THE JOURNEY

By the time I graduated from my doctoral program, the racialized experiences taking place during my doctoral studies and their consequences—as I perceived it—had destroyed me. After being unable to secure a job of any kind in a shrinking field that has become even more resistant to practices of equitable hiring, I decided to leave an academia that had psychologically beaten me and go in search of my sense of personal well-being and peace of mind. Over time and with a whole lot of personal and professional healing, however, I learned to see myself as not being destroyed by my academic efforts to have what others led me to believe was not initially intended for me—the PhD and a career in Italian. When I graduated, I perceived my graduate studies as a shipwreck. My experiences over the last five years have led me to now see my studies instead as an inherently purgatorial process, that, as in the case of Dante's *navicella*, was necessary to my liberation from the beliefs and behaviors that only worked to keep me from the fullness of self-knowledge. Leaving academia was not a failure, then, but a radical act of self-preservation carried out in the tradition of my ancestors who jumped ship during the Middle Passage and dove into the womb of Atlantic Ocean rather than live a life of bondage anchored in the indignities born from other human beings' treacherous use of power. What on the surface looked like their physical death, was, in fact, a spiritual rebirth through which they were able to transform into a new way of being in the world and, inevitably, find their way back home.

Born anew and with the full awareness of who I am outside of the psychological, emotional, and racialized stress and trauma associated with my experiences in graduate school and the everyday realities of living as a Black woman in America, I now see that language was not my Achilles heel after all. In actuality, the part of myself that doomed me to failure was rooted in my not recognizing the value of using my voice and remaining silent in the belief that it would save me. My hope that my silence would keep me from the fate of the only other Black woman known by me to graduate with a PhD in Italian caused me to let so many things go unsaid. Here, on the other side of my Middle Passage, I now understand the power that comes along with speaking myself into existence and by saying what needs to be said to more actively shape my life experience. I wish I could go back in time and speak truth to the lies of other people's ignorance. I instead will settle for more loudly advocating for and actively facilitating the development of intersectionally inclusive learning environments—work that aligns with and continues the work begun before and continued throughout my graduate studies.

Now that I recognize the value of using my voice, I would like to leverage that insight in the service of diverse students and scholars pursuing careers in the field of Italian studies and conclude with a series of suggestions meant to empower them to persist on their journey. I would particularly like to make a set of recommendations for navigating the range of situations in which racial trauma and race-based stress can happen. As Truong and Museus (2012) affirm,

> coping with racism and racial trauma is a complex process that demands mental, emotional, spiritual, and physical energy and effort. Individuals must have

> knowledge of the strategies that they can use in specific situations and must also consider how those strategies might trigger particular responses and result in being further or less oppressed [/dehumanized]. (228)

The strategies available to people of color to navigate situations triggering the race-based stress that exacerbates the trauma they have already experienced as a result of living in a racial democracy "depend on several factors including their racial socialization experiences, racial identity development, personal experiences, collective experiences, individual characteristics, and situational characteristics" (229). The strategies I emphasize speak to a particular experience. Nevertheless, I believe that students of diverse backgrounds can find value in my suggestions even if the modalities of their dynamics shaping their own experiences of race-based stress are dissimilar from mine.

The first of these suggested strategies is always to remember that in addition to accepting diverse students and scholars into Italian academic spaces in the United States, institutions, departments, and disciplines are also accepting students' historical realities, lived experiences, and the perspectives they give rise to. It is imperative that minority students create room and hold open a space for all three of these on their journey and allow themselves to be guided by them as they make their way toward, and navigate, the professoriate. Second, I encourage them to identify and explore the terms of those identity-based social contracts that will undoubtedly try to shape their experiences in the field and work to prevent their full inclusion within it. A critical understanding of how a person is racially socialized is vital insofar as it "can lead to the development of meta-analytic critical consciousness through self-knowledge and appreciation of color; [by developing] a more comprehensive sense of where they fit within the system of oppression, facilitate racial identity development [doctoral students of color can more fully] catalyze the coping process with racism" (Truong and Museus 2012, 229). Part and parcel with this recommendation comes my third suggestion to people of color in doctoral programs and disciplines where they are often the single minority: actively seek out those aspects of the discipline where their social identity is included and—more important—valued. There may be no critical discussions of racialized social alterity during coursework, comprehensive exams, or conferences. Yet there are scholars out there—some of whom participated in the Calandra Institute's diversity conference that gave birth to this collection of essays—who are dealing with issues that reflect the intersection of varying social identities (whether race, gender, class, ability, sexuality, linguistic identity, religion, etc.) with the Italian cultural experience. My fourth suggestion is to advocate on behalf of themselves and others for more culturally responsive practices of student/scholar engagement. Advocacy work could also provide students with greater insight into their research as well as a fuller understanding of the impact that their work and presence could have on the essential questions at the heart of Italian studies. The fifth recommendation I make is to intentionally seek resources and relationships that will assist you in the development of practical ways of coping with identity-based trauma and stress so that you are better enabled to resist and persist along the entire trajectory of the doctoral/junior faculty pathway. Be sure that, whatever strategies that they explore and adopt fall within all three categories for coping with racism as defined by experts—problem focused, emotion focused, and support seeking—and focus not only on reliving racial trauma/race-based stressors but also on working through their responses to these. (For an explanation of these see Mellor [2004].) Finally, I want you to know what I learned the hard way, that your silence will not save you from what you fear but only rob you of yourself and of the capacity to self-actualize in the ways you see fit. Speak up; your very life—both personal and professional—depends on it.

A BEGINNING AT THE END?

Though this essay ends, my story is to be continued. I left the academy five years ago and, somehow, I find myself with one foot back in it in large part due to the power of and response to Deborah Parker's provocative article. After agreeing to teach a course of elementary Italian in January 2019 at my alma mater, the Catholic University of America (a decision that coincides with my participation in the conference generating this volume), I was very happily poised to return to the classroom at the same institution in the fall of 2019 when I taught three courses, two of which I designed myself. Though it is a contingent position that remains professionally precarious, I am looking forward to having an opportunity to create the impact I desired to make at the outset of my doctoral program. I am especially grateful to carry out my work from a perspective anchored in the profound sense of personal power that could only be gained by my leaving academia. It was an act that forced me to creatively eke the means of my survival with the substantial support of my community of care and stints in the fields of secondary education, nonprofit youth development, unemployment, and social entrepreneurship. Leaving academia also provided me an opportunity to learn what I failed to realize as I initially made my way to it: The authority to develop my intelligence and enact my intellectual agency in the world could not be given to me from the outside, it had to be developed from the inside. Cultivating this sense of personal power and professional prowess, however, is only possible when the seeds of both are sown in soil that facilitates its growth, not stifles it. Even the most barren of fields can bear the choicest fruits as long as it is intentionally fertilized and the weeds that grow up to choke its crops are accounted for and removed. With this insight and the keys to my personal power nestled safely under my belt, I return to the classroom with everything I need to thrive—both personally and professionally—and to survive the slings and arrows of academia that I no longer see myself as having to accommodate at the expense of my own psychological and spiritual well-being. These tools, however, will not only be of benefit to me but also my students insofar as they will allow me to open up for them doors to a world of opportunity that extends beyond the bounds of the college campus. They have already proven themselves to be useful—at least that is what students said in last semester's evaluations. They seem to have appreciated how I brought my own experiences as a nonheritage Italian-language learner to bear on those of my students and used them to create engaging learning experiences that modeled for learners how to more fully explore—and connect with—a culture quite different from their own. At the same time, they express gratitude for my having brought their study of Italian language and culture into conversation with their own professional and personal interests. This allowed them to (1) engage *italianità* on its terms as well as (2) discover and chart the contours of Italian culture themselves, moving beyond the stereotypes they erroneously associate with the peninsular nation. Most importantly, my newfound insights help me to leverage my experiences as a student and an aspiring professional in the service of promoting students' active development of the twenty-first-century global competencies necessary to their being competitive in current and future job markets. Five of nine students saw such value in my approach that they returned to my language class in the fall. It is a testament not to my teaching but the power of diversity, equity, and inclusion (DEI) work. Rather than using all their energy to psychologically self-protect and intellectually self-defend, DEI programming helps minority students to redirect their attention to the very purpose for their being in the classroom and leveraging it to power their academic, personal, and professional development. While these efforts may look like they focus on a few, when explored more deeply we can see that, in reality, they generate greater well-being for us all.[8]

Notes

1. For more on the nature of this race-based trauma and stress see Comas-Diaz, Hall, and Neville (2019).
2. I refrain from using terms typically utilized to describe nonwhite peoples in the United States and other contexts. My inclusion of them in this essay is only for clarity's sake.
3. The title of a groundbreaking memoir written by two African American centenarian educators and activists.
4. As stated in Amienne (2017), these discriminatory and abusive mechanisms are normalized in the academy and are often cited as the reason for diverse students and scholars' departure.
5. Not all aspects of the Italian racial contract with Black women I briefly described above were a part of my experience. I was not inappropriately sexualized, but I was expected to pick up after departmental lectures along with the other female graduate students.
6. There is nothing wrong with being white and proud of your culture. There is, however, as Representative Steve King reminds us, everything is wrong with being a White supremacist (when race/privilege meets power).
7. In 2012, 51,000 doctoral degrees were awarded that year. Of these, 473 were conferred in the foreign languages.
8. For a greater understanding of the social benefits of personal well-being see the United Nations Sustainable Development Solutions Network's (2019) World Happiness Report (sponsored, ironically, by the Ernesto Illy Foundation).

Works Cited

American Psychological Association. 2006. "Stereotype Threat." Research in Action. https://www.apa.org/research/action/stereotype (accessed May 1, 2019).

Amienne, K. A. 2017. "Abusers and Enablers in Faculty Culture." *The Chronicle of Higher Education,* November 2. https://www.chronicle.com/article/abusers-and-enablers-in-faculty-culture/ (accessed June 20, 2019).

Bhabha, Homi K. 2004. *The Location of Culture*. London and New York: Routledge.

Bennet, Laura. 2015. "The First-Person Industrial Complex." *Slate*, September 14 (accessed June 20, 2019).

Caponetto, Rosetta Giuliani. 2012. "Blaxploitation Italian Style." In *Postcolonial Italy: Challenging National Homogeneity*, edited by Cristini Lombardi-Diop and Caterina Romeo, 191–203. New York: Palgrave Macmillan.

Chae, D. H., S. Clouston, M. L. Hatzenbuehler, M. R. Kramer, H. L. F. Cooper, S. M. Wilson, and B. G. Link. 2015. "Association between an Internet-Based Measure of Area Racism and Black Mortality." *PLoS ONE* 10(4): e0122963. http://dx.doi.org/10.1371/journal.pone.0122963 (accessed July 18, 2019).

Cipriani, Lidio. 1935. *Un assurdo etnico: L'impero etiopico*. Florence: R. Bemporad & Figlio.

Comas-Díaz, L., Hall, G. N., & Neville, H. A. 2019. "Racial trauma: Theory, research, and healing: Introduction to the special issue." *American Psychologist, 74*(1), 1-5. http://dx.doi.org/10.1037/amp0000442 (accessed September 12, 2019).

Coppola, Manuela, and Sonia Sabelli. 2012. "'Not a Country for Women, nor for Blacks' Teaching Race and Gender in Italy between Colonial Heritages and New Perspectives." In *Teaching "Race" with a Gendered Edge,* edited by Brigitte Hipfl and Kristin Loftsdòttir, 143–159. Budapest: Central European Press.

Cottom, Tressie McMillan. 2019. *Thick and Other Essays*, Kindle ed. New York: New Press.

DiAngelo, Robin. 2018. *White Fragility: Why It's So Hard for White People to Talk about Racism*, Kindle ed. New York: Beacon.

Endo, Rachel. 2015. "From Unconscious Deficit Views to Affirmation of Linguistic Varieties in the Classroom: White Preservice Teachers on Building Critical Self-Awareness about Linguicism's Causes and Consequences." *Multicultural Perspectives* 17(4): 207–214.

Fanon, Frantz. 1967. *Black Skin, White Masks*. New York: Grove Press.

Gomm, Roger, and Martin Hammersley. 2001. "Thick Ethnographic Description and Thin Models of Complexity." www.leeds.ac.uk/educol/documents/00001820.htm (accessed June 15, 2019). June 15.

Liu, William Ming, Rossina Zamora Liu, Yunkyuong Loh Garrison, Ji Yuon Cindy Kim, Laurence Chan, Yu C. S. Ho, and Chi W. Yeung. 2019. "Racial Trauma, Microaggressions, and Becoming Racially Innocuous: The Role of Acculturation and White Supremacist Ideology." *American Psychologist* 74(1): 143–155.

Lorde, Audre. 2007. *Sister Outsider*. Berkeley, CA: Crossing Press.

Mellor, D. 2004. "Responses to Racism: A Taxonomy of Coping Styles Used by Aboriginal Australians." *American Journal of Orthopsychiatry* 74(1): 56–71.

Mills, Charles W. 1997. *The Racial Contract*, Kindle ed. Ithaca, NY: Cornell University Press.

National Science Foundation. 2012. *Survey of Earned Doctorates*. https://www.nsf.gov/statistics/srvydoctorates/#tabs-2&tools&tabs-2 (accessed September 11, 2019).

O'Healy, Áine. 2009. "'[Non] è una somala': Deconstructing African Femininity in Italian Film." *The Italianist* 29: 175–198.

Parker, Deborah. 2018. "Race and Foreign Language." www.insidehighered.com (accessed June 21, 2019).

Sartre, Jean-Paul. 1976. *Black Orpheus*. Paris: Présence Africaine.

Skutnabb-Kangas, Tove. 1989. "Multilingualism and the Education of Minority Children." *Estudios fronterizos* 8(18–19): 36–67.

Strazza, Michele. 2012. "Faccette nera dell'Abissinia: Madame e meticci dopo la conquista dell'Etiopia. *Humanities* 2: 116–133.

Tolentino, Jia. 2017. "The Personal-Essay Boom Is Over." www.newyorker.com (accessed May 18, 2019).

Truong, Kimberly A., and Samuel D Museus. 2012. "Responding to Racism and Racial Trauma in Doctoral Study: An Inventory for Coping and Mediating Relationships." *Harvard Educational Review* 82(2): 226–255.

United Nations Sustainable Development Solutions Network. 2019. *World Happiness Report*. https://worldhappiness.report (accessed August 20, 2019).

Verga, Giovanni. 1993. *I Malavoglia*. Milan: Feltrinelli.

Welz, Claudia. 2014. "A Voice Crying Out from the Wound—With or without Words: On Trauma, Speech, and Silence." *Dialogue: A Journal of Theology* 56(4): 412–427.

Hybridize or Decline: Practical Solutions toward a Sustainable Future for Italian Studies

VETRI NATHAN

The challenges faced by the field of Italian studies in post–Great Recession academia closely align with those being encountered by the humanities in general. In other ways, structural, cultural, and institutional specificities of doing research and teaching in or about Italy present their own unique obstacles to change, growth, and renewal. The very timely symposium on diversity held in New York[1] in January 2019 made me conclude, yet again, that immediate hybridization of the field of Italian studies will be fundamental for its continuing existence and growth in institutions of higher education. I also believe that this conclusion can be extrapolated and applied to all of the humanities, and while my observations and recommendations are U.S.-specific, they are applicable to many global situations.

In this essay, I will briefly define what I mean by the term *hybridity* and then elaborate upon some of the practical paths individuals and institutions could take in order to move toward future sustainability. I have been fortunate to have tried and tested these paths at my current institution, the University of Massachusetts Boston, and my work is bearing fruit thanks also to an excellent team of colleagues and some helpful administrators. I am glad and very aware that many people are doing great work in several institutions to combat the seemingly perpetual *crisi*, but have also witnessed how others continue to follow older approaches that do not work. My task here is to quickly present my toolbox of initiatives and thoughts that may be added to a growing chorus of other individuals doing some brilliant work in their respective institutions.

In the wake of the 2008 financial crisis, panicked universities, parents, and students abandoned majors and sturdy general education requirements in the humanities in favor of "professional" courses that were believed to create more employment opportunities. Conveniently forgotten was one root cause of the crisis: a lack of thorough grounding in liberal arts education in the general populace, that wonderful contemporary American iteration of age-old way of learning so fundamental in providing the lateral- and critical-thinking skills needed to sustain an informed democratic polity and needed also to sustain personal long-term career success whatever the chosen field of work. Only an individual aware of his or her civic rights and duties and who understands how people, societies, and cultures operate can fully exercise oversight of political and financial representatives for any short-sighted or destructive policies or expertly manage the politics and culture of a competitive office environment. The rise of chauvinistic nationalism, authoritarian leaders on both the right and the left, a more recent emerging global crisis in democratic institutions, and general mistrust of global cooperation have also contributed to the steady decline of important educational experiences for students that I consider to be "keystone" college experiences: the study of second or third languages and meaningful study abroad. All the approaches to possible solutions I discuss here can be subsumed under two themes: hybridity and adaptation.

I use the term *hybridity* on purpose: Indeed, it is one of my long-term career goals to create a space that will instill a different understanding of multiple identities through this word—a term that stands in contrast to those such as *multiculturalism* and *diversity*. I use *hybridity* specifically as defined by Homi K. Bhabha; instead of a melting-pot notion of separate cultures coming together in harmony, a vision that unwittingly serves to indirectly reestablish a difference of identities, Bhabhian hybridity is the less-comforting yet far more rewarding unlocatable and always shifting "in-between" of all cultural and national identities (Bhabha 1994). Through this formulation, *all identities* are chronically and permanently hybrid, and the understanding of these shifting sands beneath even seemingly monolithic identities exposes the wondrous (or to some scary) similarities between the center and its peripheries, between the Self and the Other.[2] Rather than reactively containing or managing the ever-mutable qualities of identity, the understanding and teaching of Bhabhian hybridity and other such conceptualizations of fluid identity can allow individuals, institutions, and cultures to be open to the past and future of all such formations (religion, gender, caste, class, nationality, etc.) and step "through the looking-glass" to view themselves as being not quite so different from so-called "diverse," "minority," or liminal sections of society.

If the adoption of hybridity is the key to sustaining Italian studies for future generations, then hybridizing the field does not simply amount to introducing token coursework in "diversity" subjects. Undoubtedly, there is much material that can be categorized as such and will reap more interest in students and administrators due to their relevance and profitability—courses that discuss migration, for example, can fit into this group of new and updated "diverse" programming. What I am suggesting is a more rewarding big-picture renewal of the field, where even more traditional topics such as Dante or the Risorgimento become foci of understanding how hybrid identities work through time and space in the Italian nation. Such an approach to "diversity" will serve to include "multicultural" material not as a separate section within the Italian major or minor but by rearranging the picture to make students aware of the implications of cultural identity in whatever their own lived personal, academic, and career experiences in the future may be, Italian or not. Transformed in this way, Italian studies becomes hybrid and relevant to students whether it will be central to their future lives or not. Questions of Italian national culture become explicitly pertinent to students of any nation. Every course becomes relatable and practically usable to the many different lived experiences of an increasingly complex student body.

To describe one example of this approach: My course in Italian American culture not only celebrates the specific histories, failures, and accomplishments of the Italian American community but also challenges students to explore the patterns in other times and societies where new groups of migrants or outsiders have been met with fear and disdain. I ask students to analyze canonical works such as Mario Puzo's *The Godfather* and John Fante's *Dago Red* in order to gain a deeper insight into how literary or cinematic representation in itself poses many problematic questions about identity and power. Films such as Spike Lee's *Do the Right Thing* allow students to discuss the complex relationship of Italians in America with other communities. I also use films such as Emanuele Crialese's *Nuovomondo* (Golden Door) in order to highlight the important roles played by Italian American women in the construction of a diasporic identity. Throughout the course, I guide students to recalibrate conventional, fixed popular stereotypes of Italian ethnicity, gender, and sexuality by examining representations in television, cinema, literature, public discourse, and popular culture. Rather than writing a final paper, students create videos that explore hybrid migrant identities and notions of ancestry within their own families. Several faculty members at other universities are working on similarly creating relevant connections within courses, and this can only serve to bolster the field at large. At UMass Boston (the city's only public university) such an approach becomes overtly important as my classes always contain a mind-boggling mélange of hybrid identities, both Italian American and not. Continually urging students to connect specific histories and topics to more general questions of identity and hybridity allows them to truly explore cultural studies as a field, learn its methodologies, and—why not—actually *enjoy* courses. This in turn promotes retention in a field that always seems to be in jeopardy of becoming a service program for language and Gen-Ed requirements rather than majors or minors. Retention in turn opens the door to further hiring, hopefully in the more financially secure kind of positions.

Most of what I discuss here is not new information, but this all needs to be articulated often and in different venues for the message to become mainstream in academia, especially in the humanities. Besides hybridizing the curriculum, some of the other useful ways to successfully hybridize Italian studies are to:

1. Embody Hybridity: Our students are increasingly hybrid. They come from increasingly complex racial, national, religious, and cultural backgrounds. Faculty bodies in Italian should also mirror this richness of experience. I do not intend to state that hiring should only look at any one aspect, but I have witnessed the positive effect on students of the embodied presence of visibly different faculty in the Italian classroom. A visibly "out of place" body can allow faculty to discuss questions of hybridity that go beyond the visible and into everyone's lived experiences of identity. While I initially did not want to face the unpleasant truth, I have learned through my work in personnel committees that faculty of color can have many conscious and unconscious biases working against them. From personal experience, I have frequently experienced how these biases transform into outright prejudice when faculty or students of color travel to Italy to teach or undertake research.[3] I believe the only direct solution to this is to foster visible difference in classroom and cultural venues so that a newer vision may slowly form about who is allowed to be an accepted authority or learner of Italian cultural knowledge.

2. Work with Administrators: Faculty often (semi) jokingly refer to the administrators as the "dark side." Like any other group of managers, chairs, deans' offices, provosts, and so forth can be either effective and willing, or not, in promoting the humanities. The most useful approach is to identify allies and work with them on practical ways to accrue visibility and importance for a relatively small program. A supportive chair, dean, or "higher-ups" can provide insights on institutional pathways that may be less clear to instructors. This is not due to faculty inability to understand institutional pressures but rather to the nature of the job of administrators, who must inherently look at the big-picture situation across the institution.

3. Get outside Italian Studies: Italianists tend to be a very inward-looking group of teachers and researchers, and this is both a pity and an understatement. I, too, am guilty of presenting most often in purely "Italian" panels and conferences, but I have realized the benefits of going beyond the field and discussing my work in venues that have a more global scope. Also, within the confines of our institutions, the field is ripe for cross-connections with both popular and smaller departments. This is already being done by some and needs to be done more. Linking up with—I'm going to say it—management or science, or even other nation-focused programs, will only help Italian studies become stronger rather than dilute its relevance. The key is to modify and adapt course syllabi to make them relevant to these fields and then to "slip in" some old-fashioned reading of books in the schedule. Yes, no one wants to read books in college anymore, but there are sneaky ways to get students to move away from their gadgets and skim-reading to some more thoughtful and deeper reading. The important part is to adapt and create new hybrid course titles and points of entry into the material. In my department (Modern Languages, Literatures and Cultures) at UMass Boston, the faculty have spearheaded an initiative to create a new global studies major. We did this because, if it comes to fruition, it promises to be a major that students can accept and also render acceptable to their parents and future employers without having to worry or convince anyone else how it will help them secure a stable future. Most important, faculty members in our department also believe that it is not a zero-sum game—that French, Italian, Chinese, or Arabic studies can only gain from a global studies major rather than lose students. We believe that courses that have a more global approach can act as feeders into more nation-specific language courses and subjects. Crucially, rather than simply pay lip service to the importance of global cultural awareness, the major will have a strong two-language requirement, making foreign languages a key part of the puzzle toward true cultural competency.

4. Fundraise: This again can seem like anathema to many faculty: "It's not my job." However, as education becomes a deliberate pawn in partisan political battles and state funding declines for public learning, it is up to faculty to work with advancement offices to become more entrepreneurial. There are many programs, nonprofits, government leaders, and influential donors who are supportive of STEM education. Where are

those who support the humanities? They do exist, and it is our task to find them. At UMass Boston, I was fortunate to get the opportunity to cultivate a relationship with a visionary donor who has provided a substantial endowment to set up an Italian Culture Center.[4] Such foresight and generosity do still exist, and it is again our task to work with parts of the administration that know how to reach out to alumni or community elite to support Italian studies and the humanities. Learning how to communicate about the importance of our field to laypersons and "hybridizing" academic discourse to reach people beyond our own small circle are key to successfully accomplishing this. It takes practice, as I have learned myself.

5. Promote Meaningful Study Abroad: The emphasis would lie on the "meaningful" part. Italy is still a prime study-abroad destination, but unfortunately many programs generate only short-term results and do not promote deep and long-term interest in Italian studies. The commercialization of study abroad is a big problem, with private companies building trips that are little more than glorified tourism in disguise. The solution to this is to actively build and promote faculty-led programs, thus ensuring some continuity and connection with the professors in the home campus and the study-abroad experience. While this may be a very time-consuming enterprise, faculty-led programs allow for a personal incentive for students to go with their professor and make connections with academic work before and after their journey to Italy. Another issue in some more prestigious institutions that have campuses in Italy is the dilution of the Italian-focused programming to include teaching in other subjects. To combat this, I believe Italian studies faculty need to offer more of the hybrid content courses described above. These courses that have an interdisciplinary approach should be more attractive to all students attending a semester in the Italian location. Another important aspect is working with others in the university to make the wider academic community realize the importance of culturally specific programming in such a location.

All the pathways mentioned above focus on hybridizing Italian studies to make more explicit connections between it and other fields of study, to other departments and programs, and to the wider cultural ecosystem, both academic and non. Diversity for the sake of maintaining the intellectual quality of a liberal arts education is important, but hybridity is a deeper and more urgent redress for the survival and sustainability of the field. I am sure that my conclusions are shared by many, yet resistance to change or just plain inertia are also widespread. It is my hope that those who share these thoughts will work quickly, efficiently, and collaboratively with each other to create a united, mutually supportive, and hybrid community of academics, administrators, and students.

Notes

1. The symposium on Diversity in Italian Studies was organized by the John D. Calandra Italian American Institute in New York City on January 17 and 18, 2019. I would like to thank the organizers for this excellent initiative, especially Dean Anthony Tamburri.
2. For a more detailed description of Bhabha's concept of hybridity see Vetri Nathan (2017).
3. For a groundbreaking and thought-provoking article on the issues facing faculty of color in Italian studies, read Parker (2018).
4. At the time of writing, the Catherine Frisone Scott Italian Cultural Studies Center, in memory of John B. Frisone, is scheduled to open at the University of Massachusetts Boston in the fall of 2019.

Works Cited

Bhabha, Homi. 1994. *Location of Culture*. London: Routledge.

Nathan, Vetri. 2017. *Marvelous Bodies: Italy's New Migrant Cinema*. West Lafayette, IN: Purdue University Press.

Parker, Deborah. 2018. "Race and Foreign Language." Inside Higher Ed. https://www.insidehighered.com/views/2018/06/21/paucity-asians-and-other-minorities-teaching-and-studying-italian-and-other-foreign (accessed May 7, 2019).

Transforming Italian Studies

DEBORAH PARKER

I would not be addressing the subject of transforming Italian studies had matters gone otherwise at the University of Virginia. After getting my PhD from Harvard in 1985, I was on the job market for two years. While I had about eight interviews, I received no offers. Hiring committees were visibly surprised when they saw I was Asian. After Dante Della Terza, my adviser at Harvard, wrote to Tibor Wlassics, the senior Italianist at the University of Virginia, Wlassics hired me as a lecturer for one year. The following year the department converted the line to tenure track and invited three candidates to campus, one woman and two men. The department offered the job to the two men, both of whom turned down the offers.

The dean at the time informed the department that he would not fund any more on-campus interviews. At that point, Wlassics decided to offer me the position. One of my colleagues quipped, "So, we've hired a Chinese woman from Canada to teach Italian." The comment was meant to be funny, but it also reveals just how much of an anomaly an Asian Italianist was.

For the next six years, I gave papers at the Kalamazoo International Conference on Medieval Studies, Medieval Academy meetings, the Modern Language Association (MLA), and the American Association for Italian Studies (AAIS). It was at the AAIS that I felt most out of place. My experiences were mixed—friendly encounters alongside periods of isolation. What I remember most, however, is how very different my experiences were at the first Renaissance Society of America (RSA) meeting I attended in 1991. The organizers put me on a panel with William J. Kennedy (Cornell) and Daniel Javitch (NYU), two comparatists working on Renaissance commentaries, both of whom reached out to me after my talk. In successive years, I befriended many scholars from different disciplines at the RSA. All responded to my work rather than to me as a curiosity or an anomaly.

Henceforth, I attended ever fewer AAIS meetings and soon stopped going altogether. The point here is obvious: We gravitate to where we find affinities and support. Whereas learned societies such as the RSA, the Sixteenth Century

Society, and the Medieval Academy of America include historians, art historians, musicologists, neo-Latinists, and foreign-language specialists, members of Italianist societies are largely literature specialists. There is little diversity in fields encompassed by Italian studies and even less among its members. As Konrad Eisenbichler (professor of Italian, University of Toronto) sees the field:

> So many Italian departments are made up nearly exclusively of Italians or hyphenated Italians. There are very few (if any) "non-visible" minorities in Italian (I think of myself as an example of the very few: I am not Italian, but Austrian by birth and now Canadian). Where are the non-Italian Europeans (whites) in Italian departments? My point is that if Italian departments are made up only of people who are Italian or hyphenated Italians, these departments risk becoming (or have already become) small ethnic enclaves that are relevant only to an immigrant group in the area and not to the wider scholarly community of the humanities. They lose credibility and validity as a scholarly discipline and become filiopietistic entities that eventually fall into oblivion (as we constantly see when Italian departments are either dramatically reduced or even closed down across North America—in the 1990s the University of Toronto had 22 professors in Italian (all but me of Italian extraction), now it has 14 (and I'm still the only non-Italian). By comparison, the University of Toronto's Spanish and Portuguese Department has 16 professors, and 3 of them have non-Spanish names, the University of Toronto French Department has 45 faculty members of which 25 have non-French names (over half!)[1]

Eisenbichler's observation echoes my own sentiment—and that of many others. A failure to diversify has deleterious effects.

The decision to attend RSA meetings estranged me from Italian. I continued to teach Italian literature, especially Dante, the author who drew me to Italian, but my interactions for the last twenty years have largely been with art historians. As a Renaissance specialist with a particular interest in early modern artist-writers, I never had to prove myself or be subjected to gatekeeping behaviors, tests of my Italian or kneejerk reactions to my ethnicity. Amid the world of Renaissance scholars—at the RSA, I Tatti, or Florentine archives—people responded to my work and not my ethnicity.

My scholarly trajectory as an Asian-Canadian in Italian, a field that was inhospitable to minorities in the 1980s and 1990s, is one story among many that involve exclusion, identity, and transformation. It was also buried. I didn't realize how many other minorities had had similar experiences until I interviewed roughly forty professors and graduate students for my 2018 *Chronicle of Higher Education* article "Race and Foreign Languages." There is a remarkable consistency to observations made by the Others among us. Gaoheng Zhang (assistant professor of Italian, University of British Columbia) notes the tendency of some Asian scholars to identify themselves in terms of their "originary" cultures and to the [fields] in which they specialize. We see this in Asians and Asian Americans who work on Chinese history, language, or film. Yet Asians who do not work on their originary culture self-identify differently. As Zhang puts it, "[While] I'm Chinese-born, raised, and trained at the high school and college-level, I'm not nationalistic. I know an awful lot about Italy because of my research. I wish people could focus more on the bigger issues rather than on the national contexts so much."

Zhang has sought out other scholarly venues, ones he finds less "provincial" such as those that focus on migration studies, mobility studies, gender studies, and masculinity studies. Roughly twenty-five years separate Zhang's experiences and mine on the job market. Yet, as he remarked when we met in Toronto in 2016 to discuss our respective interests, hiring tendencies in Italian studies have not changed much. The treatment of minorities in the field remains ambivalent and inhospitable—perhaps unconsciously so in the latter case. The more it remains resistant to hiring minorities, the more we risk alienating minorities and hyphenated members—and the faster the field will collapse.

Moisés Park (assistant professor of Latin America studies, Baylor) also spoke to me about the frustrations of being obliged to address one's minority status:

> I am frequently asked my point of view or opinion as an Asian, rather than as a Latin Americanist in U.S. and Latin America. It is frustrating that I try to address an issue and immediately the follow up deals with my phenotype. There is an expectation that I should also be an expert in East Asian history, politics, culture, and language. The main challenge is breaking the phenotypical influence in others' view of who I am; in other words, often I am viewed as an Asian, *then* as a Latin Americanist, Latino or American.[2]

There are consequences to alienating minorities in the field, not to mention scholars perceived as outsiders: They leave Italian, as Wuming Chang (PhD in Italian, Brown), Arthur Lei (MA in Italian, Berkeley), and Kenyse Lyons (PhD in Italian, Yale) have done, and these departures diminish a field in profound ways. Excluding minorities shuts out new fields of inquiry and approaches: As Konrad Eisenbichler put it, exclusionary practices foreclose membership in the wider scholarly community of a dwindling field that has systematically excluded the very people who might reanimate it.

Within Italianist spaces minorities are often obliged to address their Otherness, to disrupt the phenotypical influence in the way in which they are regarded by others. As long as peninsular Italianists subject minorities and the Others among us to language tests, the practice of speaking Italian pointedly to seemingly close ranks, the more difficult it becomes to make Italianistica more inclusive. Many people speak a foreign language with an accent; virtually all make occasional grammar mistakes. But this phenomenon can become a way of testing a minority's or non-native speaker's bonafides. At times, the intent may not be harmful, but at others it is offensive, weaponized if somewhat unconsciously. *What* we say should prevail over *how* we say it.

Minorities are not the only groups within Italian who find themselves alien presences in the world of Italian studies. While the online responses to my article came from minorities, others contacted me privately. This latter group includes Italo-Americans, Italo-Canadians, non-Italian Europeans, and peninsular Italian women. One American Italianist who was trained as a comparatist recalls: "I was repeatedly lectured by (male) Italians in the local community and told how lucky I was to have gotten a job and it was only because I am a woman and the department was under pressure to hire a woman, since the previous female 'token' had left."[3] Such aggressions speak for themselves. In summing up the harm done not only to the target but to the field at large, Mary Ann Carolan (professor of Italian, Fairfield University) observes: "An intellectual endeavor should not be limited to any particular ghetto if it aspires to be a serious field of inquiry."[4]

By far the most poignant response to my article came from Catherine Adoyo (adjunct lecturer in Italian, Georgetown), whose comment was posted online:

> This is so real. I have developed the sense that one of the greatest shortcomings in "Languages and Literatures" scholarship, especially in Italian, is in defining such disciplines according to national boundaries and the attendant identity politics. I have seen countless iterations of the "how Italian are you?" litmus test frame many an interaction by establishing an undeclared pecking order of *priority of authority*, with peninsular Italians holding pride of place, their American descendants readily leveraging their ancestral bonafides to be heard, others of European descent claiming authorizing proximity, and then the rest. Reading this article makes me wonder honestly whether Africans even have a place at this table.

In a private communication, Adoyo added: "I sincerely believe that the lack of diversity in disciplines like Italian is only just a symptom of a much deeper problem; the provincial attitude that Italian literature is *about* Italians with the corollary that it is *for* Italian readers, Italian scholars, Italian thinkers, Italian people and them alone." Qi Chen (assistant professor of Italian, Beihang University, China) outlines the repercussions succinctly: "If Italian studies were confined in the West, it may have difficulty achieving truly international status. This is especially true for large countries like China, with great potential. Researchers in Italian studies should be more open to minority researchers and understand that different views about the same topics are possible." A striking number of themes reverberate in these voices—provincialism, exclusion, nationalism, identity. The repercussions of unmindful, discriminatory, and paternalistic behavior have affected Italian studies for decades, creating a culture that has not been receptive to hiring minorities.

WHAT CAN WE DO?

I ended "Race and Foreign Languages" with this question: "Virtually everyone I queried deemed this topic 'important and timely.' Can this sentiment be converted to action? Can Italian enact a bold and more inclusive vision for its future—or will we be left managing a decline?" Information available on Italian studies websites shows how entrenched the field has become. I examined the composition and number of tenure-track faculty by gender and race on the departmental websites of twenty-six American doctoral programs and tried to determine the approximate number of auxiliary general faculty (non-tenure-track lines), the number of graduate students, and whether or not there are minorities among them.[5] While the information may not be accurate, since some of the data could be out-of-date, it nevertheless offers a panorama of the current composition of departments that have a graduate program in Italian. The largest departments are those at the University of Toronto (12–14), Rutgers (7), NYU (9), and the University of Wisconsin (7). Since many Italian studies programs include colleagues from other departments, I limited my count to the number of tenure-track faculty in Italian. The institutions with a preponderance of male colleagues are UCLA, Toronto, Stony Brook, Notre Dame, and Indiana. The gender composition has been unchanged, at times for decades, in these institutions.

While there are no minorities in these institutions, there are a small number in other places, which include myself and Hiromi Kaneda at the University of Virginia (Kaneda was hired as a lecturer in 2018). Vetri Nathan, Veena Kumar, and Aileen Feng are tenured at, respectively, the University of Massachusetts,

Dominican University, and the University of Arizona. As of January 2019, there appear to be four minority students enrolled in PhD programs—at Notre Dame, Harvard, UCLA, and University of Toronto. In 2017, the University of British Columbia, an institution with a large number of Asian and Asian Canadian students, offered Gaoheng Zhang a tenure-track position. Akash Kumar is currently a visiting professor at Indiana University.

These are dismal numbers: Over the last fifty years, Italian programs have hired only five minorities in tenure-track positions—myself, Veena Kumar Carlson, Vetri Nathan, Aileen Feng, and Gaoheng Zhang. There are no Afro-Americans in tenure-track jobs in the field: Ray Fleming retired from Florida State University a few years ago. Catherine Adoyo is an adjunct lecturer at Georgetown University. As of 2019 Kenyse Lyons is a lecturer at Catholic University. To provide more context for evaluating these numbers, I will offer one point of comparison: There are currently two Asians and two Black people in the French Department at the University of Virginia. Given the paucity of minorities in Italian, the task before us is formidable. Of the roughly twenty Italianists I contacted working in departments with graduate programs, only three acknowledged that Italian is "not very diverse at all." Many people, notably at UCLA and Berkeley, the two programs that have produced the highest number of minority PhDs in Romance language classes, didn't answer my query or sidestepped my questions by mentioning minority undergraduates they had taught. Silence, in this instance, speaks for itself.

We should not underestimate the commitment required to combat decades of intransigence and complacency. With the bleak state of the job market and collapse of the humanities, many of our peers do not consider this an opportune moment for hiring. Nor should we underestimate the resistance we will encounter. On January 11, 2019, an article appeared in the *Chronicle of Higher Education* on an ugly racial incident that took place at the annual meeting of the Archaeological Institute of America and the Society of Classical Studies. A White independent scholar told Dan-el Padilla, a Black assistant professor of classics, that he had gotten this job at Princeton only because he was Black. In a response Padilla declared that it is incumbent on established figures within a profession to take a position when disruptive incidents occur: In his view academics who have been the beneficiaries of power or the patronage system "must surrender that power" (Pettit 2019). Given that no minorities have been hired in Italian in a tenure-track position over the last three years, the likelihood of such an incident happening at an Italianist scholarly meeting is small. No minorities were hired in 2019 to tenure-track positions in Italian although two, Akash Kumar and Catherine

Adoyo, were finalists for positions at UC Santa Cruz and UC Davis. Given the prominence of diversity in the national discourse, this is a propitious time to make Italian more diverse. More important, deans and provosts are receptive to making target-of-opportunity hires.

To make Italian more inclusive we need to actively adopt a number of measures. Addressing the problem directly is one step. In 2018 Valerio Ferme, until recently the president of the AAIS, created a committee for inclusivity and diversity. In February 2019 the Department of Italian Studies at Yale organized a symposium on the Future of Italian Studies. We must change the pipeline at every level—from providing undergraduates with a transformative study abroad experience, to offering fellowships for minority students applying to graduate programs, to offering them grants to give papers at scholarly meetings, to diversifying the professoriate itself.[6] Other measures include improving the preparation of minority graduate students, exploring the study of Italian in China, improving the experiences of minority students studying abroad in Italy, Clorinda Donato's outreach to Spanish speakers, and diversifying the professoriate.

We need to provide better mentoring for foreign minority graduate students and be more attuned to the obstacles they face. If we value the training we give here in the United States, then we should seek to make it available to everyone who can do the work and make English easier to manage for foreign students. What many do not see is how much additional effort must be made to become Italianists for non-native speakers of English here—learning both Italian and English, acquiring a mastery of the canon of Italian literature, and mastering different critical approaches are but some of the challenges. The teaching of literature in East Asia is different from that practiced in Anglo-European institutions. Wuming Chang, who recently received his doctorate from Brown, describes the difficulties he encountered:

> As a person entering a field where one is a demographic minority, either due to race, gender, sexual orientation, or economic status, one would face immense challenges even if discrimination on a personal level were not a problem. One of the most crippling ones is an information disparity that often exists between the majority and the minority. What often separates the minority from the others is the lack of unwritten "know-how" that most people in the field know simply by virtue of belonging to a social group.
>
> Being a minority in my field can feel like migrating to a new world, or multiple worlds, each of which operates on different assumptions. Chinese ideas of Italian, Latin, and Dante differ from Italian ones, which in turn differ from how

people view them in America. In the U.S. I struggled with the academic neglect of meter and style, which I have as the core of my research because, among other reasons, I come from more traditionalist China. In China, there is a long-held view that literature must have a moral and political value.[7]

If we know more about the way Chinese universities prepare their students for advanced study, we will have a better sense of how to mentor them. In China, there are eighteen universities with undergrad programs in Italian studies, each of which has no more than thirty new students per year. There are four universities with master's programs (Beijing Foreign Studies University, University of International Business and Economics, Shanghai International Studies University, and Beijing Language and Culture University). In addition, there are seven universities with undergrad programs in European literature that accept students in Italian studies (Beijing Foreign Studies University, Beijing Language and Culture University, Graduate School of Chinese Academy of Social Sciences, Shanghai International Studies University, Nanjing Normal University, Hunan Normal University, and Xi'an International Studies University).[8] Each of these universities has no more than four students in master's programs a year, no more than half of whom continue in academia as doctoral students. This list may be helpful to American institutions with agreements with Chinese universities. More dialogue with Chinese colleagues can help them better prepare Chinese students seeking to enter American graduate programs.

The experience of minority undergraduate students studying in Italy represents another challenge. On October 23, 2018, *New York Times* journalist Nicole Phillip published "My Very Personal Taste of Racism Abroad," about her experiences in Florence while enrolled in NYU's study abroad program five years ago. I was in Florence in November 2018 when responses to Phillip's article appeared in *La Nazione* and *La Repubblica*.[9] In interviews Dario Nardella, Florence's mayor, declared that "Firenze non è stata, non è, e non sarà mai una città razzista" (Florence has not been, is not, and will never be a racist city). (Minority soccer players might disagree.) Many of us have witnessed blatant and subtle examples of racism in Italy or been the victims of microaggressions. There is a solution to this problem: The roughly forty American study abroad programs based in Florence, not to mention other member programs of the Association of American College and University Programs in Italy (AACUPI), can seek an audience with Nardella or Italy's foreign minister, remind them of the considerable revenue these programs add to the local economy, and ask them to launch a campaign to treat foreigners, especially foreign students, with civility.

France offers a ready model: Since 1996 France has launched periodic national campaigns, the most recent of which was in 2015, to urge citizens to be friendlier to tourists (i.e., 1995's Do you speak touriste? 2015 Bonjour).[10] Measures undertaken include a nationwide advertising campaign, booklets on how to treat visitors from different cultures, more English signage, and an extensive renovation of the Gare du Nord. These measures have succeeded: France is listed as one of the most visited countries in tourism surveys. AACUPI could urge the Italian government to do the same, especially in places like Florence with a high concentration of study abroad programs—or threaten to send their students elsewhere.

Sometimes solutions to obstacles are surprisingly low tech and low cost. Our department recently made posters featuring minority celebrities such as Kobe Bryant, Jhumpa Lahiri, and Venus and Serena Williams (all of them speakers of Italian) with the caption "Did you know Kobe Bryant speaks Italian? Why don't you?" Clorinda Donato (2018) (professor of French and Italian, California State University) has attracted Italian majors by doing outreach to Spanish speakers. Donato has written a grammar, using a method of intercomprehension, to fast-track students who know Spanish into Italian or another Romance language. This strikes me as one of the most effective forms of outreach given how many communities throughout the United States have large numbers of Spanish speakers.

My last words concern the importance of diversifying the professoriate. Institutions in California and large East Coast cities have significant numbers of Latinx and Asian students. Andrea Mouddares (assistant professor, UCLA) told me that UCLA has "more and more Asian students taking classes in Italian. Last fall in a course on Venice in the Renaissance, 11/13 were minority students; 30–40% of UCLA's Italian majors are students of color, 80/175 students in a spring 2018 Dante class were Asian." At the same time, he acknowledges, "it is very difficult to translate this interest in our classes into a higher number of Italian majors. The attraction of majors such as Economics, Computer Science, and Engineering is strong."[11] Guy Raffa has encountered the same phenomenon at the University of Texas, where he is an associate professor: He teaches two Dante courses, one on the *Inferno* made up mostly of first-year students, and one on the *Divine Comedy* consisting of upper-division students; both attract many students of Hispanic and Asian origin, but few of them go on to major in Italian.

Numerous studies show that minority students are especially receptive to minority teachers.[12] UCLA and Berkeley are the institutions that have produced the most minority PhDs in the United States in Romance languages. Yet none of these institutions has any minorities among their teaching staff. Given the importance of identity politics to this generation of students, diversifying the professoriate at these two institutions could attract more Asians to the study of Italian. Christina Lee, an associate professor of Spanish at Princeton University, reports that Asian students have told her, "I want to be like you."[13]

Italian departments with large numbers of minorities could also invite Italianists of color to give talks or as visiting professors. An Asian or African American speaker could present a current research topic and meet with students to discuss why they chose to study Italian. Joint appointments with departments such as African American studies and East Asian studies are another option worth pursuing.

Qi Chen told me that the most popular Italian authors in China are Dante, Machiavelli, Vico, and Calvino. The first two names do not surprise me, but the latter two do—and this in itself is worth investigating. What aspects of Chinese students' culture and subjectivity make Vico and Calvino engaging? To what features in these authors' works are Chinese especially receptive or are particularly fitted to pursue? These are new research topics. Such subjects demonstrate the advantages of a more global engagement in Italian, but the acquisition of this information must be actively pursued. Over many email exchanges, Qi Chen and I became friends. I befriended Xiaoyi Zhang via email after I sent a link to my article to Zygmunt Baránski at Notre Dame. Both Qi Chen and Xiaoyi Zhang participated in Gaoheng Zhang's recent conference on Italy/East Asia. Establishing connections requires effort, but the rewards are manifest: We learn more about global interest in Italian and add new subjects to the field through global contacts. I've been the beneficiary of just this kind of contact. About five years ago I met Kenichi Nejime (professor of history, Gakushuin Women's University, Tokyo, and president of the Japanese Society of Renaissance Studies) at Villa I Tatti, whose director, Lino Pertile, effected outreach to Japan and China. Pertile put me in touch with Japanese and Chinese scholars who work on the Italian Middle Ages and Renaissance. When I visited Japan three years ago, Nejime connected me with Japanese Renaissance specialists. Last November I met Morhihisa Ishiguro (professor of Italian history, Kanazawa University), whom I had first met in Kanazawa three years earlier, in Florence where we spoke in Italian on Renaissance subjects.

Texts intervene differently in different cultures. Modes of understanding and modes of intervention vary in fascinating ways. We can approach this subject traditionally, examining instances in which Italianists look into the Other. Two examples include Eric Salerno's 2018 *Dante in Cina* or Marco Medugno's dissertation on African authors who grew up in Italian Somaliland. Or we can adopt a more expansive approach and look at how prominent contemporary Chinese authors such as Ba Jin, Lao She, and Can Xu have adapted Dante. Pursuit of such a subject would likely be collaborative, since very few works by Ba Jin and Can Xu have been translated into English. Such a project would enhance the understanding of Dante as a global author and of the dynamics of cultural appropriation.

I've touched on the limitations of a nationalistic attitude toward the study of Italian. Is there really an "inside" perspective available only to peninsular Italians? A more expansive view of who teaches and studies Italian would welcome approaches from "without"—from the place of another culture. Moreover, the "inside" here—especially when discussing scholarship that addresses the remote past—is an ambiguous construction. Any present-day Italian speaks at a remove from a medieval or Renaissance writer or artist. The constructed nature of the privilege asserted by some peninsular Italians warrants as much scrutiny as that of the so-called outsider. It is only when we learn to question our relation to the past rigorously and reflexively that we can continue to provide scholarship relevant to our multicultural and multinational world. The Other here is a reminder of our essential alterity to every figure in the past.

While among the Envious in Purgatory, Guido del Duca asks, "O gente umana, perché poni 'l core / là v'è mestier consorte divieto" ("Oh humankind, why do you set your hearts / there where our sharing cannot have a part") (*Purg.*14.86–87). These words address the difference between earthly and divine love, where the former is divisive (desiring different goods means fewer for all), the latter increases each soul's share of love. We might see the benefits of enlarging the field of critical inquiry in Italian studies in analogous terms. The more voices we have, the greater the number of subjects for all to explore.

Notes

1. Konrad Eisenbichler in a private communication. Cited with Eisenbichler's permission.
2. Moises Park, cited in Parker (2018).
3. Private email communication from an American Italianist who does not wish her identity to be revealed.
4. Mary Ann Carolan, cited with her permission.
5. I looked at Italian program websites of Berkeley, UCLA, University of Wisconsin, Notre Dame University, University of Chicago, Indiana University, University of Texas, Columbia, New York University, Johns Hopkins, University of North Carolina, Duke, Harvard, Yale, Florida State, Georgetown, SUNY Stony Brook, Stanford, Rutgers, University of Oregon, Cornell, University of Pennsylvania, University of Toronto, Ohio State University, University of Washington, Princeton, and Rutgers.
6. I've adapted here an observation made by Deanna Shemek in a private communication.
7. Wuming Chan in a private communication. Cited with his permission.
8. I am indebted to Qi Chen at Beiheng University for this information.

9. See, for example, http://www.ilgiornale.it/news/cronache/firenze-giornalista-afroamericana-nyt-denuncia-citt-razzismo-1602480.html.
10. See, for example, https://www.dailymail.co.uk/travel/travel_news/article-3121241/French-encouraged-nicer-tourists-France-tries-shed-reputation-one-unwelcoming-countries-world.html.
11. Andrea Moudarres in a private communication. Cited with his permission.
12. See, for example, the recent report recently published by Inside Higher Ed, *Diversifying Graduate Schools and the Faculty:* https://www.insidehighered.com/content/diversifying-graduate-schools-and-faculty?utm_source=Inside+Higher+Ed&utm_campaign=5cede4148dreports_strategic_planning_20190125_COPY_01&utm_medium=email&utm_term=0_1fcbc04421-5cede4148d-199869857.
13. Christina Lee cited in Parker (2018).

Works Cited

Donato, Clorinda, and Pierre Escudé. 2018. "Mutual Understanding with Intercomprehension." *Language Magazine*, August 21. https://www.languagemagazine.com/2018/08/21/mutual-understanding-with-intercomprehension/ (accessed July 1, 2019).

Parker, Deborah. 2018. "Race and Foreign Languages." *Inside Higher Ed*, June 21. https://www.insidehighered.com/views/2018/06/21/paucity-asians-and-other-minorities-teaching-and-studying-italian-and-other-foreign (accessed July 3, 2019).

Pettit, Emma. 2019. "My Merit, My Blackness Are Fused Together. *Chronicle of Higher Education.* https://www.chronicle.com/article/My-MeritMy-Blackness/245462 (accessed January 11, 2019).

Phillip, Nicole. 2018. "My Very Personal Taste of Racism Abroad." *New York Times*, October 23. https://www.nytimes.com/2018/10/23/travel/racism-travel-italy-study-abroad.html (accessed July 3, 2019).

Diversity and Inclusion in Italian Studies Curricula

DEANNA SHEMEK

The strength of Italian studies as an academic discipline in North America depends crucially—as is true for all fields of study—on our willingness, and our concrete efforts, to be as inclusive as possible. In the particular case of Italian, this means reaching well beyond the traditional demographic group to which the study of this culture has appealed—namely Italian Americans and other students of European descent—and welcoming the diverse communities that now make up university student bodies. For decades, Italian thrived as a discipline on considerable student populations descended from Italian immigrants, as Italian American communities sprang up, and held strong, mainly in the northeastern United States, the California West Coast, and the eastern region of Canada that includes Ontario. In other areas, including my native Midwest, the general prestige of European cultures afforded Italian a substantial foothold in language, literature, history, and art history curricula even without sizable heritage populations up until roughly ten years ago. The context is changing fast, and neither affordable transatlantic travel, nor Made in Italy marketing, Andrea Boccelli, Elena Ferrante, and Eataly provide sufficient counterweights to shift the trend.

Part of the field's challenge is clearly shared by the humanities in general. Persuaded that gainful employment will result reliably from STEM (science, technology, engineering, and math) and business-related degrees, and inspired by the promise of participation in the contemporary technological revolution, students are minimizing humanistic studies and flocking in overwhelming numbers toward science, technology, and business fields. Course requirements for STEM degrees, at the same time, have risen steadily, squeezing out elective options (like languages and literature classes) that, by definition, historically rounded out the liberal-arts education of students pursuing nonhumanities majors. Add to this picture the rise of global English—which has created for native Anglophone students the sense that learning other languages is now unnecessary—and we have something of a perfect storm that is not only affecting Italian enrollments but also narrowing the range of cross-cultural competencies for undergraduates generally.[1]

Humanities disciplines, for their part, have moved away from national foci toward different forms of "imagined community" that map broader regional, plural histories and cultures (Anderson 1983, Cachey 2016). Meanwhile, contemporary migration patterns are creating more global societies in all of the West, and the argument for studying European cultures in general now must be made in dialogue with postcolonial critiques of Eurocentrism and of whiteness. And yet, regardless of ethnic demographics, students of all backgrounds who do opt for the humanities are increasingly open to studies that take them beyond their own heritage. Just as students of European extraction are boosting enrollments in Arabic and Japanese, Italian should be seeking to attract students of Hispanic, Asian, African, and other backgrounds. Our task, as I see it, is to join this exciting and complex conversation, bringing Italian studies into a broader world picture and embracing the fact that Italy itself has become an increasingly multiethnic culture.

This essay offers strategies for appealing to diverse student constituencies, based on my experience in one university-level Italian program at the University of California (UC) and my barely begun participation in another. For twenty-eight years, I taught in the Department of Literature at UC Santa Cruz (UCSC), which combines both English and non-English literary studies into one academic unit. Modern languages at UCSC are taught through the Department of Languages and Applied Linguistics and have historically been staffed principally by full-time lecturers. The Literature Department, which is staffed mostly by tenured faculty, includes the options of concentrating coursework in Italian literature for a literature degree or completing an interdisciplinary major (or a minor) in Italian studies. The latter—a joint production of faculty principally in these two departments plus the History Department and the Department of the History of Art and Visual Culture—has been the overwhelming choice of students of Italian since its establishment in 1999.[2] Enrollments and majors in both Italian literature and Italian studies have been declining since the economic downturn of 2008, as is true for most humanities disciplines and for literary studies in particular (Cachey 2016).

In July 2018 I transferred to the Department of European Languages and Studies at the University of California, Irvine (UCI), which currently offers only a minor in Italian studies and where enrollments have not historically supported the mounting of upper-division courses taught in Italian.[3] As my colleagues and I consider how to build a more robust program in Italian at UC Irvine, issues of diversity and inclusion seem to me to be key. For what student population should Italian studies courses be designed? As we may see from official information published by both of these campuses and by UC as a nine-campus state system, both UCSC and UCI qualify through the U.S. Department of Education as

Hispanic Serving Institutions, meaning that at least 25 percent of their registered students self-declare as Hispanic (UCSC Office of Institutional Research 2019; UCI Office of Institutional Research 2018; University of California Office of the President 2018; UCI News 2017). These campuses thus join 290 others nationwide who share this status (Hispanic Association of Colleges and Universities 2019), while UCI also registers as an Asian American Native American Pacific Islander Serving Institution, which has a 10 percent enrollment threshold (U.S. Department of Education Programs 2016; UCI News 2017). At both UCSC and UCI, moreover, the Hispanic student population is balanced or outweighed by Asian/Asian American students, and each of these groups alone roughly equals or outnumbers White students, making these campuses exceptionally multicultural, global communities. Shifts in our student demographics include economic capacity as well as ethnicity, as the University of California welcomes increasing numbers of first-generation college students, and UC Irvine plays a recognized role at the forefront of this effort (UCI News 2017). As tuition rises within state schools, students are aiming to diminish their time to completing their degrees. This response has included less study abroad, or choosing modest-gain summer programs over yearlong programs that build substantial proficiency and deeper cultural competency. Even humanities and social sciences students are opting out of advanced language study in order to finish their degrees earlier and limit their debt, or—in a rather false connection that nonetheless fulfills requirements on some campuses—electing to study a computer programming language instead of a human one. Finally, in thinking about diversity in my classroom, I strive also to recognize gender difference, both in my text choices and in my openness to student explorations of alternative gender expressions in our materials. Thinking in terms of ethnic and racial identity, economic background, and gender and sexuality orientations, I see three general strategies as crucial to building a broader and more diverse audience for Italian. While the following is based on my personal experience as a faculty member, I hope that it may spark thinking for others in different regional and institutional settings.

RELINQUISH TERRITORIALITY

Many times I have heard colleagues complain that someone in English or film studies is teaching Italian material, thus robbing our programs of enrollments. I have even heard them lament that study abroad takes students out of our campus classrooms and should be discouraged because it diminishes our enrollment numbers or offers an inferior instructional model. I submit that moving toward, rather than away from, these attractive learning options is advisable. In literature at UCSC it was easy to invite, for example, the faculty member in Jewish studies who taught a course on Jews in Venice, or the comparatist who taught opera and film to contribute courses to Italian studies (they happily agreed); courses on ancient Rome, whether in literature, history, or art history, also earn credit in Italian studies. It may have been the case that students sacrificed my course for one of these, but on the whole, building this broader student base—also through my own courses taught in English on Italian materials—created a better foothold for Italian studies and inspired some students who would not have done so otherwise to take Italian. At UCI, as I broach the European studies context, I am reaching across departments to connect, for example, not only with Italian historians, art historians, and music and classics faculty but also, for example, with a historian specializing in food studies, migration, and Chinese American relations who teaches comparative histories of Italian and Chinese neighborhoods (and their food) in North America. I have also happily accepted the invitation to participate in UCI's summer Shakespeare festival by organizing a symposium on Shakespeare and Italy (UCI Shakespeare Center 2019). It is important to look beyond the traditional, nationally focused teaching and research communities on our campuses and to encourage our students to think about Italian culture in wider frameworks, even as we continue to evolve instruction in the traditional areas of our field.

TEACH DIVERSITY HEAD ON

In 2016, moved by daily headlines about the migration crisis in Italy, I developed a class called "Migration Italy" and secured for it the campuswide Ethnicity and Race general educational code.[4] This course's materials included the historic migrations of Italians to the United States—especially California—and elsewhere, as well as the waves of migration into Italy from Africa, the Middle East, and Central Europe since the late twentieth century. It began with readings in English on medieval migrations into Europe (Geary 2001), which helped to destabilize from the outset the concept of a historically consistent Italian race descended from the Romans. Leonardo Sciascia's short story "Il lungo viaggio" presented haunting parallels between Italian migrations to America and the human trafficking of migrants seeking entry into Europe via Italy today (Sciascia 1997). Gianfranco Norelli's documentary film *Finding the Mother Lode* (2013) focuses on Italian migration to California during the Gold Rush days and makes comparisons between how Italian and Chinese immigrants were seen by Californians at that time. The mostly Northern Italians were perceived as Whites while the Chinese, like Southern Italians who immigrated to the northeast United

States, were racialized as nonwhites. Additional documentary films offered the option of expanding on this history (*Pane amaro*, 2009; *The Italian Americans*, 2015). Norelli's film became a productive point of departure for discussions of racialization in the context of immigration, a topic on which students were eager to reflect, since they brought their own experiences to bear on their understanding of it. Supplemented by readings in English from critical literature (Jacomella 2015; Parati 2005; Pogliano 2015), the remaining readings in the course were texts by fiction and memoir writers, who recount stories of migration to Italy in the last generation from India, Senegal, Somalia, Algeria, and elsewhere (Capitani and Coen 2005; Khouma 1990; Lakhous 2006). All of them dwell, in different ways, on identity and cultural difference, language problems, racism, and in some cases gender and gender expectations as these are inflected by ethnicity and cultural heritage. A number of these texts tell stories of upward class mobility; others decidedly do not, and this difference became a topic for discussion among my students, at least one of whom was undocumented. One class each week was devoted to student presentations of media coverage about our topic. This class and all of the coursework, with the exception of the secondary readings and websites, were conducted in Italian.

I am not a specialist in migration studies, and I claim no originality for this course. I relied on the research of the many scholars working in this area to construct a course that provided a much-needed balance in our curriculum and stimulated passionate student engagement.

TEACH THE CLASSICS DIVERSELY

A third strategy regards teaching Italian literary classics. The challenge of pivoting my area of research specialization—the Italian Renaissance—toward a diverse student audience is real, but not as great as one might think. Taking a cue from the feminist critique of the literary canon, I begin simply by "making visible" the topics and players already present in early modern texts: teaching Jewish and female poets who wrote in Italian; emphasizing the instability of gender categories in chivalric and lyric texts, focusing, for example, on cross-cultural encounters and gender in Boccaccio's *Decameron* (e.g., Morosini 2010; Kirkham 1993; Migiel 2003) and on class issues like poverty and hunger in Renaissance theater (Henke 2015), as well as noting the many Arabic sources for Italian Renaissance innovations.

My course in English on Ariosto's *Orlando Furioso* (1532) has offered a particularly rich set of opportunities to open up space for diverse perspectives in reading early Italian literature. Ariosto's poem is putatively a narrative about the medieval battle for European Christendom, threatened by a pagan aggressor, but he regularly undercuts the idea of radical cultural difference and European superiority. There are surely episodes in the *Furioso* that betray anti-African and anti-Arab racism as well, and these are places in the poem that call for focus and critique (Cavallo 2013). Rather than move things along, I welcome this discussion, and students appreciate the resonance of Ariosto's world of religious and cultural conflict in our own.

The aspect of the poem that most consistently inspires student interest, however, is its portrayal of gender identities. Ariosto's female knights habitually cross dress, refuse a univocal femininity, catalyze episodes of same-sex eroticism, and argue for nonbinary conceptions of their sex (Shemek 1998; DeCoste 2009; Stoppino 2011). Male characters like Bradamante's twin brother, Ricciardetto (also a cross-dressing knight), and even the poem's epic hero Ruggiero embrace gender-bending self-transformations in famous episodes of the poem, with different moral outcomes. Then there is Ariosto's narrator, who takes up the substantial Italian Renaissance debate over gender roles and invites readers to be skeptical about cultural and racial stereotyping (Shemek 1989). This course ends with our viewing operatic works based on *Orlando Furioso* (Handel's *Alcina*; Vivaldi's *Orlando Furioso*), which give students occasion for historically informed reflection on early opera's use of the castrato and modern stagings that place female singers in trouser roles, as either continuations or distortions of sixteenth-century investments in questions of gender and identity. I have been moved by students' ready and passionate grasp of these issues in an epic poem that is nearly five hundred years old. Two students of the thirty-three in my most recent version of this course (2017) went on to earn divisionwide awards: One wrote a prize-winning thesis on the *Furioso* in comparative dialogue with contemporary transgender theory; the other won a Koret Foundation grant to conduct a transhistorical study of women in combat as portrayed in the Italian Renaissance and today, which ranged from Italian Renaissance poetry to *Game of Thrones*, the female superheroes in popular movies, and interviews with women veterans of U.S. wars.

Attention to these topics comes at a certain cost, on account of the limited time we have for any given course, but all courses must limit the material they can cover. We spend less time on the classical and medieval sources to which the *Furioso* is indebted, less time poring over intertextualities—although they are far from absent in my course. In a similar way, teaching the migration class has meant displacing, at least some of the time, courses like more general surveys. But this shift feels timely to me. While students may not gain a comprehensive sense of the Italian literary landscape (which I am not sure they have ever really obtained in such courses), they are enabled to relate to Italian literature in ways that matter to them and that, I think, may endure in their minds. If we are in the business of equipping students with a lifelong love of reading, ethical inquiry, and cultural dialogue, then the trade-offs are well worth this change, and Italian has a lot to offer. Such attention to diversity may, I hope, bring us to strategy number 4, the diversification of our PhD cohorts and our faculties, topics that others are discussing in the present volume.

Notes

1. There is the somewhat complementary issue of humanities students' poor mathematical, scientific, and technical literacy, but it is a separate one, fueled more by student gravitation than by burdensome degree requirements. This problem is corrected to some degree by general education requirements and students' general sense that STEM studies are necessary, even if they don't appeal to all sensibilities. The lack of humanities student enthusiasm for tech and science courses is, however, barely noticeable at the enrollment level, since student demand for STEM courses continues to exceed faculty and classroom capacities on many campuses. At the same time, fields like engineering also struggle to achieve diversity, particularly in the area of attracting women and underrepresented minorities to their majors.

2. In tune with the trend of remapping disciplines noted above, the Department of History of Art and Visual Culture at UCSC has replaced retiring faculty who focused substantially on Italian art with scholars from different, often exciting, arenas. The vast artistic patrimony of Italian Medieval and Renaissance art, however, is now taught not by a tenured professor but by one lecturer, who is present for only one academic quarter each year (one to two courses), supplemented by Italian units in courses of much broader scope—for example, one on museums and collecting. No faculty member in the department specializes in the huge area of Greco-Roman art history, but one concentrates research in ancient Greek, Byzantine, and Islamic art, which sometimes includes Italian materials.

3. Because the first year of my appointment was spent on leave, my actual teaching at UCI commenced in fall 2019. I am grateful to colleagues at UCI who have helped me understand the landscape there for Italian studies, including especially James Chiampi and Franca Hamber.

4. My course title was obviously borrowed from the important volume edited by Parati (2005). I also owe thanks, in particular, to Rhiannon Noel Welch, who generously shared with me her syllabus for a course she taught at UCSC as a visiting lecturer in 2011, which served as my point of departure.

Works Cited

Anderson, Benedict. 1983. *Imagined Communities: Reflections on the Origin and Spread of Nationalism*. New York: Verso.

Ariosto, Ludovico. 1973, 1977. *Orlando Furioso: A Romantic Epic*, translated by Barbara Reynolds. New York: Penguin.

Cachey, Theodore. 2016. "America amica-amara: Sugli studi di letteratura italiana nell'America del nord." *La rassegna della letteratura italiana* No. 120, series IX: 159–185.

Capitani, Flavia, and Emanuele Coen, eds. 2005. *Pecore nere. Racconti*. Rome: Laterza.

Cavallo, Jo Ann. 2013. *The World beyond Europe in the Romance Epics of Boiardo and Ariosto*. Toronto: University of Toronto Press.

DeCoste, Mary-Michelle. 2009. *Hopeless Love: Boiardo, Ariosto, and Narratives of Queer Female Desire*. Toronto: University of Toronto Press.

Finding the Mother Lode: Italian Immigrants in California. 2013. Directed by Gianfranco Norelli. IxoraFilms. DVD.

Geary, Patrick J. 2001. *The Myth of Nations: The Medieval Origins of Europe.* Princeton, NJ: Princeton University Press.

Henke, Robert. 2015. *Poverty and Charity in Early Modern Theater and Performance.* Iowa City: University of Iowa Press.

Hispanic Association of Colleges and Universities. N.D. "HACU Member Hispanic Serving Institutions" https://www.hacu.net/assnfe/CompanyDirectory.asp?STYLE=2&COMPANY_TYPE=1%2C5 (accessed April 23, 2019).

Jacomella, Gabriella. 2015. "The Silence of Migrants: The Underrepresentation of Migrant Voices in the Italian Mainstream Media." In *Destination Italy: Representing Migration in Contemporary Media and Narrative,* edited by Emma Bond, Guido Bonsaver, and Federico Faloppa, 149–163. Oxford: Peter Lang.

Khouma, Pap. 1990. *Io, venditore di elefanti. Una vita per forza fra Dakar, Parigi, e Milano,* edited by Oreste Pivetta. Milan: Garzanti.

Kirkham, Victoria. 1993. "Boccaccio's Dedication to Women in Love." In *The Sign of Reason in Boccaccio's Fiction,* 117–129. Florence: Olschki.

Lakhous, Amara. 2006. *Scontro di civiltà per un ascensore a Piazza Vittorio.* Rome: e/o.

Migiel, Marilyn. 2003. *A Rhetoric of the Decameron.* Toronto: University of Toronto Press.

Morosini, Roberta, ed. 2010. *Boccaccio geografico. Un viaggio nel Mediterraneo tra le città, i giardini, e il 'mondo' di Giovanni Boccaccio.* Florence: Polistampa.

Pane amaro. 2009. Directed by Gianfranco Norelli. Eurus Productions. DVD.

Parati, Graziella. 2005. *Migration Italy: The Art of Talking Back to a Destination Culture.* Toronto: University of Toronto Press.

Pogliano, Andrea. 2015. "Framing Migration: News Images and (Meta-) Communicative Messages." In *Destination Italy: Representing Migration in Contemporary Media and Narrative,* edited by Emma Bond, Guido Bonsaver, and Federico Faloppa, 125–148. Oxford: Peter Lang.

Sciascia, Leonardo. 1997. In *Il lungo viaggio. Racconto integrale tratto da Il mare colore del vino,* edited by Maria Antonietta Covino Bisaccia and Maria Rosaria Francomacaro. Perugia: Guerra Edizioni.

Shemek, Deanna. 1989. "Of Women, Knights, Arms, and Love: The Querelle des Femmes in Ariosto's Poem." *Modern Language Notes* 104: 68–97.

Shemek, Deanna. 1998. *Ladies Errant: Wayward Women and Social Order in Early Modern Italy.* Durham, NC: Duke University Press.

Stoppino, Eleonora. 2011. *Genealogies of Fiction: Women Warriors and the Dynastic Imagination in the Orlando furioso.* New York: Fordham University Press.

The Italian Americans. 2015. Directed by John Maggio. PBS Series, four episodes.

UCI Office of Institutional Research. 2018. "Undergraduate Admissions." https://www.oir.uci.edu/Undergraduate-Admissions-Dashboard.php (accessed May 1, 2019).

UCI News. 2017. "Doing the Most for the American Dream." https://news.uci.edu/2017/06/09/doing-the-most-for-the-american-dream/ (accessed May 1, 2019).

UCI Shakespeare Center. 2019. "Shakespeare in Italy." https://www.humanities.uci.edu/shakespeare/calendar/events.php?recid=7485&dept_code_val=987&event_cat=current&file_name=events (accessed June 1, 2019).

UCSC Office of Institutional Research, Assessment, and Policy Studies, University of California, Santa Cruz. 2019. "New, Continuing, and Returning Students by Ethnicity 2018 Fall Quarter." https://diversity.ucsc.edu/diversity/images/student_demo2018.pdf (accessed April 23, 2019).

University of California Office of the President. 2018. "Fall Enrollment at a Glance." https://www.universityofcalifornia.edu/infocenter/fall-enrollment-glance (accessed April 23, 2019).

U.S. Department of Education Programs. 2019. https://www2.ed.gov/programs/aanapi/faq.html#q2 (accessed May 2, 2019).

Reflections of and on Diversity: (Re)Discussing Course Materials

ALESSIA VALFREDINI

This essay is informed by the view that world language (WL) learning is relevant and central in education to the extent it demands the learners to engage, as critical thinkers, with a diverse range of ways of thinking and making meaning that expand the ones rooted in their background (Valfredini 2018b). In order not to be viewed as a commodity, language learning must position itself at the center of the educative goals for which Banks (2007) advocates: to prepare students with "the knowledge, skills, and values that will enable them to live, interact, and make decisions with fellow citizens from different racial, ethnic, cultural, language, and religious groups" (3). The encounter with a different language is an opportunity to observe and engage with diversity, not just the diversity observable in the contexts where the language being learned is spoken, but by transposition and the mediation of the language, the complex actualizations of diversity in contexts familiar to the learner.

The engagement with diversity in the WL classroom is inherently an encounter with privilege and marginalization, for "differences do not exist independently of how they are perceived in the general society" (Nieto and Bode 2008, 84). Recognizing this reality, as part of the WL community, educators of Italian face an imperative to reflect on their role in "prepar[ing] students to be reflective, moral, caring, and active citizens in a troubled world" (Banks 2007, 3) and on the treatment of diversity and social justice in the Italian curriculum and classroom (Fabbian and Zanotti Carney 2018a, 2018b). As we language instructors, curriculum designers, and program administrators ponder over the extent to which concerns of inclusiveness and social engagement belong in an Italian classroom, we must recognize the unjust burden suffered by those who are disadvantaged and subordinated while also acknowledging that oppression has "consequences for all" (Bell 2016, 15). Once we recognize that the losses caused by living in an unjust society affect everyone, then it is no longer a matter of whether we should embrace the cause of diversity in Italian studies, but how we can actively respond to it by promoting awareness, inclusiveness, and critical engagement. The Italian classroom becomes a model for committed democratic engagement, where multivocality paired with engaged dialogue (as opposite to indoctrination) constitutes the core of the curriculum.

At a time when decline in language enrollment and budget cuts present a particularly pressing concern for Italian programs,[1] recognizing and acting on our roles and responsibilities is for language educators and program developers a necessity for surviving and prospering (Hipwell and Melucci 2018). How can language learning be recast in order to be strategically central in the current educational landscape? How is it relevant? Meyer and Land (2003) discuss the idea of *threshold concept* to indicate an essential type of transformative disciplinary learning that leads to "a transformed way of understanding, or interpreting, or viewing something, without which the learner cannot progress" (1). Threshold concepts constitute a higher type of learning, in contrast with other core disciplinary concepts that are not transformative in nature. While I acknowledge that addressing the concerning trends in Italian studies is a complex matter that requires multiple lines of change, I argue that one essential threshold concept that Italian programs can offer is the critical and responsible engagement with multiple perspectives and a range of worldviews, thus asserting the centrality of our discipline in the educational landscape.

While WL classrooms have a remarkable potential to offer exposure to diverse perspectives via the exploration of cultural themes and the very process of learning the language—a process that Osborn (2006) considers central for democracy because languages encapsulate worldviews—it takes intentional scrutiny and action to actualize this potential. In fact, the language classroom can feed ideas of "foreignness" and "Otherness" (Kramsch 1987; Osborn 2000, 2006; Reagan and Osborn 2002), and studies indicate that language learners may retain prejudices and biased views of the target language and culture (Kubota, Austin, and Saito-Abbott 2003). Intentional action must be taken to promote *critical multiculturalism* (Kubota 2004a), in contrast with *liberal multiculturalism*, one that emphasizes flattening communalities, essentializes the Other, and is oblivious to power and privilege. Language instruction often risks validating inequalities via the following means: its accessibility (or lack thereof) to diverse groups of learners (Moeller and Abbott 2018; Ortega 1999; Reagan and Osborn 1998);[2] its classroom practices and the enactment of power in the class dynamics (Freire 1970/2005; Nieto 2010); and its content selection and the adopted study approach. This essay will focus on the last of these three areas.

While acknowledging that challenging inequalities requires changes at a systemic level, thus engaging stakeholders beyond the individual classroom or language program, this essay addresses the question: How can educators promote critical engagement, inclusiveness, and representation of diversity when designing the content of the language classroom/curriculum, both in the selection of material and the approach to studying it? In the context of this essay linguistic instruction and cultural content are conceived as systemic and inseparable and both included in the more general term *content*. Additionally, the term *critical* refers to a rigorous intellectual analysis that dissects the topic under examination from a variety of perspectives and is aware of the role of power and ideology in cultural representations.

Instructors and curriculum designers need to be intentional when seeking to be inclusive and equitable. I will highlight three overlapping areas for action, areas that afford opportunities to critically engage with diversity in designing the content of the language curriculum: the representation of a multifaceted idea of Italy and Italianness, the critical scrutiny of materials, and the explicit discussion of social justice.

REPRESENTING A VARIETY OF EXPERIENCES AND VOICES

For a variety of reasons, not least of them being tradition, convenience, and the necessity to achieve some level of standardization, it is common for language curricula to be structured around textbooks. This is a potentially problematic aspect of WL instruction, given the "tendency among language textbooks to represent cultures to be different from one another but as each of them being homogeneous [*sic*]" (Canale 2016, 236). Textbooks of Italian are not exempt from shortcomings (Fabbian, Zanotti Carney, and Valfredini 2019). Studies on a variety of disciplinary textbooks found that they have a tendency to legitimize hegemonic views and imbalanced power relationships (Anyon 2011; Apple and Christian-Smith 1991; Sleeter and Grant 2011). That is true also for WL textbooks, which nevertheless remain a central source of information on the worldviews associated with the studied languages and on which roles are appropriate for different groups within that worldview (Bori 2018; Azimova and Johnston 2012; Canale 2016; Chapelle 2016; Herman 2007; Kidd 2016; Risager 2018; Curdt-Christiansen, Lan, and Weninger 2015). The representations common in textbooks "do not favour students' understanding of culture from a more modern or poststructuralist viewpoint: as the complex coexistence of conflicting ideologies, discourses and identities which operate in time and space, and which are embedded in wider historical processes" (Canale 2016, 236).

We, language educators and instructors of Italian specifically, are called to actively seek instead the curricular reflection of a variety of voices that reflect a complex and multifaceted view of Italy. If a multivocal representation is not in the textbook, then we can replace or integrate the textbook with a range of purposefully selected materials. The intent is twofold. On the one hand, it is to provide an encounter with a multitude of experiences and realities related to Italianness, some of which will be beyond what students have encountered in their personal lives, so that we enlarge the horizon of the students. On the other hand, by representing a multitude of experiences we are being "mindful of reproducing knowledge hierarchies in their classrooms" (Becker 2014, 17), and we refuse to erase the experiences of our students from the curriculum based on their financial means, lifestyle, social and cultural capital, sexual orientation, gender identity, race, ethnicity, religious beliefs, physical and mental health and ability, immigration and citizenship status, or political views: We are being inclusive, validating the lived experiences of our own students.[3] Very much like educators in other disciplines, educators in language studies need to create spaces in the curriculum to value funds of knowledge (Moll et al. 1992) and acknowledge variations in ways of learning.[4]

As we strive to represent diversity and be inclusive, we need to be wary of the dangers of essentialism and question any assumptions about the students' imagined communities (Carrol, Motha, and Price 2008; Norton 2001), favoring instead inquiry and complexity, asking questions and contemplating an array of answers. To this end, Kubota (2004b) offers a helpful framework to inform the teaching of culture: adopting a *descriptive* rather than prescriptive approach, acknowledging the *diverse* nature of cultures (in terms of their inherent variability and complexity), offering a *dynamic* view of culture across history, and embracing a *discursive* nature of construction of knowledge. Kubota's framework can coexist in addition to, and not necessarily replace, the widely adopted American Council on the Teaching of Foreign Languages model of culture as comprised of product, practices, and perspectives[5] and address some of its limitations (Ennser-Kananen 2016).

Acknowledging the diversity of our students in the curriculum means also making course materials accessible to people with a range of different abilities and being cognizant of principles of universal design for learning for accessibility, an approach that aims at increasing the experience of *all* students by offering multiple modalities of access and of participation.

EXAMPLES: DIVERSE REPRESENTATIONS OF ITALIANNESS

In order to offer a multivocal view of Italy and Italians, as we review and select our course materials, we can ask ourselves: How does the course depict the everyday, average Italian? What is implicitly set as the norm? Asking these questions allows us to be mindful of the choices we make: to be intentional in including a diverse range of characters that reflect the reality of contemporary Italy (not equated to its national borders) when writing examples and exercises; to select images that reflect the ethnic and racial variability of Italians; to revise and integrate vocabulary lists for inclusiveness and equity; to expose heteronormative assumptions; and to knowingly represent a range of family models, abilities, and spiritual beliefs. Statistical data is a powerful tool to raise awareness of the complex makeup of contemporary Italy and has the added benefit of being generally accessible at the very early stages of language studies and across educational levels: As students learn how to introduce themselves, they can also search for the most common names among newborns in Italy, or, when talking about school, they can read statistics on the diversity in contemporary Italian classrooms (and most likely very early on come across the issue of citizenship rights, which will prepare them for later conversations on national belonging) and search data on the languages studied and those spoken in Italy.

We should also be aware of the implications of the choices we make in representing exceptional Italians: writers, musicians, politicians, scientists, artists, and so on. Are all the successful people, the visionaries, and the heroes we present of the same race, ethnicity, gender, religious belief? Are they all able bodied? Are marginalizing aspects of the identity of famous Italians hidden or sanitized to minimize controversies? While ready-made materials tend to reflect groups in power, we need to be intentional in showcasing the achievements of women, LGBTQIA+ people, Italians of color, Italians denied citizen rights, and people with a range of religious beliefs and abilities. This can be done by replacing or integrating the material in the textbook: A reading on Italian scientists may name only White, able-bodied, male inventors, maybe sanitizing potentially controversial aspects of the scientist's identity, but we can open up to our students an inspiring world of diverse Italian scientists who left or are leaving their mark in the world's scientific community.

EXAMPLES: STRIVING FOR INCLUSIVITY

When we strive to include the lived experiences of all students in the curriculum, we should consider the voices we represent in materials such as vocabulary lists, illustrations, examples, grammar-focused exercises, conversation and writing prompts, and readings. Routinely actively scrutinizing the course materials helps identify areas where we may inadvertently erase the experiences of nondominant groups. If we are learning about hobbies or traveling, are we mindful of socioeconomic diversity, rather than working under a middle-class/

upper-middle-class assumption (Herman 2007)? When learning the language for shopping, are we implicitly promoting a consumerist view and excluding students from participation based on their financial means? When talking about sports, leisure, art, music, means of transportation, and so on, are we thinking from the perspective of a diverse range of abilities? Are we working from an able-bodiedness assumption? When we discuss health and well-being, which messages are we sending on mental illness? Are we assuming following a healthy diet is solely a matter of choice, without considerations of access based on socioeconomic status and cultural capital, and as a result shaming some of our students?

Additionally, we need to be wary of exclusionary views of Italianness or national belonging in respect to students who sit in our classes: We must try to legitimate the experiences of students of Italian heritage, students who speak dialects, and students experiencing the historical or contemporary trauma of being hurt by Italians by making those voices visible, and therefore valid, in the curriculum.

MAKING VISIBLE THE INVISIBLE THROUGH INQUIRY

The previous section argued that the representation of a variety of voices is the result of intentional design. The reality of most of the cultural products to which the students are routinely exposed, from textbook to original sources, within and outside the classroom, is that they do not reflect such diversity, and occasional representations of marginalized perspectives that students will encounter will often originate from sources imbued with power and ideology. On the one hand, textbook discourse does not favor "poststructuralist and critical views of culture in which subjective, historical, and ideological factors are at stake" (Canale 2016, 239); on the other hand, original sources reflect the standpoint of the author and present reality from perspectives that reflect power and privilege. In response, advance language courses in secondary and higher education settings can explicitly include, among the course materials, theoretical writings on critical theory, but all of the courses, regardless of their linguistic or educational level, can foster critical inclusion by simply dissecting, in age-appropriate fashion, the textbook and original materials.

In order to make visible the perspectives of different groups and realities among the interpretative frameworks, we have the powerful tools of inquiry and critical reflection: We can, as Kubota (2004b) argued in her theory of culture, embrace the discursive nature of knowledge construction:

> The meanings of cultural difference can be seen as politically and ideologically constructed by discourses in which certain worldviews are produced to reinforce,

maintain, or subvert unequal relations of power. Unlike a common view that cultural difference exists as a neutral and objective fact, this perspective conceptualizes cultural difference as socially, politically, and historically produced. Through a discursive construction of cultural difference, social and institutional practices as well as our views of cultural identities of the Self and the Other are given particular meanings. This perspective implies that cultural difference has multiple meanings, serving various political and ideological purposes. The concept of cultural difference and/or similarity is appropriated and strategically used for different aims, such as domination, accommodation, resistance, and so on, and its meaning is constantly in flux. (29)

Through inquiry and critical reflection, we question reductionist views of culture and avoid the trap of simplistic cultural comparisons. When culture is seen as discourse, we adopt a postmodern poststructuralist pedagogy that addresses ideology and power as a topic (Crawford and McLaren 2003). By politicizing the conversation of cultural differences and seeing cultural differences as constructed discursively, binary or reductionist views of cultural difference are averted and its meanings are understood within relationships of power: "[C]ultural difference needs to be viewed as relational and as a construct shaped by discourses and power" (Kubota 2004b, 21). Once we start seeing differences as discursive practices, we move beyond the dualism of either *othering* or *emphasizing similarities*, to instead problematize both and see a new, higher value in difference (Kubota, 2004b).

In her work on "painful topics" in the language curriculum, topics often associated with marginalization and injustice, Ennser-Kananen (2016) suggests questions to guide reflection and inquiry: "We must ask ourselves: What is absent? Who resides in the margins, footnotes, and outs? Who is described in derogatory language? Who is tokenized and stereotyped?" (561).[6]

EXAMPLES: QUESTIONS TO GUIDE CRITIQUE

One of the areas that we can dissect in class about the Italian language itself: Which are the assumptions and implications of grammar and language choice? As we cast grammar as inherently linked to meaning making and reflective of the dominant perspective, reflections on grammar can help observe how power is instilled in language: Questions on gender expression and sexism are apparent from the first lessons for beginners and can be further explored when learning about professions; even the choices made by the textbook to provide the masculine or feminine of certain lexical items are rich material for discussion.[7] Opinion articles and essays are easily available for more in-depth study.

Approaching the study of lexical items through inquiry and interlanguage comparisons also offers insights on different cultural perspectives, providing an entry point for complex, nuanced thinking. Osborn (2006) argues that the lack of one-to-one correspondence between words in different languages is one of the reasons why teaching languages is a necessity. Words and their suggested translation can be entered in image search engines; comparing the resulting images, as Barnes-Karol and Broner (2010) demonstrated, is a rich opportunity to question monolithic worldviews and see the world from different angles.

In reading literary texts, song lyrics, or newspaper articles, word choices can be contextualized and problematized for their inclusivity and their connotations in terms of representations of gender, race, age, ability, and so on. At more advanced linguistic levels and in secondary/higher education, sociolinguistic analysis of the implications hidden beyond the surface of linguistic utterances is possible. As students hypothesize what is the subtext, which are the assumptions and implications of dialogues from a movie, a commercial, or the textbook, they develop awareness and sensitivity for intercultural communication and derive a critical framework that they can apply to virtually any verbal exchange.

Another way to question representations is by critiquing the materials. Often exclusionary or prejudicial, textbooks and many cultural products provide an excellent opportunity to demonstrate ideology in action. A critique can start with very concrete and simple questions, requiring us to observe who's visible and who's absent, to notice what those represented are like and what they do. It is possible to tally the answers and gain a sense of the extent of any imbalance in representations or create concept maps with the connotations associated with different characters.

Using concrete, simple language and visual representations makes critical inquiry within reach to novice learners. If working with original materials, cultural comparisons may emerge or even be encouraged; in order to avoid simplistic overgeneralizations or stereotyping, it is helpful to examine a variety of examples of the same type of cultural product so that a hypothesis can be refined or confuted.[8]

ENGAGING WITH THEMES OF DIVERSITY AND SOCIAL JUSTICE

We have so far identified two parallel lines of action: intentionally representing a multitude of experiences in the curriculum and approaching course materials with critical inquiry, identifying omissions, partial representations, and stereotyping. The explicit inclusion in the syllabus of themes of inclusiveness, equality, and social justice is the third area of action I want to suggest to continue the path toward *critical multiculturalism* (Kubota 2004a). Building on Osborn (2006),

Randolph and Johnson (2017) conceptualize social justice as "the equitable sharing of social power and benefits within a society" (100). Bell (2016) frames it as simultaneously a goal and a process, in a way that's particularly fit for a discussion on the teaching of languages. According to Nieto (2010), it is "a philosophy, an approach, and actions that embody treating all people with fairness, respect, dignity, and generosity" (46).

Inclusiveness and social-justice-focused learning units can be designed for different levels of linguistic proficiency and adapted to be developmentally appropriate. In discussing the political nature of language study, Randolph and Johnson (2017) point out that learning goals related to diversity, inclusiveness, and social justice need not detract from language-related learning goals; rather, they work in synergy with them. Working within the framework of the World Readiness Standards and the five areas that they identify (communication, cultures, connections, comparisons, and communities) (National Standards Collaborative Board 2015), Randolph and Johnson (2017) "imagine the scope of social justice to include any aspects of the language classroom through which participants (students, teachers, and other stakeholders) come to a greater understanding of or make progress towards equity in society" (101), from course content to community-based learning.

EXAMPLES: PROMOTING AWARENESS OF DIVERSITY AND SENSIBILITY TO PREJUDICE

At lower proficiency levels, themes related to critical inquiry and social justice can be approached by asking concrete questions, letting students inductively notice patterns (Valfredini 2018a), and facilitating comments by pointing out cognates such as *controversia, discriminazione, razzismo, sessismo, classismo, pregiudizio, stereotipo,* and so on (Randolph and Johnson 2017). Students at higher proficiency levels can also engage in research on the history and legislation of the fights for social justice, access theoretical texts, and comprehend more complex opinion pieces.

In the introductory classroom, when students can understand everyday related questions in the present tense, we can provide them with a list of different names and ask them to guess where the characters come from, how they look, what they do, which music they listen to, how they spend their free time. The activity can be done also with illustrations rather than verbal answers. Answers are better kept anonymous: We don't want to shame our students; rather, we want to expose the pervasiveness and automaticity of prejudices. We can then counter stereotypical or biased portrayals by providing real-life profiles of people with those names that question dominant narratives. Finally, as suggested above, we can retrieve statistical data on common newborn names in contemporary Italy.[9]

Another simple activity to bring awareness of different perspectives is playing association games. For example, if we are learning about leisure time, students may individually brainstorm in writing what they think of when they see the word *domenica* (Sunday) or *estate* (summer). Answers can be posted on walls, and students can walk past them and reflect on similarities and differences in experiences. Responses can be anonymous or not. In classes that are homogenous in many aspects, in order to sensitize students to the dangers of being entrenched in one's single-sided perspective, we can rely on perspectives from outside the classroom. The danger of essentialization can be addressed by following up with more questions or more information, modeling inquiry and openness to dialogue.

EXAMPLES: INTRODUCING SOCIAL JUSTICE THEMES IN THE ITALIAN CLASSROOM

Virtually any thematic unit in the textbook can be reframed to learn about social justice. Additionally, we can design units fully focused on a social justice theme or centered on learning about social justice leaders and initiatives. An excellent resource for ideas and their practical implementation within a World Readiness Standards framework is Glynn, Wesley, and Wassell (2014). The volume provides an appendix that suggests ways to approach topics such as disability, environment, family structures, access to healthy food, gender, immigration, and poverty.

Adopting a pedagogy of inquiry, students can approach case studies drawing on a variety of sources (statistical, literary, filmic, interviews, media, legislation, etc.) and perspectives. For example, in a secondary- or higher-education setting, a study of poverty can start with researching thresholds and definitions in Italy and in the local context; data can offer insights of the socioeconomic composition of the school or university (including, if available, its social mobility rankings), of the local community, of larger communities, and the nation. Guest speakers or student research can provide information on the history and policies that explain disparities among those communities. In parallel, literary texts can provoke; provide insights into the lived experience of others, avoiding essentialism; and bring a deep, dignified human component to the study. Interviews with local advocates on personal experiences may be available or may be conducted by the students and further enrich the complexity of perspectives available while connecting at a human level. Educators can reasonably expect issues of racial disparities, crime and organized crime, and migrations to emerge in a learning experience that is centered on inquiry and discovery, not on finding a final, single answer.

While such an approach to studying poverty is more appropriate for intermediate or advanced courses, other social justice case studies can be accessible at lower proficiency levels and in primary-education settings. For example, an excellent opportunity to discuss gender and sexuality, a topic that arguably permeates the curriculum, is when learning about the family. Search-engine image results provide rich opportunities to engage with simple language. Students can describe the pictures. After several repetitions, the instructor can ask whether some families are absent from the results and ask students to describe what those absent families may look like. Websites of advocacy groups will validate a wider range of experiences. The discrepancy between the two (the search-engine results and advocacy-oriented websites) will raise awareness of the hegemony of views in widely adopted sources of information, a dominance that extends to textbooks. At the same time, focusing the questions on absence or invisibility allows educators to center the discussion on the representation of a wide range of existing experiences as equally valid, rather than discussing conflicting and apparently irreconcilable worldviews, hardly an entry point conducive to transformative dialogue.

Finally, social justice also means opening up the borders of the school or university to the community around it. From simple explorations of the local context beyond the classroom, to the inclusion of materials originated from or connected to that context, to community-based learning partnerships, there's a wealth of opportunities to engage with complex perspectives and histories if we enter that world.

ADDRESSING CHALLENGES

When taking action to confront issues of exclusion, ideology, and injustice, it is expected that one will encounter resistance—whether conscious or unconscious—and discomfort. To start with, students, parents, and administrators may perceive that time spent on critical discussions of cultural themes is less time spent on language learning. This concern is unfounded if lesson planning integrates organically the various course objectives in well-designed units and we can dismantle it by sharing examples of the work done in the classroom.

Additionally, some students, parents, and administrators may also be concerned that the Italian classroom becomes a site of indoctrination, a real concern if we fail to model inclusiveness and critical engagement. Adopting an approach of inquiry means modeling democracy and dialogue in the classroom: The goal is not to change minds so that they agree with each other; rather, it is to offer minds the opportunity to contemplate a multitude of perspectives and voices.

Yet another challenge to consider: Even the students who are most open to the exploration of topics connected to marginalization and power may feel uncomfortable in a classroom setting that addresses diversity and exclusion via inquiry. Discomfort is likely and conflict is possible. There is a vast body of research that gives us tools for understanding, preventing, mitigating, and addressing such issues, in the classroom and as an institution: See, for instance, the scholarship on *brave spaces* (Arao and Clemens 2013); Singleton's (2005) framework for *courageous conversations* together with Kay's (2018) suggestions on how to talk about race; and Ennser-Kananen's (2016) arguments in favor of the inclusion of *painful topics* in language curricula. Helpful suggestions for establishing norms of engagement for the classroom are available on several university websites, such as UCLA Excellence in Pedagogy and Innovative Classrooms (EPIC 2019), CSU Monterey Bay (Office of Inclusive Excellence 2019), and Yale University (Poorvu Center for Teaching and Learning 2019). A simple Italian source, accessible to students with lower linguistic proficiency levels, is the bilingual *Manifesto della comunicazione non ostile/Manifesto of Non-Hostile Communication* (Associazione Parole O_Stili 2019; CAST 2019), which can act as a starting point to establish a classroom climate conducive to exchange and which itself represents an interesting initiative to discuss.

Based on their study of students of Japanese, Swahili, and Spanish, Kubota, Austin, and Saito-Abbott (2003) warn us that students may be uninterested or believe that the WL class is not a proper venue to engage with ideas of diversity and social justice.[10] But, as these scholars argue, the educator's job is also to expose students to ideas and perspectives that they may not seek on their own. In order for learning to happen and to avoid perpetuating existing patterns, educators "must expand [the students'] awareness" (22). Well-established pedagogical practices can sustain participation of reluctant groups or students: giving students time and venues to prepare ideas and language before sharing with a larger group; using the think-pair-share protocol; setting up a predictable, structured environment and routines so that students are familiar with the expected format for pair work, small-group work, reports to full class, turn taking, and so on; offering a variety of options in terms of modalities of expression; and creating ground rules for class conversations and debates.

CONCLUSIONS

As the work of WL education is scrutinized in light of pressing questions on diversity and inclusion, Italian studies faces a remarkable opportunity to reflect on its role and to effect curricular changes aimed at reasserting the relevance of studying Italian. When learning the language is sustained by a conviction of its value for democracy (Osborn, 2006), we offer students the chance to engage with a multitude of life experiences and perspectives; when our epistemological approach to the course materials entails critical reflection, justice becomes an active concern.

While any effort toward the overt discussion of social justice is commendable, condensing the discussion of equality and inclusion in an isolated unit or part of a unit risks positioning them as peripheral.[11] In contrast, I argued for an Italian curriculum where themes of diversity and social engagement are recurrent lenses applied critically to any type of knowledge students encounter in the course. I suggested three areas of action: the intentional representation of a diverse Italy and a diverse range of manifestations of Italianness paired with a sensitivity to the diversity our students bring to the classroom; the critique of the textbook and of original materials, seen as discursively constructed and imbued with power, as a way of thinking and critically approaching knowledge; and the direct inclusion of themes connected to social justice in the language curriculum. Intentionally organizing the Italian curriculum with these three areas in mind makes it a transformative learning experience: It offers our students "a new and previously inaccessible way of thinking about something" (Meyer and Land 2003, 1); promoting the acquisition of this key threshold concept is a way for Italian studies to respond to calls for relevancy and responsibility.

Notes

1. See 2013 and 2016 MLA reports (Goldberg, Looney, and Lusin 2015; Looney and Lusin 2019).
2. Reagan and Osborn (1998) argue that WL education has historically had a tracking-and-sorting function.
3. Delpit (1995) argued that educators should act at two levels: teach those who are marginalized the hegemony's tools and give value to the tools they bring from their own experience and turn them into assets.
4. See the concepts of *funds of pedagogy* (Zipin 2009) and of *multimodal pedagogies* (Stein 2004).
5. Glynn, Wesley, and Wassell (2014) offer a critical revision of the Three P's model.
6. Ennser-Kananen (2016) suggests second and third steps in which participants in the reflection address their own discomfort and question their roles in privilege and oppression.
7. For an in-depth discussion of problematic aspects of textbooks and classroom practices to address them, see Fabbian, Zanotti Carney, and Valfredini (2019).

8. For an exemplification of this technique applied to the study of commercials, see Valfredini 2018a.

9. For a critical pedagogy activity on names in the Spanish classroom, see Randolph and Johnson (2017, 111–112).

10. Some students in their study also disagreed that the class material should be made relevant to their ethnic background.

11. See Sadker and Zittleman (2007) for the concept of fragmentation and isolation.

Works Cited

Anyon, Jean. 2011. "Ideology and United States History Textbooks." In *The Textbook as Discourse: Sociocultural Dimensions of American Schoolbooks*, edited by Eugene. F. Provenzo, Jr., Annis N. Shaver, and Manuel Bello, 109–139. New York: Routledge.

Apple, Michael W., and Linda K. Christian-Smith. 1991. "The Politics of the Textbook." In *The Politics of the Textbook*, edited by Michael W. Apple and Linda K. Christian-Smith, 1–21. London: Routledge.

Arao, Brian, and Kristi Clemens. 2013. "From Safe Spaces to Brave Spaces: A New Way to Frame Dialogue around Diversity and Social Justice." In *The Art of Effective Facilitation: Reflections from Social Justice Educators*, edited by Lisa Landreman, 135–150. Sterling, VA: Stylus.

Associazione Parole O_Stili. 2019. *Manifesto della comunicazione non ostile*. https://paroleostili.it (accessed April 6, 2019).

Azimova, Nigora, and Bill Johnston. 2012. "Invisibility and Ownership of Language: Problems of Russian Language Textbooks." *Modern Language Journal* 96(3): 337–349.

Banks, James A. 2007. "Multicultural Education: Characteristics and Goals." In *Multicultural Education. Issues and Perspectives*, 6th ed., edited by James A. Banks and Cherry A. McGee Banks, 3–32. Hoboken, NJ: John Wiley & Sons, Inc.

Barnes-Karol, Gwendolyn, and Maggie A. Broner. 2010. "Using Images as Springboards to Teach Cultural Perspectives in Light of the Ideals of the MLA Report." *Foreign Language Annals* 43(3): 422–445.

Becker, Ava. 2014. "Funds of (Difficult) Knowledge and the Affordances of Multimodality: The Case of Victor." *Journal of Language and Literacy Education* 10(2): 17–33.

Bell, Lee Anne. 2016. "Theoretical Foundations for Social Justice Education." In *Teaching for Diversity and Social Justice*, edited by Maurianne Adams, Lee Anne Bell, with Diane J. Goodman and Khyati Y. Joshi, 3–27. New York: Routledge.

Bori, Paul. 2018. *Language Textbook in the Era of Neoliberalism*. London: Routledge.

Canale, Germán. 2016. "(Re)Searching Culture in Foreign Language Textbooks, or the Politics of Hide and Seek." *Language, Culture and Curriculum* 29(2): 225–243.

Carroll, Sherrie, Suhanthie Motha, and Jeremy N. Price. 2008. "Accessing Imagined Communities and Reinscribing Regimes of Truth." *Critical Inquiry in Language Studies* 5(3): 165–191.

CAST. 2019. *Universal Design for Learning* http://www.cast.org/our-work/about-udl.html?utm_source=udlguidelines&utm_medium=web&utm_campaign=none&utm_content=homepage#.XKiiGutKiqA (accessed April 6, 2019).

Chapelle, Carol A. 2016. *Teaching Culture in Introductory Foreign Language Textbooks*. London: Palgrave Macmillan.

Crawford, Linda, and Peter McLaren. 2003. "A Critical Perspective on Culture in the Second Language Classroom." In *Culture as the Core: Interdisciplinary Perspectives on Culture, Teaching, and Learning in the Second Language Curriculum*, edited by Dale L. Lange and R. Michael Paige, 127–157. Greenwich, CT: Information Age.

Curdt-Christiansen, Xiao Lan, and Csilla Weninger, eds. 2015. *Language, Ideology and Education: The Politics of Textbooks in Language Education*. London: Routledge.

Delpit, Lisa. 1995. *Other People's Children: Cultural Conflict in the Classroom*. New York: New Press.

Ennser-Kananen, Joanna. 2016. "A Pedagogy of Pain: New Directions for World Language Education." *The Modern Languages Journal*, 100: 556–564. https://doi.org/10.1111/modl.1_12337 (accessed March 18, 2019).

EPIC. 2019. *Inclusive Classrooms.* https://epic.ucla.edu/ste/inclusive-classrooms/ (accessed April 8, 2019).

Fabbian, Chiara, and Emanuela Zanotti Carney. 2018a. "Critical Pedagogy, Social Justice, and Prosocial Identities in the Italian Classroom. Part I." *Italica* 95(2): 241–271.

Fabbian, Chiara, and Emanuela Zanotti Carney. 2018b. "Critical Pedagogy, Social Justice, and Prosocial Identities in the Italian Classroom. Part II." *Italica* 95(3): 417–433.

Fabbian, Chiara, Emmanuela Zanotti Carney, and Alessia Valfredini. 2019. "What's in a Book? A Social Justice Approach to FL Textual Contents (and Discontents)." In *Pathways to Paradigm Change: Critical Examinations of Prevailing Discourses and Ideologies in Second Language Education,* edited by B. Dupuy and K. McNichols, AAUSC. Boston: Cengage Learning.

Freire, Paulo. 1970/2005. *Pedagogy of the Oppressed: 30th Anniversary Edition.* New York: Continuum.

Goldberg, David, Dennis Looney, and Natalia Lusin. 2015. *Enrollments in Languages Other Than English in United States Institutions of Higher Education, Fall 2013,* Febraury. https://apps.mla.org/pdf/2013_enrollment_survey.pdf (accessed April 6, 2019).

Glynn, Cassandra, Pamela Wesley, and Beth Wassel. 2014. *Words and Actions: Teaching Languages through the Lens of Social Justice.* Alexandria, VA: The American Council on the Teaching of Foreign Languages.

Herman, Deborah M. 2007. "It's a Small World After All: From Stereotypes to Invented Worlds in Secondary School Spanish Textbooks." *Critical Inquiry in Language Studies* 4(2–3): 117–150.

Hipwell, Louise, and Donatella Melucci, eds. 2018. *Innovation in Italian Programs and Pedagogy. Special Issue of TILCA.* Teaching Italian Language and Culture Annual. http://tilca.qc.cuny.edu/wp-content/uploads/2018/TILCA%202018%20Special%20Issue.pdfl (accessed April 6, 2019).

Kay, Matthew R. 2018. *Not Light, But Fire: How to Lead Meaningful Race Conversations in the Classroom.* Portsmouth, NH: Stenhouse.

Kidd, Jenny. 2016. *Representation.* New York: Routledge.

Kramsch, Claire. 1987. "Foreign Language Textbooks' Construction of Foreign Reality." *Canadian Modern Language Review* 44(1): 95–119. http://utpjournals.metapress.com/content/120329/?sortorder=asc (accessed October 10, 2014).

Kubota, Ryuko. 2004a. "Critical Multiculturalism and Second Language Education." In *Critical Pedagogies and Language Learning,* edited by Bonny Norton and Kelleen Toohey, 30–52. Cambridge: Cambridge University Press.

Kubota, Ryuko. 2004b. "The Politics of Cultural Difference In Second Language Education." *Critical Inquiry in Language Studies* 1(1): 21–39.

Kubota, Ryuko, Theresa Austin, and Yoshiko Saito-Abbott. 2003. "Diversity and Inclusion of Sociopolitical Issues in Foreign Language Classrooms: An Exploratory Survey." *Foreign Language Annals* 36(1): 12–24.

Looney, Dennis, and Natalia Lusin. 2019. "Enrollments in Languages Other Than English in United States Institutions of Higher Education, Summer 2016 and Fall 2016." https://www.mla.org/content/download/83540/2197676/2016-Enrollments-Short_report.pdf (accessed April 6, 2019).

Meyer, Jan, and Ray Land. 2003. "Threshold Concepts and Troublesome Knowledge: Linkages to Ways of Thinking and Practising within the Disciplines." In *Improving Students' Learning—Ten Years On,* edited by Chris Rust, 412–424. Oxford: Oxford Center for Staff and Learning Development.

Moeller, Aleidine J., and Martha G. Abbott. 2018. "Creating a New Normal: Language Education for All." *Foreign Language Annals* 51: 12–23.

Moll, Luis, Cathy Amanti, Deborah Neff, and Norma Gonzalez. 1992. "Fund of Knowledge for Teaching: Using a Qualitative Approach to Connect Homes and Classrooms." *Theory into Practice* 31(2): 132–141.

National Standards Collaborative Board. 2015. *World-Readiness Standards for Learning Languages,* 4th ed. https://www.actfl.org/publications/all/world-readiness-standards-learning-languages/standards-summary (accessed April 6, 2019).

Nieto, Sonia. 2010. *Language, Culture, and Teaching: Critical Perspectives.* New York: Routledge.

Nieto, Sonia, and Patty Bode. 2008. *Affirming Diversity: The Sociopolitical Context of Multicultural Education,* 5th ed. Boston: Pearson Education.

Norton, Bonny. 2001. "Non-Participation, Imagined Communities and the Language Classroom." In *Learner Contributions to Language Learning: New Directions in Research*, edited by Michael Breen, 159–171. Harlow, U.K.: Pearson Education.

Office of Inclusive Excellence. 2019. *Faculty Resources*. https://csumb.edu/diversity/faculty-resources (accessed April 8, 2019).

Ortega, Lourdes. 1999. "Language and Equality: Ideological and Structural Constraints in Foreign Language Education in the US." In *Sociopolitical Perspectives in Language Policy and Planning in the USA*, edited by Thom Huebner and Kathryn A. Davis, 243–266. Amsterdam: John Benjamins.

Osborn, Terry A. 2000. *Critical Reflection and the Foreign Language Classroom*. Westport, CT: Bergin & Garvey.

Osborn, Terry A. 2006. *Teaching World Languages for Social Justice: A Sourcebook of Principles and Practices*. Mahwah, NJ: Lawrence Erlbaum Associates.

Poorvu Center for Teaching and Learning. 2019. *Inclusive Classroom Climates*. https://poorvucenter.yale.edu/ClassClimates (accessed April 6, 2019).

Randolph, Linwood J., and Stacey Margarita Johnson. 2017. "Social Justice in the Language Classroom: A Call to Action." *Dimension* March 16–18: 99–121.

Reagan, Timothy G., and Terry A. Osborn. 1998. "Power, Authority and Domination in Foreign Language Education: Toward an Analysis of Educational Failure." *Educational Foundations* 12: 45–62.

Reagan, Timothy G., and Terry A Osborn. 2002. *The Foreign Language Educator in Society: Toward a Critical Pedagogy*. Mahwah, NJ: Lawrence Erlbaum Associates.

Risager, Karen. 2018. *Representations of the World in Language Textbooks*. Bristol, U.K.: Multilingual Matters.

Sadker, David M., and Zittleman, Karen. 2007. "Practical Strategies for Detecting and Correcting Gender Bias in Your Classroom." In *Gender in the Classroom: Foundations, Skills, Methods, and Strategies across the Curriculum*, edited by David M. Sadker and Ellen S. Silber, 259–275. New York: Routledge.

Singleton, Glenn E. 2005. *Courageous Conversations about Race: A Field Guide for Achieving Equity in Schools*, 2nd ed. Thousand Oaks, CA: Corwin.

Sleeter, Christine E., and Carl A. Grant. 2011. "Race, Class, Gender, and Disability in Current Textbooks." In *The Textbook as Discourse: Sociocultural Dimensions of American Textbooks*, edited by Eugene F. Provenzo, Jr., Annis N. Shaver, and Manuel Bello, 183–215. New York: Routledge.

Stein, Pippa. 2004. "Representations, Rights, and Resources: Multimodal Pedagogies in the Language and Literacy Classroom." In *Critical Pedagogies and Language Learning*, edited by Bonny Norton and Kelleen Toohey, 1–17. Cambridge: Cambridge University Press.

Valfredini, Alessia. 2018a. "Developing Cultural Literacy: The Contrastive Study of TV Advertisements." *Journal of Language Teaching and Technology* 1: 2–14.

Valfredini, Alessia. 2018b. "Preparing for Life and Career in the 21st Century: A Role for Italian Courses from a Multilingual, Multicultural, Interdisciplinary, and Critical Perspective." In *Innovation in Italian Programs and Pedagogy, Teaching Italian Language and Culture Annual*, Special Issue, edited by Louise Hipwell and Donatella Melucci (Fall 2018), 139–150.

Zipin, Lew. 2009. "Dark Funds of Knowledge, Deep Funds of Pedagogy: Exploring Boundaries between Lifeworlds and Schools." *Discourse: Studies in the Cultural Politics of Education* 30(3), 317–331. doi.org/10.1080/01596300903037044 (accessed July 18, 2019).

From Roots to Routes: Italian Studies Between China and Italy via North America

GAOHENG ZHANG

When people find out that I am a professor of Italian studies, they invariably ask me why I speak Italian, being a Chinese native and living in North America. I get this question from people from all walks of life, in China, in Italy, in North America, almost everywhere I go. "Why don't you teach Italian in China? Do you teach Chinese to Italians too? Do you teach Italian language courses in Italian?" In professional settings, too, I often get asked this question by my colleagues, students, and audiences in talks, as well as during job interviews. "Can you tell us about the differences in teaching Italian between China and the United States? Why did you study Italian as an undergraduate major in China?" People are massively curious about the seemingly odd connection between my chosen profession and my cultural, ethnic, and national identity. After responding to the same question so often, I decided to come up with two options to spice up my reply with humor: "Would you like to hear the romantic or the unromantic version of how I learned to speak Italian?" People usually smile and beg to know both: "I want to hear the romantic one first!"

For the romantic story, I relate how I was inspired and nurtured by my hometown's close historical and affective ties with Italy: In his travelogue, *Il Milione*, Marco Polo lauds Hangzhou as the most splendid city on Earth. The most extensive and praiseworthy description Polo has lavished on any Chinese city in his writing is about Hangzhou (transliterated as Kinsay or Quinsai in various versions of *Il Milione*). Shortly before Polo visited China, the Mongol emperor had moved the capital to Beijing from Hangzhou, an old capital basking in the glory of the Southern Song Dynasty's achievements in urbanization, arts, and crafts. An average Chinese would easily make the association between Italy and China through Hangzhou and Polo. My fondness for Italian culture therefore was firmly grounded in this historical encounter. Turning to the unromantic story, I narrate how, because of China's extremely competitive university entrance exams, there existed a system in which elite universities were able to select students for specially designated fields of study by conducting their own exams. In the year I graduated from my high school, it was granted two language options by Beijing Foreign Studies University (BFSU), widely considered the most prestigious Chinese university for training language specialists and diplomats. Between the Italian and Thai languages, my mother chose Italian for me and I passed BFSU's self-administered exams and was successfully admitted to the Italian program. I often hasten to add that the unromantic story is about Chinese tiger parenting and how children come to terms with it. Only through this storytelling can I then establish a legitimate desire from my part to pursue a PhD in Italian studies at New York University. My interlocutors often seem to be happy with either version, having their curiosity satisfied, though they rarely ask why I chose to go to NYU, for which, incredibly, I have another funny story to tell.

This anecdote contains a central idea about diversity in Italian studies that I wish to address in this short essay: a perceived oddity or uniqueness given my language of research and teaching (Italian) and my native tongue (Chinese) in a place where neither is the official language (English). I will offer my observations about the challenges faced by researchers who do not have an Italian background and my solutions to them in relation to ideas about cultural roots and routes. I shall do so within the context of my academic and professional trajectory in Italian studies. After earning a BA in Italian language and literature from BFSU and a PhD in Italian studies from NYU, I then worked as a provost's postdoctoral fellow at the University of Southern California and as an assistant professor of Italian cinema at the University of Toronto. Currently I am a tenure-track assistant professor of Italian studies at the University of British Columbia in Vancouver. I have conducted extensive archival research in several Italian cities and specialized collections; I have attended a refresher course at the University for Foreigners in Perugia for teaching Italian; and I taught at NYU's Florence campus and at the University of Florence on a visiting-professor appointment. Between 2010 and 2016, I have done forty job interviews and diligently recorded the questions and exchanges immediately afterward for future reference.

This brief sketch of my academic journey indicates that the concept of cultural roots, often so valued in foreign language and culture education, is a rather problematic one for me, and it is often posed to me as such by people who are intrigued by my experience. For example, during job interviews in North America, my fluency in Italian was often tested in a way that suggested this was a more important component than critical thinking or teaching skills. Nonetheless, I do believe that these potential employers were also evidently curious about me and my qualifications. As puzzled as I initially was, after several tryouts it became clear to me that they were testing my performance of Italianness, and an essential component in validating it was my Italian-language ability. The same thing can be said about an appraisal of my knowledge of the Italian literary canon. For another example, when I tried to open up conversations with Chinese academics of Italian studies, particularly when I was exploring job prospects in China, they expressed mixed feelings about the values of English-language scholarship on Italy, as they seemed to seek approval mainly from Chinese and Italian readers; they appeared to think that Italians would better understand the materials thanks to a longer period of assimilation in the relevant cultural milieu.

These and other examples often made me question, if not agonize over, my place in teaching Italian and Italian studies courses in North America, being neither an Italian nor an English native speaker. Such (self-)doubting afflicted my professional self-presentation and well-being. How does one disentangle oneself from this web of doubts focused on language ability and national and cultural identity and thus move on from their debilitating effects? How do I reconstruct my own story and draw energy from it? How do I reframe my own thinking in a way that will help me act proactively for the benefit of my professional and personal lives?

My solution was to highlight even more prominently what I had been researching and teaching about "cultural routes"—that is, Italy's global networks, and in particular, Italian–Chinese communications—and illuminate for potential employers the significance of studying these dimensions of Italian cultures and transculturation. For my PhD dissertation, I worked on travel dynamics in the cinema of Gianni Amelio, who made films both in and outside Italy, including in China. In my postdoctoral years, I embarked on a different project, one focused on media debates about Italy's Chinese population. Titled *Migration and the Media: Debating Chinese Migration to Italy, 1992–2012*, it was published by University of Toronto Press in 2019. At the University of Southern California, the University of Toronto, and the University of British Columbia (UBC), I offered a course taught at both undergraduate and graduate levels about Italy and China that caters to students who wish to explore their interests in both countries but who are not aware of the links between the two. In the context of large waves of Chinese undergraduate students in North America and nonheritage students interested in China, I have noticed that this course tended to attract this population and then introduced them to Italian materials. Meanwhile, my Italian heritage students in this course often expressed their delight in learning an aspect of their history about which they knew close to nothing. Moreover, at UBC, I teach a course on Colonial and Postcolonial Italy, offering students an opportunity to study how Italy's amnesia about how colonialism has impacted its postcolonial condition. My course on Made in Italy consciously underscores how such labeled products have global influence or are influenced by global dynamics. To emphasize my research and teaching in Italy's global history and connections and to judiciously use them as a highlight in my job interviews did not mean for me disregarding accuracy in language use or a firm grasp of the canonical works. Rather, it meant reviewing and revising a discipline through my own experiences, as well as making myself feel at home in this discipline.

Another solution I employed to reroute the thorny question pertaining to my nationality and associated issues was to focus on addressing critical concepts and methodologies (e.g., migration, gender, etc.) that would resonate with humanistic scholars and students in general. In other words, I often seek my audience from outside Italian studies. For example, my book about Chinese migration to Italy is listed under their Cultural Studies book series and is cross-listed with Italian studies, Asian studies, communications studies, media studies, cultural studies, and literary studies. This is because the book draws on concepts such as Italy's multiple mobilities, Chinese migrants' flexible citizenship, culture as a framing event, and culture as a repertoire.

Through organizing two conferences on Italy and East Asia at the University of Toronto and at Stony Brook University (SBU), I was able to draw scholars from China, Australia, Europe, and North America who work on East Asia's relationships with Italy into the orbit of Italian studies in North America. Many of these scholars, like me, focus on transculturation. Transculturation refers to the process of transitioning from one culture to another and moving back and forth between them. For example, one scholar from the SBU conference examines Chinese translations of Dante's *Commedia* in order to probe the limits of the Chinese language in conveying concepts that were previously unknown in this linguistic code. Another scholar analyzed how Italy's 150th anniversary celebration of its unification and Japan's centennial celebration of its Meiji Revolution were similarly and differently staged as reaffirmations of both countries' modernization. These are examples of how academics consciously mobilize their cultural and linguistic resources in uncovering the transcultural transactions in events that contributed to the formation of Italian culture or demonstrated Italian culture's influence. In skillful analyses drawing on interdisciplinary and comparative theories and methods, the result need not be Italo-centric, as the case studies obviously pertain to some aspect of Italy, but, more significantly, help to broaden the horizons of Italian studies as a discipline by putting it into dialogue with other disciplines and cultures.

We are all bearers of cultural roots to some extent, but to look at things from a different angle, the same discourse is valid for cultural routes. My experiences told me that diversifying Italian studies means moving closer to routes than to roots. Italian history about mobilities and transculturation has also provided us with a rich array of materials to research and teach. I hope to continue exploring this exciting opportunity by way of Italian–Chinese mobilities and cultures and their articulations in North America, the longest-standing West–East relationship in written record and a significant example of global circulation of people and ideas on three continents.

Contributors

SOLE ANATRONE is an assistant professor of Italian studies at Vassar College whose research focuses on questions of gender and sexuality, race, migration, (post)colonialism, and activism in cinema, literature, and cultural studies. Her publications include: "Almeno non hai un nome da negra": Race, Gender and National Belonging in Laila Wadia's *Amiche per la pelle* for *Gender/Sexuality/Italy Journal*; and "Disciplining Narratives and Damaged Identities in Rossana Campo's *Lezioni di arabo*" for *California Italian Studies*. She is also co-editor and contributor to *Queering Italian Media* (Lexington Books, 2020). She is a cofounder, with Julia Heim, of Asterisk, a taskforce that offers workshops to university faculty, students, and staff geared toward fostering LGBTQAI+ inclusivity inside and outside the classroom; she is on the steering committee of the Consortium on Forced Migration and is a member of the advisory board to the Queer Studies Caucus of the American Association of Italian Studies. Anatrone holds a PhD in Italian studies and a designated emphasis in women, gender, and sexuality studies from the University of California, Berkeley.

NICOLINO APPLAUSO, holder of a PhD in Romance languages and literatures at the University of Oregon, is a visiting assistant professor of Italian at Loyola University, Maryland. He is also a lecturer of Italian, Spanish, and Latin at Morgan State University, where he established its first Italian program in fall 2018. This new Italian program is of historical importance because it is believed to be the only Italian program currently taught at a Historically Black College and University in the United States. He has published more than a dozen book chapters and peer-reviewed articles on various topics ranging from history and political satire to humor, music, and poetry in medieval and modern Italy. He is the author of *Dante's Comedy and the Ethics of Invective in Medieval Italy: Humor and Evil* (Lexington Books, 2019), which proposes a new approach to invective and comic poetry written in Italy during the thirteenth and fourteenth centuries and paves the way for an innovative understanding of Dante's masterpiece. He is the co-author, with Fabian Alfie, of *Dante satiro: Satire in Dante Alighieri's Comedy and Other Works* (Lexington Books, 2020), which is the first comprehensive study on Dante and satire. His forthcoming book is a history manual of contemporary Italy, co-edited with the late Mario B. Mignone, titled *Italy Today: Changes and Challenges in the Twenty-First Century from World War II to the Coronavirus Pandemic* (forthcoming from Peter Lang Publishing).

RYAN CALABRETTA-SAJDER is assistant professor of Italian at the University of Arkansas, Fayetteville, where he teaches courses in Italian, film, and gender studies. Author of *Divergenze in celluloide: Colore, migrazione e identità sessuale nei film gay di Ferzan Özpetek* with Mimesis editore and editor of *Pasolini's Lasting Impressions: Death, Eros, and Literary Enterprise in the Opus of Pier Paolo Pasolini* with Fairleigh Dickinson University Press, he focuses on research interests including the integration of gender, class, and migration in both Italian and Italian American literature and cinema. In spring 2017 he was a Fulbright Foundation of the South Scholar at the University of Calabria. He is currently working on two authored, book-length projects, one exploring the Italian American gay author Robert Ferro who died of AIDS complications in 1988, and the second on the Algerian Italian author Amara Lakhous.

ROSETTA GIULIANI CAPONETTO is associate professor of Italian studies at Auburn University. Her areas of academic interest include Italian literature and cinema of the Fascist period; Italian colonialism in the Horn of Africa; Italy's trusteeship in Somalia; food and philanthropy; postcolonial theory; and race and ethnic studies. She is the author of *Fascist Hybridities: Representations of Racial Mixing and Diaspora Cultures under Mussolini* (Palgrave Macmillan, 2016).

MARY ANN McDONALD CAROLAN is professor of modern languages and literatures and director of the Italian studies program at Fairfield University. She has written extensively on film in a variety of journals. She is the author of *The Transatlantic Gaze: Italian Cinema, American Film* (State University of New York Press, 2014), which documents the sustained and profound artistic impact of Italian cinema upon filmmakers in the United States from the postwar period to the new millennium. Carolan's current book-length project, *Orienting Italy: China through the Lens of Italian Filmmakers*, examines the ways in which Italian directors have employed documentary, historical fiction, and fictional narratives to represent China and its people both at home and in Italy.

JOHN CHAMPAGNE is professor of English at Penn State Erie, the Behrend College. Former chair of Penn State Behrend's global languages and cultures program, he was also the 2018–2019 Penn State laureate, which involved traveling around Pennsylvania to present his talk "Art and Politics: The Case of Corrado Cagli." His sixth book, published in 2019 by Peter Lang's Italian Modernities series, is titled *Queer Ventennio: Italian Fascism, Homoerotic Art, and the Nonmodern in the Modern*.

MARK CHU is senior lecturer in Italian at University College Cork, Ireland. His research and teaching address, among other topics, questions of identity and migration in Italian culture. He is currently working on a book project on the representation of the Chinese in Italian culture. He served as head of the Department of Italian from 2003 until 2018. He has published widely on Sicilian literature and was editor in chief of the first three issues (2011–2013) of *Todomodo*, the international journal of Sciascia studies, published by leading Italian academic publisher Leo S. Olschki in collaboration with the Associazione degli Amici di Leonardo Sciascia.

SIÂN GIBBY is writer/editor at the John D. Calandra Italian American Institute (Queens College, CUNY). She earned a BA from Indiana University in Italian language and literature and an MSArch from the University of Cincinnati. Beginning in 1998 she has worked as an editor and writer, including stints at *Slate* magazine, *Tablet*, and the Jewish Theological Seminary before coming to the Institute in 2010. She is the translator of Quinto Antonelli's *Intimate History of the Great War: Letters, Diaries, and Memoirs from Soldiers on the Front* (2016), Francesco "Kento" Carlo's *Resistenza Rap* (2018), and Luigi Fontanella's *God of New York* (forthcoming). She is currently writing a play about Italian American poet Pascal D'Angelo.

SHELLEEN GREENE is an associate professor of cinema and media studies in the Department of Film, Television, and Digital Media at the University of California, Los Angeles. Her research interests include Italian cinema, Black European studies, and postcolonial studies. Her book *Equivocal Subjects: Between Italy and Africa—Constructions of Racial and National Identities in the Italian Cinema* (Bloomsbury/Continuum, 2012) examines the representation of mixed-race subjects of Italian and African descent in the Italian cinema. Her work has also been published in *Terrone to Extracommunitario: New Manifestations of Racism in Contemporary Italian Cinema* (Troubador Press, 2010); *Postcolonial Italy: Challenging National Homogeneity* (Palgrave Macmillan, 2012); and *California Italian Studies* (8.2, 2018).

KRISTI GRIMES is associate professor of Italian and co-director of the Italian Program at Saint Joseph's University, where she teaches courses in Italian language, culture, literature, and art history. Dr. Grimes holds a BA from the College of the Holy Cross, an MA from the University of Notre Dame, and a PhD from the University of Chicago. Her research focuses on Petrarch and the lyric tradition, interdisciplinary relations between literary and visual traditions, the iconography of female saints, and the history of humanism. Her work has been published in *Italian Culture*; *Latomus: Revue d'Études Latines*; *Lectura Petrarce*; *The Medieval Feminist Forum*; and *The Journal of the Midwest Modern Language Association*. Dr. Grimes regularly teaches in the SJU Rome Summer Program and is working on a textbook on diversity and study abroad.

JULIA HEIM is a lecturer of Italian studies at the University of Pennsylvania and a translator of queer theory, art criticism, and the children's book series Geronimo Stilton. Dr. Heim holds a PhD in comparative literature from the CUNY Graduate Center. She is a cofounder of Asterisk, a higher education LGBTQIA+ inclusivity task force, and her own research focuses on LGBTQIA+ representation in contemporary Italian television. Most recently she has co-edited the volume *Queering Italian Media*, which was published in 2020 by Lexington Press.

KENYSE LYONS is a dedicated global educator, intersectional feminist, visual studies enthusiast, and decolonial scholar. She completed her doctoral studies at Yale University in 2012 and has taught at a range of secondary and undergraduate institutions, including Montgomery College, Yale University, Fairfield University, and Prince George's County Schools. She has a passion for leveraging her teaching and research in the service of the identification, analysis, and correction (*à la* Giambattista Vico) of those colonial modes of thinking, seeing, being, and relating that continue to plague how Italy perceives of and engages the sexualized, gendered, and racialized Other. Her publications include an article titled "'Pro o Contro La rabbia': Elsa Morante, Pier Paolo Pasolini and the Work of Art in the Atomic Age," published in *Elsa Morante's Politics of Writing: Rethinking Subjectivity, History, and the Power of Art* and edited by Stefania Lucamante (Fairleigh Dickinson University Press, 2014). She is currently working on an article anchored in her recent talk at the University of Calgary on the latent (and most likely unintentional) Black feminism of Bernardo Bertolucci's 1998 film *Besieged*. She is also in the process of preparing a book project that explores the role of photography in the organization and alternative reimagining of social, cultural, and political life in Italy in the light of late modernity. She is currently an adjunct faculty member at The Catholic University of America in Washington, D.C.

AKASH KUMAR is a visiting assistant professor of Italian at Indiana University, Bloomington, and associate editor of Digital Dante. His research has two main strands: the crossing of poetry, philosophy, and science in early Italian poetry of the thirteenth century and in Dante;

and the interactions between Western and non-Western cultures in popular activities like game playing and storytelling. Some recent projects include a collaboration with Richard Lansing on *The Complete Poetry of Giacomo da Lentini* (University of Toronto Press, 2018) and the essay "Walls of Inclusivity: Dante's Divine Comedy and World Literature" for the *Wiley-Blackwell Companion to World Literature* (2020). This essay stems in part from a work in progress "Vernacular Hybridity Across Borders: Dante, Amir Khusro, and Sandow Birk."

VETRI NATHAN is associate professor and head of the Italian studies program in the Department of Modern Languages, Literatures and Cultures at the University of Massachusetts Boston. Nathan received an MA and PhD in Italian from Stanford University in 2009. His research interests include immigrant cultures and globalization in contemporary Italy, European colonialism and postcoloniality, Italian cinema, and food studies. He has published various articles on these topics, and his book *Marvelous Bodies: Italy's New Migrant Cinema* was published by Purdue University Press in 2017.

DEBORAH PARKER is professor of Italian at the University of Virginia. She is the author of *Commentary and Ideology: Dante in the Renaissance* (Duke UP, 1993), *Bronzino: Renaissance Painter as Poet* (Cambridge UP, 2000), and *Michelangelo and the Art of Letter Writing* (Cambridge UP, 2010) and the general editor of *The World of Dante* website. She is the co-author, along with Mark Parker, of *The Attainable Text: The Special Edition DVD and the Study of Film* (Palgrave Macmillan, 2011), *Inferno Revealed: From Dante to Dan Brown* (Palgrave Macmillan, 2013), and most recently, *Sucking Up, A Brief Consideration of Sycophancy* (University of Virginia Press, 2018). Reviews have appeared in the *Washington Post*, *Kirkus*, and *Salon*.

DEANNA SHEMEK is professor of Italian and European studies at the University of California, Irvine. She is the author of *Ladies Errant: Wayward Women and Social Order in Early Modern Italy* (1998). Her collaborative editing includes *Phaethon's Children: The Este Court and Its Culture in Early Modern Ferrara* (2005) and *Writing Relations: American Scholars in Italian Archives* (2008). She edited and cotranslated Adriana Cavarero's *Stately Bodies: Literature, Philosophy, and the Question of Gender* (1995). Her edition and translation of the *Selected Letters* of Isabella d'Este (2017) won the Society for the Study of Early Modern Women's 2018 prize for the best translation of a woman's work. She codirects IDEA: Isabella d'Este Archive, an online project for study of the Italian Renaissance.

ANTHONY JULIAN TAMBURRI is dean of the John D. Calandra Italian American Institute (Queens College, CUNY) and distinguished professor of European languages and literatures. He is co-founder of Bordighera Press and past president of the Italian American Studies Association and of the American Association of Teachers of Italian. He has authored 16 books and more than 120 peer-reviewed essays and book chapters concentrating on literature, cinema, and semiotics. His books include: *Of* Saltimbanchi *and* Incendiari*: Aldo Palazzeschi and Avant-Gardism in Italy* (1990); *To Hyphenate or Not to Hyphenate* (1991); *A Semiotic of Ethnicity: In (Re)cognition of the Italian/American Writer* (1998); *Italian/American Short Films & Videos: A Semiotic Reading* (2002); *Semiotics of Re-reading: Guido Gozzano, Aldo Palazzeschi, and Italo Calvino* (2003); *Narrare altrove: diverse segnalature letterarie* (2007); *Re-viewing Italian Americana: Generalities and Specificities on Cinema* (2011); *Re-reading Italian Americana: Specificities and Generalities on Literature and Criticism* (2014); *Scrittori*

Italiano[-]Americani: trattino sì trattino no (2018), *Un biculturalismo negato: La scrittura "italiana" negli Stati Uniti* (2018); and *Signing Italian/American Cinema: A More Focused Look* (2021). He is executive producer and host of the Calandra Institute's TV program, *Italics*, which is produced in collaboration with CUNY TV. He also writes a column for *La Voce di New York*, entitled "The Italian Diaspora." For more information see his website, www.anthonyjuliantamburri.org.

ALESSIA VALFREDINI is a senior lecturer at Fordham University, where she coordinates the Italian language program and serves as assessment coordinator for the Department of Modern Languages and Literatures. She earned a PhD in language, learning, and literacy at the Graduate School of Education of Fordham University. She studies world language education in higher education contexts, with a focus on higher order cognitive functions, interdisciplinarity, social justice, and civic engagement.

GAOHENG ZHANG is assistant professor of Italian studies at the University of British Columbia in Vancouver. He is a humanities scholar of migration, mobilities, multiculturalism, media, rhetoric, ethics, and masculinity. Zhang is the author of *Migration and the Media: Debating Chinese Migration to Italy, 1992–2012* (University of Toronto Press, 2019), which is the first detailed media and cultural study of the Chinese migration from both Italian and Chinese migrant perspectives, as well as one of the few book-length analyses of migration and culture.

Index

#MeToo, 39

Abbot, Martha G., 178, 188
able-bodied, iv, 133, 137, 181, 182
ableness, ii
acculturation, 132
activists, 18, 37, 67, 95, 99, 147n3; José Donoso, 33; Medhin Paolos, 94; Vito Russo, 41n12
advocacy, 37, 145, 187
African Americans, iv, 13–24, 132; and Italian Americans, 38–39, 93; YouTube blogs, 20
African Italian filmmakers, 22n9, 95n3
African Italian, 19–20; subjects in film, 94
AIDS, in Italian and Italian American Canon, 25–43
Aleramo, Sibilia (Rina Raccio), 26; *Una donna*, 26–27, 31; *Il passaggio*, 26
Alighieri, Dante, 5, 21, 28, 39, 41n15, 60–62, 109–122; 131, 143, 151, 157, 158, 163, 165–167, 196; adapted by Chinese authors, 166–167; *Divina Commedia*, 109–122; importance to Bengali Renaissance, 111–112
Amelio, Gianni, *La stella cheon c'è*, 60, 195
American Association for Italian Studies (AAIS), 67, 94, 157
American Association of Teachers of Italian, 37
American Council on the Teaching of Foreign Languages, 180
American Psychological Association, 141
Anatrone, Sole, 35–36, 41n4, 94
Anderson, Benedict, 53n9, 170
Antonioni, Michelangelo, *Cina/Chung Kuo*, 60–61
Anyon, Jean, 179
Applauso, Nicolino, 53n2
Apple, Michael W., 179
Arabic, 47, 59, 115, 173; studies, 153, 170

Arao, Brian, 188
Ardizzoni, Michela, 48
Ariosto, Ludovico 6, 173, 174
Arnaudo, Marco, 42n16
Asian Italian, 19
Association of Departments of Foreign Languages (ADFL), 58, 98, 101, 104
Avanza, Martina, 48
Azimova, Nigora, 179

Banks, James, 177
Baraka, Amiri, 39
Baránski, Zygmunt, 166
Barnes-Karol, Gwendolyn, 184
Barolini, Teodolinda, 110, 114
Bassani, Giorgio, *Il giardino dei Finzi-Contini*, 85
Becker, Ava, 180
Bedarida, Raffaele, 74, 77
Bell, Lee Anne, 177, 185
Bengali Renaissance, 111–112
Bellezza, Dario, 39, 40
Belotti, Elena Gianini, *Adagio un poco mosso*, 83; 85
Benadusi, Lorenzo, 73, 74
Benjamin, Walter, 71
Benozzo, Francesco, 103, 111
Bersani, Leo, 27, 38–39
Bertolucci, Bernardo, *L'ultimo imperatore*, 60
Bhabha, Homi, 92, 98, 105n8, 136, 150, 155n2
Bhopal, Kalwant, 81, 88n3
Birk, Sandow, 121, 122
bisexuality, 11; in Cagli, 74–75
Bissell, William Cunningham, 49
Black European/Mediterranean studies, 95
Black man, 48, 49–51, 53n6, 105n9
Black opera singers, 17
black Venus, 47, 49–50, 53n5
blackness, 47, 125–148
Blanco, José A., 20
Boccelli, Andrea, 169

Bondanella, Peter, 38, 92
Borges, Jorge Luis, 122
Bori, Paul, 179
Bossi, Umberto, 48
Botterill, Steven, 116
Boym, Svetlana, 49, 50
Braghetti, Anna Laura, *Il prigioniero*, 83
Brioni, Simone, 105n12
Broccia, Lillyrose Veneziano, 9
Broner, Maggie, 184
Bronzino, Angelo, 103
Brooks, Rayshard, iv
Brown-Harvard Conference, Queering Italian Studies, 67
Brown, Wendy, 69
Brugnolo, Furio, 118
Bullaro, Grace Russo, 94
Burdett, Charles, 87
Busi, Aldo, 40

Cachey, Theodore, 170
Cagli, Corrado, 74–77
Calandra Institute, see John D. Calandra Italian American Institute
Calandra, John D., vn3
Calvino, Italo, 60, 86, 166; *Il barone rampante*, 5; *Invisible Cities*, 28, 60; *If on a Winter's Night a Traveler*, 28
Campo, Rossano, 36, 40
Canale, Germán, 179, 182
Cantonese, 80
Capitani, Flavia, 173
Caponetto, Rosetta Giuliani, 53n4, 53nn5–7, 135
Cappozzo, Valerio, 39
Carolan, Mary Ann, 160
Castiglione, Giuseppe, 60
Catholic University of America, 145
Cavallo, Jo Ann, 174
Cavani, Liliana, *Technologies of Gender*, 28; *The Night Porter*, 28
Cena, Giovanni, 41n2
Centro di Ricerca, Politesse: Politiche e Teorie della Sessualità (Università di Verona), 67–68
Chae, D. H., 127
Chapelle, Carol, 179
Charlottesville, VA, tragedy of, i

China, 60–63, 104n3, 161–165, 166; Italian studies in, 193–197
Chen, Qi, 161, 166
Chinese, 60, 61, 79; American relations, 172; contemporary authors, 166–167; culture, 60–61, 79–80; and Italian studies, 157–167, 169–172, 193–197; Italian representations of, 87; language 20, 22n11, 60; theorists, 60
Chopin, Kate, *The Awakening*, 26
Chow, Rey, 60
Christianity, in Dante, 109–112, 121
Christian-Smith, Linda K., 179
Chronicle of Higher Education, 58, 159, 162
Ciccarelli, Andrea, 42n17
cinema, 7, 28–29, 31, 38, 47, 51, 53n5, 61, 62, 68, 69, 71, 86, 101, 151, 195; Italian cinema, 38, 91–96, 142, 194; "cinema of migration," 95
Cipriani, Lidio, 135
City University of New York, The (CUNY), ii–iii, vn3, 5
classroom, atmosphere, 9–11
Clemens, Krisiti, 188
Coggeshall, Elizabeth, 41n15
collaboration, 9, 32, 37–38, 40, 61, 66, 94, 102, 103, 155, 167
College Language Association (CLA), 16, 22n3
colonialism, 69, 71–73, 80–81, 84, 86–87, 92–95, 98, 105n9, 105n12, 110, 132–142; 196; colonial logic, 130–142; Italian in Africa, 45–55, 93; postcolonial, 71, 84, 87, 92–95, 101, 170, 195–196
Columbia University, 167n5
Compagno, Dario, 71
Conte, Giuseppe, 95n2
Coomaraswamy, Ananda, 111
Coppola, Manuela, 135
Corbucci, Sergio, 62
Cornell University, 167n5
Cottom, Tressie McMillan, 125, 129, 130
courses, extramural, 58, 59–61; intramural 58, 61–62
Crawford, Linda, 183
Crialese, Emanuele, 151

Crispolti, Enrico, 76
cultural studies, 29, 32–33, 38, 40; cross-cultural studies, 57–63
Curdt-Christiansen, Xiao Lan, 179
Curie, Marie, 25

D'Azeglio, Massimo, 98
da Lentini, Giacomo, 116
Dall'Orto, Giovanni, 69–74
DalMartello, Chiara, 8
Daniel, Arnaut, 61, 116, 117, 120–121
Dante, see, Alighieri, Dante
Dawson, Andrew, 50
De Franceschi, *La cittadinanza come luogo di lotta*, 95n3
De Franchi, Marco, *La carne e il sangue*, 83
De Lauretis, Teresa, *Alice Doesn't: Feminism, Semiotics, Cinema*, 28–30; *Technologies of Gender: Essays on Theory, Film, and Fiction*, 28–30; *The Practice of Love: Lesbian Sexuality and Perverse Desire*, 29
de' Medici, Alessandro, 103
death, as metaphor, 25–43
DeCoste, Mary-Michelle, 6, 174
Deledda, Grazia, 25, 26, 41n5
Delpit, Lisa, 189n3
DeMatteo, Lydia, 48
DiAngelo, Robin, 126, 136
diaspora, African in Italy, 45, 48–49, 93–94; Italian, 7, 93, 102
Di Filippo and Di Florio, *Migrazioni contemporanee: Testi e contesti*, 105n14
Dillon, Sam, 53n1
Dini, Andrea, 8
discovery, 109, 115, 134, 187
Distefano, Antonio Dikele, *Zero*, 95n3
Doan, Laura, 71, 74
dominant culture, iv–v, 4–5, 16, 30, 75, 80, 98, 112, 128–139, 181–182, 186–187
Donato, Clorinda, 163, 165
Donley, Philip Redwine, 20
Drake, Richard, 27
Draper, Ruth, 61
Duke University, 167n5
Dutta, Michael Madhusudan, 111

Eco, Umberto, *Theory of Semiotics*, 28; *The Name of the Rose*, 28
Edelmann, Lee, 27–28, 29, 40
emigration, 81, 86, 102
Endo, Rachel, 130, 138, 139
Ennser-Kananen, Joanna, 180, 183, 188, 189n6
equal opportunity, i
ethnicity, i, ii, iii, 67, 79, 81, 86, 88n3, 100, 128, 151, 158, 171–173, 180–181; in Italian Film Studies, 91–96
Eurocentrism, 60, 170
exclusion/exclusionary, iv, 7, 11, 13, 46–48, 57, 109–110, 122, 126–128, 139, 158–161, 182–184, 187–188

Fabbian, Chiara, 177, 179, 189n7
Fanon, Frantz, 105n9, 136, 139–140
Fante, John, 151
fashionable/fashionableness, 68, 70, 71, 73
fear, 3, 4, 32, 125, 140, 145, 151; and nostalgia in Italian studies, 45–55
Frederick II, 58–59
Fellini, Federico, 91, 95; *Satyricon*, 28
feminist/feminism, 11n1, 26, 28-29, 41n7, 71, 84, 87, 129, 173
femininity, 125–148, 174; African/black, 50, 136
Ferguson, Gary, 74
Ferme, Valerio, 26, 34, 163
Ferrante, Elena, 60, 169
Ferro, Robert, 33–35, 41nn10–11; *Second Son*, 33–34, 35, 40
fetishization, 135–136
film studies, 29, 91–96, 171–173
Fiore, Teresa, 51–52
Fitzgerald, Angela Fuscia Nissoli, 17
fixation, of PhD, 38; of racial type, 136
Flaherty, Colleen, 14
Florida State University, 162, 167n5
Floyd, George, i
Folena, Gianfranco, 116
Foucault, Michel, 71, 73
Foxx, Jaime, 62
Freccero, Carla, 71
Freedman, Paul, 114
Freeman, Elizabeth, 65
Freire, Paulo, 178

French, in Dante, 112, 116, 118, 119; studies, 16, 20, 21n1, 22n5, 22n10, 57–59, 70, 153, 158, 162, 165
Fresu, Rita, 37
fundraise, 153–154

Garcia, Melissa, 9
Garrone, Matteo, *Gomorrah*, 60
Gasman M., 15
Gatson, Sophie, 49–50
Gauntlett, David, 71, 72, 76
Geary, Patrick, 172
gender, ii, iv, v, 1–12, 12n2, 12n4, 25–42, 48, 65–78, 82–90, 94, 99–101, 128, 132–134, 144, 150–151, 159–163, 171–174, 180–187, 196
Gennari, John, *Flavor and Soul*, 22n9,
Georgetown University, 167n5
German studies, 16, 21n1, 22n5, 37–38, 53n1, literature, 45
ghetto, 57, 58, 63, 160
Ginzburg, Carlo, 71, 72
Ginzburg, Natalia, 36, 41n7
Giori, Mauro, 68–76; *Homosexuality and Italian Cinema, From the Fall of Fascism to the Years of Lead*, 68–72, 73–74
Girard, Rene, 34
Global Languages and Cultures, 66
Glynn, Cassandra, 186, 189n5
Goldberg, Jonathan, 71
Gomm, Roger, 130
Goucher College, 21n1
Gozzoli, Benozzo, 103
Gramsci, Antonio, 93
Grant, Carl A., 179
Grumley, Michael, 33, 41n10, 41n11
Guglielmo, Jennifer, 93
Guglielmo, Jennifer and Salvatore Salerno, *Are Italians White? How Race Is Made in America*, 93
Guiducci, Armanda, *Due donne da buttare*, 83

Halperin, David, 71
Hammersley, Martin, 130
Harvard University, 21, 67, 157, 162, 167n5

Hayes, Michael, 81
Heim, Julia, 1–12, 35–36, 41n4, 94
Heng, Geraldine, 112
Henke, Robert, 173
Herman, Deborah M., 179, 182
Hilhorst, Sacha, 49
Hipwell, Louise, 178
hiring process, i–ii
historically Black colleges and universities, 13–24; teaching Italian at, 15–16; 45
homosexuality, 68–69, 73, 75–76; Palazzeschi, 41n8
hooks, bell, 87, 92
humanities, 39, 41n15, 63, 82, 84, 131, 149, 152, 154, 158, 162, 169–175, 175n1
hybridity, 73, 115–121, 149–155

Ibsen, Henrik, *A Doll's House*, 26
identity, 82, 87, 98–103, 105n7, 105n9, 115, 150–152, 173–174, 181; cultural, 193–195; gender, 2–5, 10–12, 12n2, 32–36, 69, 76, 180; politics, 46–49, 92, 158–161, 166; racial, 94, 125–148, 171; trauma, 125–148, 158
immigration, iii, 20, 66, 80, 81, 86, 92, 94, 135, 173, 180, 186
immigrants, 48, 51, 52, 169, 172
imperialism, 110, 112, 131–133
Indiana University, 38, 94, 161, 162, 167n5
inferiority, 135, 138, 140
injustice, 2, 51, 126, 183, 187
Italian Americanist, 93
Italian Americans, ii, iii, vn3, 18, 25–43, 92, 93, 126, 151, 169, 173
Italian Consulate, Washington, D.C., 19; Philadelphia, 19
Italianists, 18, 21, 25, 28, 35, 57, 62–63, 68, 73, 127, 133, 141, 153, 157–168
Italian literature, 1, 26, 58, 87, 158, 161, 163, 170, 173, 175; and culture courses, 4–7
Italian textbooks, 7–9, 19–20, 22n12, 179; heteronormative, 7–8
Italian-language classes, 7–9, 10, 15, 19, 20, 33, 45, 130

italianità, 98, 133, 137, 146
Italianness, 46–47, 51, 53n7, 179, 180, 182, 189, 195
Iyob, Ruth, 49

Jacomella, Gabriella, 173
Japanese, scholars, 166; studies, 57, 170, 188
Jewish, iv; Italian experience, 85; studies, 172; poets, 173
Jin, Ba, 167
John D. Calandra Italian American Institute, iii, 9, 21, 28, 45, 79, 86, 88n3, 91, 94, 100, 145, 155n1
Johns Hopkins University, 167n5
Johnson, Stacey Margarita, 185
Johnston, Bill, 179
Journal of Blacks in Higher Education, 17

Kalamazoo International Conference on Medieval Studies, 157
Kay, Matthew, 188
Khouma, Pap, iii, 51, 173
Kidd, Jenny, 179
Kinoshita, Sharon, 113
Kinsey, Alfred, *Sexual Behavior in the Human Male*, 27
Kirkham, Victoria, 173
Kitzmiller, John, 93
Kramsch, Claire, 178
Kubota, Ryuko, 178, 180, 182–184, 188
Kwornu, Fred, 22n9; *Blaxploitation*, 18
ius soli, 95n3

La Greca, Antonella Tavassa, *La guerra di Nora*, 83
Lakhous, Amara, iii, 39, 105n14, 173
Lan, Xiao, 179
Land, Ray, 178, 189
Lavender Society, The, 40
Lazzarino, Graziana, 8
Lee, Spike, 93, 151
Lerner, Gad, 48
Lessing, Doris, 25
Levi, Primo, 84, 85, 87
LGBTQ studies, 65
LGBTQIA+, iv, 1–12, 100, 181; content in the classroom, 3–4, 29–30

LGBTQIAA+, 29, 31, 33–35, 40
linguicism, 138–139
Liu, William Ming, 126, 127, 142
Looney, Dennis, 15, 22n9, 25, 27, 33, 35–36, 39, 57–58, 86, 110
Lorcin, Patricia, 49
Lorde, Audre, 126, 127
Love, Heather, 76
Luraghi, Silvia, 37
Lusin, Natalia, 15, 25, 33, 57, 58

Mac Giolla Chríost, Diarmait, 81
Machiavelli, Niccolò, 166
Manguel, Alberto, 109
Manzini, Gianna, *Tempo innamorato*, 83
Marcus, Millicent, 93, 96n4, 142
marginalization, 1–12, 57, 67–68, 83, 85, 92, 99, 125–148, 177–192, 189n3; of LGBTQIA+ people, 1–12; of queer Italian studies, 67–68; racial, 125–148
Martin, Joanna Brett, 20
Mazzantini, Margaret, *Non ti muovere*, 83
Medugno, Marco, 166
Mellor, D., 145
Melucci, Donatella, 178
Mercer, Kobena, 73
Messina, Maria, 26
Meyer, Jan, 178, 189
Michelangelo, 60
Migiel, Marilyn, 173
migrant writers, 105n14
migration, iii, 20, 66, 80, 81, 82, 86, 92, 94, 102, 105n14, 135, 150–151, 170, 172–174, 187, 195, 196; cinema of, 95; migration studies, 101, 159, 173; African migration, 133
Mills, Charles, 133–134
Modern Language Association (MLA), 15, 25, 57, 94, 157
Moeller, Aleidine J., 178
Moll, Luis, 180
Montgomery County, 19, 22n10
Moravia, Alberto, 84; *La romana*, 83
Morgan State University, 13–24, 53n2
Morosini, Roberta, 173
Morrison, Toni, 25, 39
Muldoon, James, 87
Mullen, Sarah, 20

multiculturalism, 84, 150; critical, 178, 184–185
Museus, Samuel, 128, 143, 144
Muslim, iv, 47

Nathan, Vetri, 92; *Marvelous Bodies: Italy's New Migrant Cinema*, 95, 105n14
National Standards Collaborative Board, 185
Native American, 171
native speakers, 19–20, 61, 68, 73, 138, 140–141, 160, 163, 169, 194, 195
Naylor, Gloria, 39
Nero, Franco, 62
New York University, 167n5, 194
Nieto, Sonia, 177, 178, 185
Nietzsche, Fredrich, 71
Nobel Prize, 25; to non-European, 111–112; to women, 25
Norton, Bonny, 180, 105n11
nostalgia, 45–55
Notari, Elvira, 30–31
Notre Dame University, 161, 162, 167n5

O'Brien, Catherine, 88n6
O'Healy's, Áine, 51, 91, 94, 95, 135; *Migrant Anxieties: Italian Cinema in a Transnational Frame*, 95
Okot, Bellamy, 22n9
O'Leary, Alan, 92
O'Neill, Kevin, 88n1
O'Rawe, Catherine, 92
Ohio State University, 167n5
Olita, Anna, 37

oppression, 1, 4, 99, 140, 144, 177, 189n6; homophobic, 4
Ortega, Lourdes, 178
Osborn, Terry A., 178, 184, 189
otherness, 30, 102, 105n9, 120, 160, 178
Ozpetek, Ferzan, 7, 105n12

Paolos, Medhin, *Asmarina*, 95n3
Palazzeschi, Aldo, 32, 41n8; *Il codice di Perelà*, 32
Palumbo, Patricia, 92
Panizza, Letizia, 41n1

Papa, Mauro, 76
Parati, Graziella, 105n11, 105n14, 173, 175n4
Pardini, F.S., *In the Name of the Mother*, 22n9
Parker, Deborah, ii, iii, vn1, 13, 21, 46, 79, 88, 125, 127, 145, 155n3
Pasolini, Pier Paolo, 7, 93; *A Cinema of Poetry*, 28; *Oedipus Rex*, 29; *Salò, or the 120 Days of Sodom*, 28
Peccianti, Maria Christina, 8
Pederiali, Giuseppe, 85
Penna, Sandro, 40
Petrow, Steven, 1, 2
Pettit, Emma, 162
Phillip, Nicole, 20, 53n3, 164
Picano, Feline, 33, 41n9
Pickering-Iazzi, Robin, 92
Pinkus, Karen, 92; *Bodily Regimes: Italian Advertising under Fascism*, 92
Pirandello, Luigi, *Enrico IV*, 74
Pogliano, Andrea, 173
Polo, Marco, 60, 113, 115, 193
Portuguese, 16, 118, 158
poverty, 86, 173, 186–187
power, iv, 1, 10, 11, 32, 34, 40, 72, 73, 85, 98, 102, 125–148, 151, 162, 177–192
prejudice, ii, 20, 32, 152, 178, 185–186
Prince George's County, 19, 22n10, 22n11
Princeton University, 166, 167n5; Art Museum, 102
privilege, iv, v, 3, 52, 77n1, 79, 83, 88n3, 99, 110, 125–128, 133–138, 147n6, 167, 177–178, 182, 189n6
Puccini, Giacomo, *Turandot*, 60
Puzo, Mario, 151

queer studies, 65–78
Queer Studies Caucus (AAIS), 67, 68, 94

race, i–iv, 4, 13, 29, 48, 67, 79–81, 87, 88n3, 99–103, 105n18, 125–148; and ethnicity in Italian film studies, 91–96
racism, systemic, iv; intersectional racial contracts, 135–142; racial trauma, 125–148
Raffa, Guy, 41n15, 165
Ramey, Lyn, 112

Randolph, Linwood J., 185
Rapport, Nigel, 50
Reagan, Timothy G., 178, 189n2
Reay, Diane, 80
religion, 52, 88n2, 99, 111, 144
Renaissance, Black college, 16, 21
Renaissance, Italian, 41n1, 60, 71, 102–103, 105n18, 111, 134, 157, 158, 165, 166–167, 173, 174, 175n2
Renaissance Society of America (RSA), 157–158
reductionist views, 183
Ricci, Matteo, 60
Riga, Larase, 8
Risager, Karen, 179
Rivers, Napoleon, 22n4, 22n7
Robustelli, Cecilia, 37
Romance language programs, 13, 162, 165
Romeo, Caterina, 47, 51
Ross, Cecilia, vn2
Ross, Silvia, 82–87
Rutgers University, 161, 167n5

Sabatini, Alma, 37
Sabelli, Sonia, 135
Sachs, Nelly, 25
Sahota, G.S., 112
Saiber, Arielle, 41n15
Said, Edward, 60, 110
Salerno, Eric, *Dante in Cina*, 166
Salerno, Salvatore, 93
Sapegno, Maria Serena, 37
Sartre, Jean-Paul, 125
Schildgen, Brenda Deen, 110, 112
Sciascia, Leonardo, 172
Scott, Joan Wallach, 71
Scott, Ridley, *Hannibal*, 61
sestina, 116–119
sexuality, ii, iv, 1–12, 11n1, 12n2, 26–27, 29, 32, 34, 39, 40, 65, 68, 69, 79, 86, 94, 100, 128, 144, 151, 171, 187
Shadyac, Tom, *Bruce Almighty*, 61
Shapiro, Marianne, 116
She, Lao, 167
Silent Sam, statue, 2
Singleton, Glenn, 188
Skutnabb-Kangas, Tove, 138
Sleeter, Christine E., 179

Smythe, S.A., 94
social justice, 99, 177, 179, 184–189
Somalia, 46–47, 53n4, 135, 173; National Assembly of, 47; Somaliland, 166
Spanish, 16, 20, 22n5, 22n10, 57–58, 121, 158, 163, 165, 166, 188, 190n9
spaghetti western, 62
Spicer, Joaneth, 102
Spivak, Gayatri Chakravorty, 71, 92
statistical data, ii, 57, 97, 181, 186
stereotypes, 8, 11, 115, 127, 134–142, 146–151, 183
Stanford University, 167n5
Stony Brook University, 161, 167n5, 196
Stoppino, Eleonora, 174
Strazza, Michele, 135
study abroad, 18–20, 97–105, 150, 154, 163–165, 171
Sukubo, Grazia, 22n9
superiority, European, 174; racial, 135
Swahili, 188

Tagore, Rabindranath, 111
Tamburri, Anthony Julian, i–v, 21, 29–30, 41n8, 79, 88, 155n1
Tarantino, Quentin, *Django Unchained*, 62
Tarchetti, Ugo, *Fosca* 83
Tawfik, Younis, *La straniera*, 83
Taylor, Breonna, iv
Tellini, Gino, 32
textbooks, 7–9, 19–20, 22n12, 179, 184, 187, 189n7
Thirteenth Annual World Congress of Families, 11n1
threshold concepts, 3–4, 12n2
Title ix, 1–3
Tolentino, Jia, 129
Tondelli, Pier Vittorio, 31–32, 34–35
transgender, 2, 36–37, 174
Traub, Valerie, 71
trauma, 182; racial, 125–148; semiotic, 70; theory, 36
Truilzi, Alessandro, 49
Truong, Kimberly, 128, 143, 144
Tudico, Christopher L., 15

U.S. Department of Education, 2, 19, 170–171

U.S. Department of State, 97
University, St. Joseph, 97, 98, 99, 102
University College Cork (UCC), 79; Athena SWAN Charter, 82; Equality, Diversity & Inclusion (EDI) Unit, 81; Sanctuary Scholarships, 81; Rainbow Alliance-Allies Scheme, 81–82
University for Foreigners in Perugia, 194
University of California, Berkeley, vn2, 162, 165, 167n5
University of California, Davis, 163
University of California Irvine, 92, 170, 171
University of California Los Angeles, 161–162, 165, 167n5, 188
University of California, Santa Cruz, 163, 170
University of Chicago, 167n5
University of Massachusetts, Boston, 149, 151, 153, 154, 155n4, 161
University of North Carolina, Chapel Hill, 2, 167n5
University of Oregon, 167n5
University of Pennsylvania, 22n5, 167n5
University of Southern California, 194, 195
University of Texas, 165, 167n5
University of Toronto, 158, 161–162, 167n5, 194, 195, 196
University of Virginia, 157, 161–162
University of Washington, 167n5
University of Wisconsin, 161, 167n5

Valdman, Albert, 66
Valesio, Paolo, 77n1
VanPatten, Bill, 20
Verdicchio, Pasquale, *Bound by Distance: Rethinking Nationalism through the Italian Diaspora*, 93
Vespucci, Amerigo, 62
Vico, Giambattista, 166
Villa I Tatti, 165
Violet Quill, 33–35, 41n10

Wagner, Thomas, 80
Ward, David, 51
Wassel, Beth, 186, 189n5
Watson, Jamal, 15–16
Watson, James, 81, 88n1

Weber-Fève, Stacy, 20
Weigel, Robert, 52
Welz, Claudia, 127
Weninger, Csilla, 179
Wesley, Pamela, 186, 189n5
White, Hayden, 71
whiteness, iv, v, 51, 93, 102, 133, 140, 170
Wilson, David, 17
Wing Sue, Derald, 10–11
women, iv; authors, 25–27; marginalized in Italian studies, 27–31; Nobel Prize winners, 25; outside literary canon, 36
Wong, Wynne, 20
World Readiness Standards, 185

Xiao, Jiwei, 60, 61
Xu, Can, 167

Yale University, 159, 163, 167n5, 188

Zanotti Carney, Emanuela, 177, 179, 189n7
Zhang, Gaoheng, 159, 162, 166
Zhang, Longxi, 60
Zhang, Xiaoyi, 166

www.ingramcontent.com/pod-product-compliance
Lightning Source LLC
Chambersburg PA
CBHW080440170426
43195CB00017B/2832